When should I travel to get the best airfare?

Where do I go for answers to my travel questions?

What's the best and easiest way to plan and book my trip?

frommers.travelocity.com

Frommer's, the travel guide leader, has teamed up with **Travelocity.com,** the leader in online travel, to bring you an in-depth, easy-to-use resource designed to help you plan and book your trip online.

At **frommers.travelocity.com**, you'll find free online updates about your destination from the experts at Frommer's plus the outstanding travel planning and purchasing features of Travelocity.com. Travelocity.com provides reservations capabilities for 95 percent of all airline seats sold, more than 47,000 hotels, and over 50 car rental companies. In addition, Travelocity.com offers more than 2,000 exciting vacation and cruise packages. Travelocity.com puts you in complete control of your travel planning with these and other great features:

> **Expert travel guidance from Frommer's** - over 150 writers reporting from around the world!
>
> **Best Fare Finder** - an interactive calendar tells you when to travel to get the best airfare
>
> **Fare Watcher** - we'll track airfare changes to your favorite destinations
>
> **Dream Maps** - a mapping feature that suggests travel opportunities based on your budget
>
> **Shop Safe Guarantee** - 24 hours a day / 7 days a week live customer service, and more!

Whether traveling on a tight budget, looking for a quick weekend getaway, or planning the trip of a lifetime, Frommer's guides and Travelocity.com will make your travel dreams a reality. You've bought the book, now book the trip!

Here's what the critics say about Frommer's:

"Amazingly easy to use. Very portable, very complete."

—Booklist

♦

"The only mainstream guide to list specific prices. The Walter Cronkite of guidebooks—with all that implies."

—Travel & Leisure

♦

"Detailed, accurate and easy-to-read information for all price ranges."

—Glamour magazine

P O R T A B L E

Boston
1st Edition

by Marie Morris

IDG Books Worldwide, Inc.
An International Data Group Company
Foster City, CA • Chicago, IL • Indianapolis, IN • New York, NY

ABOUT THE AUTHOR

Marie Morris grew up in New York and graduated from Harvard, where she studied history. She has worked for the *Boston Herald, Boston* magazine, and *The New York Times,* and she covers Boston for *Frommer's New England.* She lives in Boston, not far from Paul Revere.

IDG BOOKS WORLDWIDE, INC.

An International Data Group Company
909 Third Ave.
New York, NY 10022

Find us online at **www.frommers.com**

ISBN 0-7645-6350-5
ISSN 1531-748X

Editor: Amy Lyons
Production Editor: Todd A. Siesky
Photo Editor: Richard Fox
Design by Michele Laseau
Cartographer: Elizabeth Puhl
Production by IDG Books Indianapolis Production Department
Front Cover Photo: Trinity Church and the John Hancock Tower

SPECIAL SALES

For general information on IDG Books Worldwide's books in the U.S., please call our Consumer Customer Service department at 1-800-762-2974. For reseller information, including discounts, bulk sales, customized editions, and premium sales, please call our Reseller Customer Service department at 1-800-434-3422.

Manufactured in the United States of America

5 4 3 2 1

Contents

List of Maps

AN INVITATION TO THE READER

In researching this book we discovered many wonderful places—hotels, restaurants, shops, and more. We're sure you'll find others. Please tell us about them, so we can share the information with your fellow travelers in upcoming editions. If you were disappointed with a recommendation, we'd love to know that, too. Please write to:

Frommer's Portable Boston, 1st Edition
IDG Books Worldwide, Inc.
909 Third Avenue
New York, NY 10022

AN ADDITIONAL NOTE

Please be advised that travel information is subject to change at any time—and this is especially true of prices. We therefore suggest that you write or call ahead for confirmation when making your travel plans. The authors, editors, and publishers cannot be held responsible for the experiences of readers while traveling. Your safety is important to us, however, so we encourage you to stay alert and be aware of your surroundings. Keep a close eye on cameras, purses, and wallets, all favorite targets of thieves and pickpockets.

WHAT THE SYMBOLS MEAN
✪ Frommer's Favorites

Our favorite places and experiences—outstanding for quality, value, or both. The following abbreviations are used for credit cards:

AE	American Express	EC	Eurocard
CB	Carte Blanche	JCB	Japan Credit Bank
DC	Diners Club	MC	MasterCard
DISC	Discover	V	Visa
ER	EnRoute		

FIND FROMMER'S ONLINE

www.frommers.com offers up-to-the-minute listings on almost 200 cities around the globe—including the latest bargains and candid, personal articles updated daily by Arthur Frommer himself. No other Web site offers such comprehensive and timely coverage of the world of travel.

Planning Your Trip: The Basics

*T*his chapter addresses the practical issues that arise after you decide to visit Boston. One topic you probably won't need to address is renting a car. If you plan to visit only Boston and Cambridge, public transportation is cheap, safe, and reliable, and a car is far more trouble than it's worth. Should you need to drive beyond the immediate area, you'll find branches of the national chains at the airport and downtown. They include **Alamo** (☎ 800/327-9633), **Avis** (☎ 800/831-2847), **Budget** (☎ 800/527-0700), **Dollar** (☎ 800/800-4000), **Hertz** (☎ 800/654-3131), and **National** (☎ 800/227-7368).

1 Visitor Information

The **Greater Boston Convention & Visitors Bureau,** 2 Copley Place, Suite 105, Boston, MA 02116-6501 (☎ **888/SEE-BOSTON** or 617/536-4100, 0171/431-3434 in the U.K.; fax 617/424-7664; www.bostonusa.com), offers a comprehensive visitor information kit and a "Kids Love Boston" kit. Each costs $6.25 and includes a complete travel planner, guidebook, map, and coupon book with shopping, dining, attraction, and nightlife discounts. Smaller planners that concentrate on specific seasons or events often are available free. Call the main number to gain access to **"Boston by Phone,"** a service that provides information on attractions, dining, performing arts and nightlife, shopping, and travel services.

The **Massachusetts Office of Travel and Tourism,** 100 Cambridge St., 13th floor, Boston, MA 02202 (☎ **800/227-6277** or 617/727-3201; fax 617/727-6525; www.mass-vacation.com), has a great Web site that even offers a "lobster tutorial." The free *Getaway Guide* magazine includes information about statewide attractions and lodgings, a map, and a seasonal calendar.

For information about Cambridge, contact the **Cambridge Office for Tourism,** 18 Brattle St., Cambridge, MA 02138 (☎ **800/862-5678** or 617/441-2884; fax 617/441-7736; www.cambridge-usa.org).

2 When to Go

Boston attracts large numbers of visitors year-round. Between April and November, there are hardly any slow times. The periods around college graduation (May and early June) and the major citywide events (listed below) are especially busy. Spring and fall are extremely popular times for conventions. Families pour into the area in July and August, creating long lines at many attractions. Foliage season (mid-September to early November) is increasingly popular, crowded, and expensive. December is less busy but still a convention time—look out for weekend bargains.

The "slow" season is January through March, when many hotels offer great deals, especially on weekends. This is also when the city is most likely to be covered in snow, and when some suburban attractions close for the winter.

CLIMATE   Spring and fall are the best bets for moderate temperatures, but spring (also known as mud season) is brief. It doesn't usually settle in until early May, and snow sometimes falls in late April. Summers are hot, especially in July and August, and can be uncomfortably humid. Fall is when you're most likely to catch a comfortable run of sunny days and cool nights. Winters are cold and usually snowy—bring a warm coat and sturdy boots. You can roast in May and freeze in June, shiver in September and wish you'd packed shorts in March. Dressing in layers is always a good idea.

BOSTON CALENDAR OF EVENTS

The **Greater Boston Convention & Visitors Bureau** (☎ **800/ SEE-BOSTON** or 617/536-4100; www.bostonusa.com) operates a regularly updated hotline that describes ongoing and upcoming events. The **Mayor's Office of Special Events & Tourism** (☎ **617/635-3911**) can provide information about specific happenings.

January

- **Martin Luther King, Jr., Birthday Celebration,** various locations. Events include speeches, musical tributes, gospel celebrations, and panel discussions. Check special listings in the

Thursday *Boston Globe* "Calendar" section for specifics. Third Monday of the month.

- **Chinese New Year,** Chinatown. Dragon parade (which draws a crowd no matter how cold it is), fireworks, and raucous festivals. Special programs at the Children's Museum (☎ **617/426-8855**). Depending on the Chinese lunar calendar, the holiday falls between January 21 and February 19. In 2001, January 24; in 2002, February 12.

- **Boston Wine Festival,** Boston Harbor Hotel and other locations. Tastings, classes, lectures, receptions, and meals provide a lively liquid diversion in the dead of winter. Call the festival reservation line (☎ **888/660-WINE** or 617/330-9355) for details. January through early April.

February

- **Black History Month,** various locations. Programs include special museum exhibits, children's activities, concerts, films, lectures, discussions, and tours of the Black Heritage Trail led by National Park Service rangers (☎ **617/742-5415;** www.nps.gov/boaf). All month.

- **School Vacation Week,** various locations. The slate of activities for children includes plays, special exhibitions and programs, and tours. Contact individual attractions for information on special programs, extra open days, and extended hours. Third week of the month.

March

- **St. Patrick's Day/Evacuation Day.** Parade, South Boston. Celebration, Faneuil Hall Marketplace. The 5-mile parade salutes the city's Irish heritage and the day British troops left Boston in 1776. Head to Faneuil Hall Marketplace for music, dancing, and food. March 17.

April

- **Big Apple Circus** (www.bigapplecircus.org), near the waterfront. The New York–based "one-ring wonder" performs in a heated tent with all seating less than 50 feet from the ring. Proceeds support the Children's Museum. Visit the museum box office or contact TicketMaster (☎ **617/931-ARTS;** www.ticketmaster.com). Early April through early May.

- **Red Sox Opening Day,** Fenway Park. Even if your concierge is a magician, this is an extremely tough ticket. Check with the ticket office (☎ **617/267-1700;** www.redsox.com) when tickets for the season go on sale in early January, or try to see the

Patriots Day game, which begins at 11am. Middle of the month.

- **Swan Boats Return to the Public Garden.** Since their introduction in 1877, the swan boats (☎ **617/522-1966;** www.swanboats.com) have been a symbol of Boston. Like real swans, they go away for the winter. Saturday before Patriots Day.

- ✪ **Patriots Day,** statewide. Observations commemorate the events of April 18–19, 1775. In Boston, participants hang lanterns in the steeple of the **Old North Church** (☎ **617/523-6676;** www.oldnorth.com). "Paul Revere" and "William Dawes" leave the **Paul Revere House** (☎ **617/523-2338;** www.paulreverehouse.org) in the North End to Lexington and Concord to warn the Minutemen that "the regulars are out" (not that "the British are coming"—most colonists considered themselves British). Third Monday of the month.

- **Boston Marathon,** Hopkinton, Massachusetts, to Boston. International stars and local amateurs join in the world's oldest and most famous marathon. The noon start means that elite runners hit Boston around 2:00 in the afternoon; weekend runners stagger across the Boylston Street finish line as much as 6 hours later. Third Monday of the month.

- **Freedom Trail Week,** various locations in Boston, Cambridge, Lexington, and Concord. Another school vacation week, with plenty of crowds and diversions. Family-friendly events include tours, concerts, talks, and other programs related to Patriots Day, the Freedom Trail, and the American Revolution. Third week of the month.

May

- **Museum-Goers' Month,** various locations. Contact individual museums for information on special exhibits, lectures, and events. All month.

- **Street Performers Festival,** Faneuil Hall Marketplace. Everyone but the pigeons gets into the act as musicians, magicians, jugglers, sword swallowers, and artists strut their stuff. End of the month.

June

- **Boston Dairy Festival,** Boston Common. Cows grazed on Boston Common for its first 2 centuries; now they return once a year, accompanied by other farm animals, milking contests, and children's activities. The **"Scooper Bowl"** ice-cream extravaganza takes place simultaneously on City Hall Plaza. First week of the month.

- **Dragon Boat Festival,** Charles River near Harvard Square, Cambridge (☎ **617/349-4380;** www.bostondragonboat.com). Teams of paddlers synchronized by a drummer propel boats with dragon heads and tails as they race 500 meters. The winners go to the national championships; the spectators go to a celebration of Chinese culture and food on the shore. Second Sunday of the month.

✪ *Boston Globe* **Jazz & Blues Festival,** various indoor and outdoor locations. Big names and rising stars put on lunchtime, after-work, evening, and weekend performances, some of which are free. Venues include the Hatch Shell on the Esplanade, Newbury Street, and Copley Square. Call the hotline (☎ **617/267-4301;** www.boston.com/jazzfest) or pick up a copy of the paper for a schedule when you arrive in town. Some events require advance tickets. Late June.

July

✪ **Boston Harborfest,** downtown, the waterfront, and the Harbor Islands. The city puts on its Sunday best for the Fourth of July, which has become a gigantic weeklong celebration of Boston's maritime history and an excuse to get out and have fun. Events surrounding **Harborfest** (☎ **617/227-1528;** www.bostonharborfest.com) include concerts, children's activities, cruises, fireworks, the Boston Chowderfest, guided tours, talks, and the annual turnaround of USS *Constitution.* First week of the month (June 28 to July 4, 2001).

- **Boston Pops Concert and Fireworks Display,** Hatch Shell on the Esplanade. Spectators wait from dawn till dark for the music to start (overnight camping is not permitted). They also show up at the last minute—the Cambridge side of the river, near Kendall Square, is a good spot to watch the spectacular aerial show. The program includes the *1812 Overture,* with actual cannon fire. For details, check the Web site (www.july4th.org). July 4.

August

- **Italian-American Feasts,** North End. These weekend street fairs begin in July and end before Labor Day with the two biggest, the Fishermen's Feast and the Feast of St. Anthony. The sublime (fresh seafood prepared while you wait, live music, and dancing in the street) mingles with the ridiculous (carnival games and fried-dough stands) to leave a lasting impression of fun and indigestion. Weekends, all month.

- **August Moon Festival,** Chinatown. A celebration of the harvest and the coming of autumn. Activities include the "dragon dance" through the crowded streets, and demonstrations of crafts and martial arts. Middle of the month.

September

- **Boston Film Festival** (☎ 781/925-1373; www. bostonfilmfestival.org), various locations. Independent films continue their turn around the festival circuit or make their premiere, sometimes accompanied by a talk by an actor or a filmmaker. Most screenings are open to the public without advance tickets. Middle of the month.
- **Art Newbury Street & Fashion Walk,** Back Bay. More than 30 galleries are open, and Newbury Street from the Public Garden to Massachusetts Avenue closes to traffic. You'll find special exhibits indoors and live entertainment outdoors. Check the Web site (www.newbury-st.com) for details. Middle of the month.

October

- **Columbus Day Parade,** downtown and the North End. Beginning with a ceremony on City Hall Plaza at 1pm, the parade, appropriately enough, winds up in the city's Italian neighborhood, following Hanover Street to the Coast Guard station on Commercial Street. Second Monday of the month.
- **Ringling Brothers and Barnum & Bailey Circus,** FleetCenter (☎ 617/624-1000; www.fleetcenter.com). The Greatest Show on Earth makes its annual 2-week visit. Middle of the month.
- ✪ **Head of the Charles Regatta,** Boston and Cambridge. High school, college, and postcollegiate rowing teams and individuals—some 4,000 in all—race in front of hordes of fans along the banks of the Charles River and on the bridges spanning it. The Head of the Charles (☎ 617/864-8415; www.hocr.org) has an uncanny tendency to coincide with the crispest, most picturesque weekend of the season. End of the month.

December

- *The Nutcracker,* Wang Center for the Performing Arts. Boston Ballet's annual holiday extravaganza is one of the country's biggest and best. This is *the* traditional way for young Bostonians (and visitors) to be exposed to culture, and the spectacular sets make it practically painless. Call **TicketMaster** (☎ **617/931-ARTS;** www.ticketmaster.com) as soon as you plan your trip, ask whether your hotel offers a *Nutcracker* package, or cross your fingers and visit the box office at 270 Tremont St. when you arrive. All month.

- **Christmas Tree Lighting** and **Newbury Street Stroll,** Back Bay. Carol singing precedes the lighting of the Prudential Center's magnificent tree on Saturday. It's an annual gift from Nova Scotia—an expression of thanks from the people of Halifax for Bostonians' speedy help in fighting a devastating fire there in 1917. On Sunday, music, holiday activities, and window-shoppers take over Newbury Street. First weekend of December.
- **Boston Tea Party Reenactment,** Tea Party Ship and Museum, Congress Street Bridge (☎ **617/338-1773**). Chafing under British rule, the colonists rose up on December 16, 1773, to strike a blow where it would cause real pain—in the pocketbook. Middle of the month.
- **Black Nativity,** Converse Hall, Tremont Temple Baptist Church, 88 Tremont St. (☎ **617/723-3486**). Poet Langston Hughes wrote the "gospel opera," and a cast of more than 100 brings it to life. Music and dancing by soloists and choirs frame a rousing interpretation of the Gospel according to Luke. All month.
- **Christmas Revels,** Sanders Theater, Cambridge. This multicultural celebration of the winter solstice features the holiday customs of a different culture each year. Recent themes have included Renaissance Italy and the Romany Gypsies. Be ready to sing along. For information, contact the **Revels** (☎ **617/ 621-0505;** www.revels.org); for tickets, call the **box office** (☎ **617/496-2222**) or **TicketMaster** (☎ **617/931-ARTS**). Last 2 weeks of the month.
- ✪ **First Night,** Back Bay and the waterfront. The original arts-oriented, no-alcohol, citywide New Year's Eve celebration is Boston's. It begins in the early afternoon and includes a parade, ice sculptures, art exhibitions, theatrical performances, and indoor and outdoor entertainment. Some attractions require tickets, but for most you just need a First Night button, available for about $15 at visitor centers and stores around the city. The carousing wraps up at midnight with a spectacular fireworks display over the harbor. For details, contact **First Night** (☎ **617/542-1399;** www.firstnight.org) or check the newspapers when you arrive. December 31.

Planning Pointer

You have plane and hotel reservations, but what about restaurant reservations and tickets to that big museum show? If you've heard or read about a place or an event that you just have to check out, call ahead—a couple of minutes on the phone while you're planning everything else can be an excellent investment. And if your trip coincides (intentionally or not) with a cultural event such as the *Nutcracker* or a museum show, be sure to investigate hotel packages that include tickets. You may not save much money, but you will save time.

---

3 Tips for Travelers with Special Needs

FOR TRAVELERS WITH DISABILITIES

Boston, like all other U.S. cities, has taken the required steps to provide access for travelers with disabilities. Hotels must provide accessible rooms; museums and street curbs have ramps for wheelchairs. Some smaller accommodations, including most B&Bs, have not been retrofitted. In older neighborhoods (notably Beacon Hill and the North End), you'll find many narrow streets, cobbled thoroughfares, and brick sidewalks.

An excellent source of information is **Very Special Arts Massachusetts,** 2 Boylston St., Boston, MA 02116 (☎ **617/350-7713;** fax 617/482-4298; TTY 617/350-6836; www.vsamass.org). Its comprehensive Web site includes general access information and specifics about more than 200 arts and entertainment facilities in the state.

The Americans with Disabilities Act requires all forms of public transportation to provide special services to patrons with disabilities. Newer stations on the Red, Blue, and Orange lines of the MBTA **subway** are wheelchair accessible; the Green Line (which uses trolleys) is being converted. Contact the **MBTA** (☎ **800/392-6100** outside MA or 617/222-3200; www.mbta.com) or check a current system map to see if the stations you need are accessible. All MBTA **buses** have lifts or kneelers; call ☎ **800/LIFT-BUS** for more information. Some bus routes are wheelchair accessible at all times, but you may have to make a reservation as much as a day in advance for others. To learn more, call the main information number or the **Office for Transportation Access** (☎ **617/222-5438;** TTY 617/222-5854).

One taxicab company with wheelchair-accessible vehicles is **Boston Cab** (☎ 617/536-5010); advance notice is recommended. In addition, there is an Airport Handicap Van (☎ 617/561-1769).

GENERAL INFORMATION   *A World of Options,* a 658-page book of resources, covers everything from biking trips to scuba outfitters. It costs $35 ($30 for members) and is available from **Mobility International USA,** P.O. Box 10767, Eugene, OR 97440 (☎ 541/343-1284, voice and TDD; www.miusa.org). Annual membership is $35, which includes the quarterly newsletter, *Over the Rainbow.* **Twin Peaks Press,** P.O. Box 129, Vancouver, WA 98666 (☎ 360/694-2462), publishes travel-related books for travelers with disabilities.

The Moss Rehab Hospital (☎ 215/456-9600) has provided friendly and helpful advice and referrals to disabled travelers for years through its **Travel Information Service** (☎ 215/456-9603; www.mossresourcenet.org).

You can join the **Society for the Advancement of Travel for the Handicapped,** 347 Fifth Ave., Suite 610, New York, NY 10016 (☎ 212/447-7284; fax 212/725-8253; www.sath.org). Annual membership is $45, $30 for seniors and students, and gives you access to a vast network of connections in the travel industry. The society provides information sheets on travel destinations and referrals to tour operators that specialize in traveling with disabilities. The quarterly magazine, *Open World for Disability and Mature Travel,* is full of information and resources. A year's subscription is $13 ($21 outside the U.S.).

Travelers with disabilities might also want to consider joining a tour that caters specifically to them. One of the best operators is **Flying Wheels Travel,** 143 West Bridge, P.O. Box 38, Owatonna, MN 55060 (☎ 800/525-6790; www.flyingwheels.com). It offers escorted tours and cruises, as well as private tours in minivans with lifts.

For a copy of *Air Transportation of Handicapped Persons,* write to Free Advisory Circular No. AC12032, Distribution Unit, U.S. Department of Transportation, Publications Division, M-4332, Washington, DC 20590.

Amtrak (☎ 800/USA-RAIL; www.amtrak.com) and **Greyhound** (☎ 800/231-2222; www.greyhound.com) offer special fares and services for travelers with disabilities. Call at least a week in advance of your trip for details.

Vision-impaired travelers can contact the **American Foundation for the Blind,** 11 Penn Plaza, Suite 300, New York, NY 10001 (☎ **800/232-5463**), for information on traveling with Seeing Eye dogs.

FOR SENIORS

Boston-area businesses offer many discounts to seniors with identification (a driver's license, passport, or other document that shows your date of birth). Hotels, restaurants, museums, and movie theaters may offer special deals. Restaurants and theaters usually offer discounts only at off-peak times, but museums and other attractions offer reduced rates at all times.

Seniors with a special pass can ride the MBTA **subways** for 25¢ (a 75¢ savings) and **local buses** for 15¢ (a 60¢ savings). On zoned and express buses and on the commuter rail, the senior citizen fare is half the regular fare. The Senior Pass is available for a nominal fee weekdays from 8:30am to 5pm at the Back Bay MBTA station, or by mail from Office for Transportation Access, 145 Dartmouth St., Boston, MA 02116-5162 (☎ **617/222-5438;** TTY 617/222-5854; www.mbta.com).

Membership in the **American Association of Retired Persons,** 601 E St. NW, Washington, DC 20049 (☎ **800/424-3410;** www.aarp.org), gets you discounts on car rentals, accommodations, airfares, and sightseeing. It's open to anyone 50 or older, retired or not.

A **Golden Age Passport** ($10) gives you free lifetime admission to all federal recreation areas, including parks and monuments. It's available at any National Park Service site that charges admission.

FOR GAY & LESBIAN TRAVELERS

Overall, Boston is a gay- and lesbian-friendly destination, with a live-and-let-live attitude that long ago replaced the city's legendary Puritanism.

The **Gay and Lesbian Helpline** (☎ **617/267-9001**) offers information Monday through Friday from 6 to 11pm, weekends 5 to 10pm. The weekly newspaper *Bay Windows* (☎ **617/266-6670;** www.baywindows.com) covers events, news, and features. The weekly *Boston Phoenix* publishes a monthly supplement, "One in 10," and has a gay-interest area in its Web site (www.bostonphoenix.com). You can also contact the **Boston Alliance of Gay and Lesbian Youth** (☎ **800/422-2459;** www.bagly.org).

The *Pink Pages,* 66 Charles St. #283, Boston, MA 02114 (☎ 800/338-6550; www.pinkweb.com/boston.index.html), is a guide to gay- and lesbian-owned and gay-friendly businesses. Check the comprehensive Web site or order a copy for $11 (including shipping).

GENERAL INFORMATION   Two good biannual English-language guidebooks focus on gay men and include information for lesbians. You can get the *Spartacus International Gay Guide* or *Odysseus* at most gay and lesbian bookstores, or order them from Giovanni's Room (☎ 215/923-2960) or A Different Light Bookstore (☎ 800/343-4002 or 212/989-4850). Both lesbians and gay men might want to pick up a copy of *Gay Travel A to Z* ($16).

Out and About, 8 W. 19th St. #401, New York, NY 10011 (☎ 800/929-2268 or 212/645-6922), offers guidebooks and a monthly newsletter packed with information on the global gay and lesbian scene. A year's subscription to the newsletter costs $49. *Our World,* 1104 N. Nova Rd., Suite 251, Daytona Beach, FL 32117 (☎ 904/441-5367), is a slick monthly magazine that highlights travel bargains and opportunities. An annual subscription costs $35 ($45 outside the U.S.).

4 Getting There

BY PLANE

The major airlines that serve **Logan International Airport** are **AirTran** (☎ 800/247-8726; www. airtran.com), **American** (☎ 800/433-7300; www.aa.com), **America West** (☎ 800/ 235-9292; www.americawest.com), **Continental** (☎ 800/ 525-0280; www.flycontinental.com), **Delta** (☎ 800/221-1212; www.delta.com), **Frontier** (☎ 800/432-1359; www. frontierairlines. com), **Midway** (☎ 800/446-4392), **Northwest** (☎ 800/225-2525; www.nwa.com), **TWA** (☎ 800/221-2000; www.twa.com), **United** (☎ 800/241-6522; www.ual.com), and **US Airways** (☎ 800/428-4322; www.usairways.com).

The discount airline **Southwest** (☎ 800/435-9792; www. iflyswa.com) serves suburban Providence, RI, and Manchester, N.H., and has enticed several other carriers to do likewise. Fares can be considerably cheaper than those to Boston. **T. F. Green Airport** (☎ 888/268-7222; www.pvd-ri.com) is in Warwick, RI, about 60 miles south of Boston. **Manchester International**

Airport (☎ 603/624-6556; www.flymanchester.com) is about 56 miles north of Boston.

BY CAR

Check carefully before assuming that driving is cheaper than flying. Between the outrageous cost of parking and the hassle of downtown traffic, the negligible savings may not be worth the annoyance.

The **Massachusetts Turnpike** or **Mass. Pike** (I-90) is an east-west toll road that runs to downtown Boston. The **Central Artery** (I-93) runs north-south through downtown; it's the object of the **"Big Dig,"** the enormous construction project that's worsening Boston's already deplorable traffic. The **Southeast Expressway** (I-93/Rte. 3) connects Boston with the south, including Cape Cod. **I-95** (Mass. Rte. 128) approaches Boston and detours into a beltway that intersects the Mass. Pike (to the west) and I-93 (north and south).

The approach to Cambridge is **Storrow Drive** or **Memorial Drive,** on either side of the Charles River. Storrow Drive's Harvard Square exit leads across the Anderson Bridge to John F. Kennedy Street and into the square. Memorial Drive intersects Kennedy Street; turn away from the bridge to reach the square.

The **American Automobile Association** (☎ 800/AAA-HELP; www.aaa.com) provides its members with maps, itineraries, and other travel information, and arranges free towing if you break down. The Mass. Pike is a privately operated road that arranges its own towing; if you break down there, wait in the car until one of the regular patrols arrives.

Important tip: When you reach your hotel, leave your car in the garage and walk or use public transportation. Save the car for day trips; before you set out, ask at the front desk for a route away from the construction area.

BY TRAIN

Amtrak (☎ **800/USA-RAIL** or 617/482-3660; www.amtrak.com) serves South Station, on Atlantic Avenue downtown, and Back Bay Station, on Dartmouth Street across from the Copley Place mall. In 2000, it instituted **Acela** high-speed rail service (www.acela.com) from New York. The new route is designed to compete with the airline shuttles in time (downtown to downtown, about 3 hours).

BY BUS

South Station is also the bus terminal. Consider long-distance bus travel a last resort except from New York, a route so desirable that **Greyhound** (☎ **800/231-2222** or 617/526-1801; www. greyhound.com) and **Peter Pan** (☎ **800/237-8747** or 617/ 426-8554) have drastically upgraded service. It's relatively fast (4 to 4½ hours), and the price is about half the regular train fare. Express buses, which make only one stop, are worth the extra $5 or so.

5 For Foreign Visitors

ENTRY REQUIREMENTS

The following requirements may have changed somewhat by the time you plan your trip. Check at any U.S. embassy or consulate for current information and requirements, or visit the U.S. State Department's Web site (www.state.gov).

DOCUMENTS   The State Department's **Visa Waiver Pilot Program** allows citizens of some countries to enter the United States without a visa for stays of up to 90 days. At press time they included Andorra, Argentina, Australia, Austria, Belgium, Brunei, Denmark, Finland, France, Germany, Iceland, Ireland, Italy, Japan, Liechtenstein, Luxembourg, Monaco, the Netherlands, New Zealand, Norway, San Marino, Slovenia, Spain, Sweden, Switzerland, and the United Kingdom. Citizens of these countries need only a valid passport and a round-trip air or cruise ticket in their possession on arrival.

Canadian citizens may enter the United States without visas; they need only proof of residence.

Citizens of all other countries must have a tourist visa, available free from any U.S. consulate, and a valid passport that expires at least 6 months after the scheduled end of the visit to the United States.

Obtaining a Visa   The traveler must submit (in person or by mail) a completed application form with a 1½-inch-square photo, and demonstrate binding ties to a residence abroad. Contact the nearest U.S. embassy or consulate for directions on applying by mail. Your travel agent or airline office may also be able to supply visa applications and instructions. Usually you can get a visa right away or within 24 hours, but it could take longer during the summer rush, from June to August. The U.S. consulate or embassy that issues your visa will decide whether you receive a multiple- or single-entry visa and determine any restrictions on the length of your stay.

British subjects can call the **U.S. Embassy Visa Information Line** (☎ **0891/200-290**) or the **London Passport Office** (☎ **0990/210-410** for recorded information).

MEDICAL REQUIREMENTS   Inoculations or vaccinations are not required unless you're arriving from an area known to be suffering from an epidemic (particularly cholera or yellow fever). If you have a disease that requires treatment with a controlled substance or syringe-administered medications, carry a valid signed prescription from your physician to allay suspicions that you might be smuggling drugs (a serious offense that carries severe penalties).

For current information concerning HIV-positive travelers, contact the Centers for Disease Control's **National Center for HIV** (☎ **404/332-4559;** www.hivatis.org) or **Gay Men's Health Crisis** (☎ **212/367-1000;** www.gmhc.org).

MONEY

The American monetary system has a decimal base: 1 U.S. **dollar** ($1) = 100 **cents** (100¢). Dollar bills commonly come in $1 (a "buck"), $5, $10, $20, $50, and $100 denominations. Bills larger than $20 are not welcome for small purchases and are not accepted in most taxis or fast-food restaurants. Two designs of each bill larger than $1 are in circulation. The newer versions have larger, off-center portraits on their "faces" and are identical to old-style money in value and negotiability, with one exception: Some vending machines don't recognize the new designs and bear signs warning you not to use them.

There are six coin denominations: 1¢ (1 cent or a "penny"), 5¢ (5 cents or a "nickel"), 10¢ (10 cents or a "dime"), 25¢ (25 cents or a "quarter"), 50¢ (50 cents or a "half-dollar"), and $1. A new gold-colored $1 coin went into circulation in 2000. The quarter-size Susan B. Anthony $1 coin is not in common use and is typically dispensed only by post office vending machines when you buy more than a few stamps.

The "foreign exchange bureaus" so common in Europe are rare in the United States and nonexistent outside major cities. Try to avoid changing foreign money (or traveler's checks in currency other than U.S. dollars) at small-town bank branches.

In the Boston area, many banks and some hotels offer currency exchange. At the airport, **Citizens** (☎ **800/922-9999**) and **Fleet** (☎ **800/841-4000**) banks and **Travelex** (☎ **617/567-1087**) have outlets. **American Express** (☎ **800/AXP-TRIP;** www. americanexpress.com) has offices at 1 State St., at Washington Street, downtown (☎ **617/723-8400**); 222 Berkeley St., at Boylston Street, Back Bay (☎ **617/236-1334**); and 39 John F. Kennedy St., Harvard Square, Cambridge (☎ **617/868-2600**). **Thomas Cook Currency Services, Inc.** (☎ **800/287-7362**), has offices at 160 Franklin St., near Federal Street, downtown, and 399 Boylston St., between Arlington and Berkeley streets, Back Bay.

2

Getting to Know Boston

*B*oston bills itself as "America's Walking City," and walking is by far the easiest way to get around. Legend has it that the street pattern originated as a network of cow paths, but the layout owes more to 17th-century London and to Boston's original shoreline.

This chapter tells you how to get into town and provides an overview of the city's layout and neighborhoods. It also lists information and resources you might need while you're away from home.

1 Orientation

ARRIVING

BY PLANE **Logan International Airport** ("Logan") is in East Boston at the end of the Sumner, Callahan, and Ted Williams tunnels, 3 miles across the harbor from downtown. Terminals A through D handle domestic flights. The airport is in the throes of a massive overhaul; if you're returning a rental car, allow extra time. The Terminal C information booth is a "Visitor Service Center." Staff members who have gone through concierge training can help make hotel and restaurant reservations, plan tours, provide convention information, and buy theater and sports tickets.

The Massachusetts Port Authority (☎ **800/23-LOGAN;** www.massport.com) coordinates airport transportation. The toll-free line provides information about getting to the city and to many nearby suburbs. It's available 24 hours a day and staffed weekdays 8am to 7pm.

The ride into town takes 10 to 45 minutes, depending on traffic, your destination, and the time of day. Except at off-hours, such as early on weekend mornings, driving is the slowest way to get into central Boston.

You can get into town by subway (the "T"), boat, cab, or bus. The **subway** is fast and cheap—Government Center is 10 minutes away, and a token (good for one ride) costs $1. Free **shuttle**

buses run from each terminal to the Airport station on the Blue Line of the T from 5:30am to 1am every day, year-round. The Blue Line stops at State Street and Government Center, where you can exit or transfer to the other lines.

Note: The first Blue Line stop downtown is Aquarium, which closed in October 2000 for at least a year. Shuttle buses are expected to run in a loop between State and Aquarium, but it's not a bad walk (four blocks downhill).

The trip downtown in a weather-protected **boat** takes 7 minutes, dock to dock. The free no. 66 shuttle bus connects the airport terminals to the ferry dock. The **Airport Water Shuttle** (☎ **617/330-8680**) runs to Rowes Wharf. The one-way fare is $10 for adults, $5 for seniors, free for children under 12. **Harbor Express** (☎ **617/376-8417;** www.harborexpress.com) runs to Long Wharf. The one-way fare is $10.

A **cab** from the airport to downtown or the Back Bay costs about $18 to $24. Depending on traffic, the driver may use the Ted Williams Tunnel for destinations outside downtown, such as the Back Bay. On a map, this doesn't look like the fastest route, but often it is.

Some hotels have their own **limousines** or **shuttle vans;** ask about them when you make your reservations. To arrange private limo service, call ahead for a reservation; drivers are not allowed to cruise for fares. Your hotel can recommend a company, or try **Carey Limousine Boston** (☎ **800/336-4646** or 617/623-8700) or **Commonwealth Limousine Service** (☎ **800/558-LIMO** outside Massachusetts, or 617/787-5575).

MassPort (see above) coordinates **bus service** between the airport and Gate 25 at South Station. The one-way fare is $5.

BY TRAIN & BUS   South Station is on Atlantic Avenue at Summer Street, near the Waterfront and the Financial District. It serves Amtrak and the commuter rail, and is in the same complex as the bus station. South Station is a stop on the Red Line subway, which runs to Cambridge. At Park Street on the Red Line, you can transfer free to the Green Line and (through a pedestrian passage) Orange Line. To reach the Blue Line from Park Street, take the Green Line to Government Center.

Back Bay Station is on Dartmouth Street between Huntington and Columbus avenues, straddling the Back Bay and the South End. It serves Amtrak, the commuter rail, and the Orange Line of the T. The Orange Line connects Back Bay Station with

Boston Neighborhoods

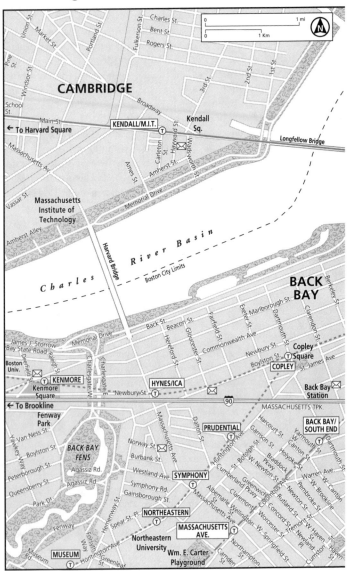

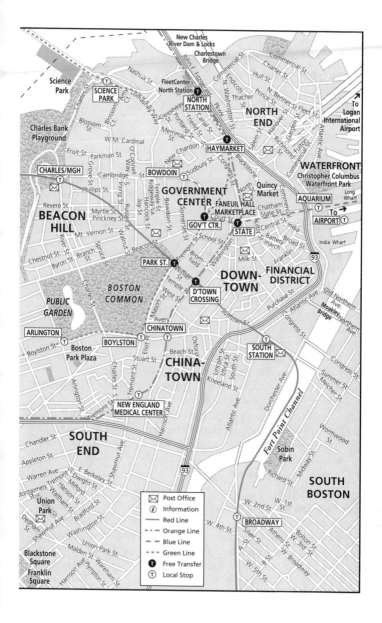

19

Downtown Crossing (where there's a walkway to Park Street station) and other points.

VISITOR INFORMATION

The **Boston National Historic Park Visitor Center,** 15 State St. (☎ **617/242-5642;** www.nps.gov/bost), across the street from the Old State House and the State Street T station, is a good place to start your excursion. National Park Service rangers staff the center, dispense information, and lead free tours of the Freedom Trail. The center is accessible by stairs and ramps and has rest rooms and comfortable chairs. Open daily 9am to 5pm except January 1, Thanksgiving Day, and December 25.

The Freedom Trail, a line of red paint or painted brick on or in the sidewalk, begins at the **Boston Common Information Center,** 146 Tremont St., on the Common. The center is open Monday through Saturday 8:30am to 5pm, Sunday 9am to 5pm. The **Prudential Information Center,** on the main level of the Prudential Center, is open Monday through Saturday 9am to 8pm, Sunday 11am to 6pm. The **Greater Boston Convention & Visitors Bureau** (☎ **888/SEE-BOSTON** or 617/536-4100) operates both centers, which dispense abundant information, pamphlets, maps, and other materials.

There's a small information booth at **Faneuil Hall Marketplace** between Quincy Market and the South Market Building. It's outdoors and staffed in the spring, summer, and fall Monday through Saturday 10am to 6pm, Sunday noon to 6pm.

In Cambridge, there's an information kiosk (☎ **617/ 497-1630**) in the heart of **Harvard Square,** near the T entrance at the intersection of Massachusetts Avenue, John F. Kennedy Street, and Brattle Street. It's open Monday through Saturday 9am to 5pm, Sunday 1 to 5pm.

PUBLICATIONS   The city's daily newspapers offer the most up-to-date information about events in the area. The "Calendar" section of the Thursday *Boston Globe* (www.boston.com/globe) lists festivals, concerts, dance and theater performances, street fairs, films, and speeches. The Friday *Boston Herald* (www. bostonherald.com) has a similar, smaller insert called "Scene." Both papers briefly list events in their weekend editions. The free weekly *Boston Phoenix* (www.bostonphoenix.com), published on Thursday and available all week, runs extensive entertainment and restaurant listings.

Where, a monthly magazine available free at most hotels throughout the city, lists information about shopping, nightlife, attractions, and current shows at museums and galleries. Newspaper boxes dispense free copies of the *Phoenix;* the weekly *Tab,* which lists neighborhood-specific event information; *Stuff@Night,* a *Phoenix* offshoot with selective listings and extensive arts coverage; and the *Improper Bostonian,* with event and restaurant listings. Available on newsstands, *Boston* magazine is a lifestyle-oriented monthly with cultural and restaurant listings.

CITY LAYOUT

When Boston was established, in 1630, it was one-third the size it is now. Much of the city reflects that original layout, a seemingly haphazard plan that leaves even longtime residents tearing their hair. Old Boston abounds with alleys, dead ends, one-way streets, streets that change names, and streets named after extinct geographical features. On the plus side, every "wrong" turn is a chance to see something interesting you might otherwise have missed.

The landfill projects of the 19th century transformed much of the landscape, altering the shoreline and creating the **Back Bay,** where the streets run parallel. After some frustrating time in the older part of the city, that simple plan will seem ingenious. The streets go in alphabetical order, starting at the Public Garden with Arlington, then Berkeley, Clarendon, Dartmouth, Exeter, Fairfield, Gloucester, and Hereford (and then Massachusetts Avenue).

MAIN ARTERIES & STREETS The most "main" street downtown is **Washington Street.** As a tribute to the first president, streets (except Mass. Ave.) change their names when they cross Washington Street: Bromfield becomes Franklin, Winter becomes Summer, Stuart becomes Kneeland.

The most prominent feature of downtown Boston is **Boston Common.** Its borders are **Park Street,** which is 1 block long (but looms large in the geography of the T), and four important thoroughfares. **Tremont Street** originates at Government Center and runs through the Theater District into the South End and Roxbury. **Beacon Street** branches off Tremont at School Street and curves around, passing the golden dome of the State House at the apex of Beacon Hill and the Public Garden at the foot, and slicing through the Back Bay and Kenmore Square on its way into

Brookline. At the foot of the hill, Beacon crosses **Charles Street,** the fourth side of the Common and the main street of Beacon Hill. Near Massachusetts General Hospital, Charles crosses **Cambridge Street,** which loops around to Government Center and merges with Tremont Street.

Boylston Street is the fifth side of the Common. It runs next to the Public Garden, through Copley Square and the Back Bay, and on into the Fenway. To get there it has to cross **Massachusetts Avenue,** or "Mass. Ave.," as it's almost always called (you might as well get into the habit now).

On the far side of Government Center, I-93 ("the Expressway") separates the North End from the rest of the city. **Hanover Street** is the main street of the North End; at the harbor it intersects with **Commercial Street,** which runs along the waterfront from the North Washington Street bridge (the route to Charlestown, also known as the Charlestown Bridge) until it gives way to **Atlantic Avenue** at Fleet Street. Atlantic Avenue completes the loop around the North End and runs more or less along the waterfront past South Station.

Mass. Ave. is 9 miles long, extending as far as Lexington, and cuts through Arlington and Cambridge before hitting Boston at Storrow Drive, then Beacon Street, Marlborough Street, and Commonwealth Avenue. **"Comm. Ave."** starts at the Public Garden and runs through Kenmore Square, past Boston University, and into the western suburbs. Farther along Mass. Ave., Symphony Hall is at the corner of **Huntington Avenue.** Huntington begins at Copley Square and passes Symphony Hall, Northeastern University, and the Museum of Fine Arts before crossing into Brookline.

FINDING AN ADDRESS   There's no rhyme or reason to the street pattern, compass directions are virtually useless, and there aren't enough street signs. The best way to find an address is to call ahead and ask for directions, including cross streets and landmarks, or leave extra time for wandering around. If the directions involve a T stop, be sure to ask which exit to use—most stations have more than one.

NEIGHBORHOODS IN BRIEF

These are the areas visitors generally frequent. When Bostonians say **"downtown,"** they usually mean the first six neighborhoods defined here; there's no "midtown" or "uptown." The numerous residential areas outside central Boston include the Fenway, South Boston, Dorchester, Roxbury, West Roxbury, and Jamaica Plain. With a couple of exceptions (noted below), Boston is generally safe, but you should still take the precautions you would in any large city, especially at night and when you're out alone.

The Waterfront   This narrow area runs along the Inner Harbor, on Atlantic Avenue and Commercial Street from the North Washington Street bridge to South Station. Once filled with wharves and warehouses, today it abounds with luxury condos, marinas, restaurants, offices, and hotels. Also here are the New England Aquarium and embarkation points for harbor cruises and whale-watching expeditions.

The North End   Between I-93 and the Inner Harbor lies one of the city's oldest neighborhoods. Home to waves of immigrants in the course of its history, it was predominantly Italian for most of the 20th century. It's now less than half Italian-American; newcomers, many of them young professionals who walk to work in the Financial District, dominate in numbers. Nevertheless, you'll hear Italian spoken in the streets and find a wealth of Italian restaurants, *caffès,* and shops. Nearby, and technically part of the North End, is the **North Station** area. With the opening of the FleetCenter in 1995, its nightspots and restaurants really started jumping. But despite the increased traffic, this area isn't a good place to wander around alone at night.

Faneuil Hall Marketplace & Haymarket   Employees aside, Boston residents tend to be scarce at Faneuil Hall Marketplace (also called Quincy Market, after the central building). An irresistible draw for out-of-towners and suburbanites, this cluster of restored market buildings is the city's most popular attraction. It lies between Government Center, State Street, the Waterfront, and the North Station area. Here you'll find restaurants, bars, a food court, specialty shops, and Faneuil Hall itself. **Haymarket,** just off the Central Artery, is home to an open-air produce and fish market on Fridays and Saturdays.

Government Center   Love it or hate it, Government Center introduced modern design into the redbrick facade of traditional Boston architecture. Flanked by Beacon Hill, Downtown Crossing, and Faneuil Hall Marketplace, it is home to state and federal office towers and City Hall.

Financial District   Bounded loosely by State Street, Downtown Crossing, Summer Street, and Atlantic Avenue, the Financial

District is the banking, insurance, and legal center of the city. Outside of some popular after-work spots, it's quiet at night.

Downtown Crossing   The intersection that gives Downtown Crossing its name is at Washington Street where Winter Street becomes Summer Street. The Freedom Trail runs through this shopping and business district between the Common, the Theater District, the Financial District, and Government Center. It hops during the day and slows down in the evening.

Beacon Hill   Narrow tree-lined streets and architectural show-pieces, mostly in Federal style, make up this residential area in the shadow of the State House. Louisburg (say "Lewis-burg") Square and Mount Vernon Street, two of the loveliest and most exclusive spots in Boston, are on Beacon Hill. Bounded by Government Center, Boston Common, and the river, it's also home to Massa-chusetts General Hospital, on the nominally less tony north side of the neighborhood.

Charlestown   One of the oldest areas of Boston is where you'll find the Bunker Hill Monument and USS *Constitution* ("Old Ironsides"), as well as one of the city's best restaurants, Olives. Yuppification has brought some diversity to what was once an almost entirely white residential neighborhood, but pockets remain that have earned their reputation for insularity.

South Boston Waterfront (Seaport District)   The city's new-est neighborhood needs a name—any suggestions? On the other side of the Fort Point Channel from the Waterfront neighbor-hood, it's home to the World Trade Center, Seaport Hotel, Fish Pier, federal courthouse, Museum Wharf, and a lot of construction.

Chinatown   The fourth-largest Chinese community in the country is a small but growing area jammed with Asian restaurants, groceries, and gift shops. As the "Combat Zone," or red-light district, has nearly disappeared under pressure from the business community, Chinatown has expanded to fill the area between Downtown Crossing and the Mass. Pike extension. The tiny **Theater District** extends about 1½ blocks from the intersection of Tremont and Stuart streets in each direction; be careful there at night after the crowds thin out.

South End   Cross Stuart Street or Huntington Avenue heading south and you'll soon find yourself in a landmark district packed with Victorian row houses and little parks. Known for its ethnic, economic, and cultural diversity, the South End has a large gay community and some of the best restaurants in the city. With the gentrification of the 1980s, Tremont Street (particularly the end closest to downtown) gained a cachet it hadn't known for almost a century.

Back Bay Fashionable since its creation out of landfill over a century ago, the Back Bay overflows with gorgeous architecture and chic shops. Its boundaries are the Public Garden, Kenmore Square, the river, and either Huntington Avenue or St. Botolph Street, depending on who's describing it. Students dominate the area near Mass. Ave. but grow scarce as property values rise toward the Public Garden. Commonwealth Avenue is largely residential, Newbury Street largely commercial; both are excellent places to walk around.

Huntington Avenue The honorary "Avenue of the Arts" (or, with a Boston accent, "Otts") is home to a number of landmarks. Not a formal neighborhood, Huntington Avenue is where you'll find the Christian Science Center, Symphony Hall (at the corner of Mass. Ave.), Northeastern University, and the Museum of Fine Arts. It touches on the Back Bay, the Fenway neighborhood, and the Longwood Medical Area before heading southwest into the suburbs. Parts of Huntington can sometimes be a little risky, so if you're leaving the museum at night, stick to the Green Line, a cab, or the car.

Kenmore Square The white-and-red Citgo sign that dominates the skyline above the intersection of Commonwealth Avenue, Beacon Street, and Brookline Avenue tells you you're approaching Kenmore Square. Its shops, bars, restaurants, and clubs attract students from adjacent Boston University. The college-town atmosphere goes out the window when the Red Sox are in town and baseball fans pour into the area on the way to historic Fenway Park, 3 blocks away.

Cambridge Boston's neighbor across the Charles River is a separate city; the areas you're likely to visit are along the Red Line of the T. **Harvard Square** is a magnet for students, sightseers, and well-heeled shoppers. A stroll southeast on Mass. Ave. brings you to **Central Square,** a rapidly gentrifying area dotted with ethnic restaurants and clubs. North along Mass. Ave. is **Porter Square,** a mostly residential neighborhood with some quirky shops like those that once characterized Harvard Square. Around **Kendall Square** you'll find MIT and many technology-oriented businesses.

2 Getting Around

ON FOOT

If you can manage a fair amount of walking, this is the way to go. It offers both a positive and the absence of a negative: Boston is best appreciated at street level, and walking the narrow, picturesque streets takes you past an awful lot of stalled cars.

Even more than in a typical large city, be alert. Look both ways before crossing, even on one-way streets, where many bicyclists and some drivers blithely go against the flow. The "walk" cycle of many downtown traffic signals lasts only 7 seconds, and some drivers apparently consider red lights optional anyway. Keep a close eye on the kids, especially in crosswalks.

BY PUBLIC TRANSPORTATION

The **Massachusetts Bay Transportation Authority,** or MBTA (☎ **617/222-3200;** www.mbta.com), is known as the "T," and its logo is the letter in a circle. It runs subways, trolleys, buses, and ferries in Boston and many suburbs, as well as the commuter rail, which extends as far as Providence, RI.

Newer stations on the Red, Blue, and Orange lines are wheelchair accessible; the Green Line is being converted. Call ahead or check a current system map to see if the stations you need are accessible. All MBTA buses have lifts or kneelers; call ☎ **800/LIFT-BUS** for more information. Some bus routes are wheelchair accessible at all times; you might have to make a reservation as much as a day in advance for others. To learn more, call the **Office for Transportation Access** (☎ **617/222-5438;** TTY 617/222-5854).

BY SUBWAY Subways and trolleys take you around Boston faster than any other mode of transportation except walking. The oldest system in the country, the T dates to 1897, and recent and ongoing improvements have made it generally reliable. The trolleys on the ancient Green Line are the most unpredictable—leave extra time if you're taking it to a vital appointment. The system is generally safe, but always watch out for pickpockets, especially around the holidays. And remember, downtown stops are so close together that it's often faster to walk.

Boston Transit

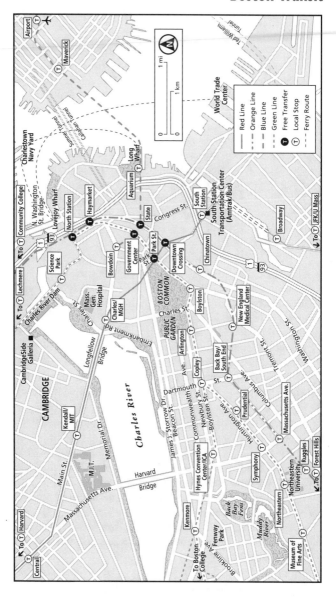

Planning Pointer

The ✪ **MBTA visitor pass** (☎ 877/927-7277 or 617/222-5218; www.mbta.com) is one of the best deals in town. You get unlimited travel on subway lines and local buses, in commuter rail zones 1A and 1B, and on two ferries, plus discounts on attractions. The cost is $6 for 1 day, $11 for 3 consecutive days, $22 for 7 consecutive days. You can order passes in advance over the phone or the Web (there's a fee for shipping), or buy them when you arrive at the Airport T stop, South Station, Back Bay Station, or North Station. They're also for sale at the Government Center and Harvard T stations; the Boston Common, Prudential Center, and Faneuil Hall Marketplace information centers; and some hotels.

The Red, Green, Blue, and Orange lines make up the subway. (The commuter rail to the suburbs is purple on system maps, and sometimes called the Purple Line.) The local fare is **$1**—you'll need a token—and can be as much as $2.50 for some surface extensions on the Green and Red lines. Transfers are free. Route and fare information and timetables are available at Park Street station (under the Common), which is the center of the system.

Service begins at around 5:15am and shuts down around 12:30am. The only exception is New Year's Eve, or First Night, when closing time is 2am and service is free after 8pm.

BY BUS   T buses and "trackless trolleys" (buses with electric antennae) provide service around town and to and around the suburbs. The local routes you're likeliest to need are **no. 1,** along Mass. Ave. from Dudley Square in Roxbury through the Back Bay and Cambridge to Harvard Square; **no. 92** and **no. 93,** which run between Haymarket and Charlestown; and **no. 77,** along Mass. Ave. north of Harvard Square to Porter Square, North Cambridge, and Arlington.

The local bus fare is **75¢;** express bus fares are $1.50 and up. Exact change is required. You can use a token, but you won't get change back.

BY FERRY   Two popular and useful routes (both included in the MBTA visitor pass) run on the Inner Harbor. The first connects **Long Wharf** (near the New England Aquarium), the **Charlestown Navy Yard,** and **Lovejoy Wharf,** off Causeway

Street behind North Station and the FleetCenter. It's a good way to get back downtown from "Old Ironsides" and the Bunker Hill Monument. The other serves **Lovejoy Wharf** and the **World Trade Center,** on Northern Avenue in South Boston near the Fish Pier and the Seaport Hotel. The fare is $1.25. Call ☎ **617/ 227-4321** for more information. Service between **Lovejoy Wharf** and **Russia Wharf,** near South Station, is scheduled to begin in 2001; call the MBTA for details.

BY WATER TAXI   From April to mid-October, there's on-call service in small boats that connect 11 stops on the Inner Harbor, including the airport. The flat fare at press time was $10. Call ☎ **617/422-0392.**

BY TAXI

Taxis are expensive and not always easy to find—seek out a cab stand or call a dispatcher. Cabs licensed in Boston are white; stringent regulations call for acceptable maintenance of both vehicle and driver. Always ask for a receipt in case you lose something and need to call the company.

Cab stands are usually near hotels. There are also busy ones at Faneuil Hall Marketplace (on North Street), South Station, Back Bay Station, and on either side of Mass. Ave. in Harvard Square, near the Coop and Au Bon Pain.

To call ahead for a cab, try the **Independent Taxi Operators Association** (☎ 617/426-8700), **Boston Cab** (☎ 617/ 536-5010), or **Town Taxi** (☎ 617/536-5000). In Cambridge, call **Ambassador Brattle** (☎ 617/492-1100) or **Yellow Cab** (☎ 617/547-3000). Boston Cab will dispatch a wheelchair-accessible vehicle; advance notice is recommended.

The fare structure: The first quarter-mile (when the flag drops) costs $1.50, and each additional eighth of a mile is 25¢. Wait time is extra, and the passenger pays all tolls, as well as the $1.50 airport fee (on trips leaving Logan only). Charging a flat rate is not allowed within the city; the police department publishes a list of distances to the suburbs that establishes the flat rate for those trips. If you want to report a problem or have lost something and can't find your receipt, call the Boston Police Department's **Hackney Hotline** (☎ **617/536-8294**).

BY CAR

You do not need a car to get around Boston and Cambridge. Traffic is wild, particularly in Boston, and parking even worse. If you arrive by car, park at the hotel and use the car for day trips. If you decide to rent a car, see the introduction to chapter 1 for names and numbers of national firms that operate in the area. Pick up the car when you need it, not before, and return it as soon as you're done.

If you must drive into town, you'll need to reach your hotel. Call the day before you arrive and ask the person answering the phone for directions that incorporate traffic patterns *as of that morning.* Especially in downtown Boston, detours can spring up overnight. Don't expect your fellow drivers to cut you any slack, either—even though the truly reckless are a tiny minority, Boston drivers deserve their notoriety. Buckle up, and pay close attention. Look both ways, even on one-way streets.

FAST FACTS: Boston

American Express   The main local office is at 1 State St. (☎ **617/723-8400**), opposite the Old State House. It's open weekdays 8:30am to 5:30pm. The Back Bay office, 222 Berkeley St. (☎ **617/236-1334**), is open weekdays 9am to 5:30pm. The Cambridge office, off Harvard Square at 39 John F. Kennedy St. (☎ **617/868-2600**), is open weekdays from 8:30am to 7:30pm, Saturday 11am to 5:30pm, Sunday noon to 5pm.

Convention Centers   **Hynes Convention Center,** 900 Boylston St. (☎ **617/954-2000** or 617/424-8585 for show info; www.jbhynes.com); **World Trade Center,** 164 Northern Ave. (☎ **800/367-9822** or 617/385-5000, or 617/385-5044 for show info; www.wtcb.com); **Bayside Expo Center,** 200 Mt. Vernon St., Dorchester (☎ **617/474-6000;**www.baysideexpo. com).

Dentists   The desk staff or concierge at your hotel might be able to provide the name of a dentist. The Massachusetts Dental Society (☎ **800/342-8747** or 508/651-7511; www. massdental.org) can point you toward a member.

Doctors   The desk staff or concierge at your hotel should be able to direct you to a doctor. Among the many area hospital referral services are Brigham and Women's Hospital (☎ **800/ 294-9999**) and Massachusetts General Hospital (☎ **800/ 711-4MGH**). The **Boston Evening Medical Center,** 388 Commonwealth Ave. (☎ **617/267-7171**), offers walk-in service, honors most insurance plans, and accepts credit cards.

Area code alert

As of April 2001, eastern Massachusetts has eight area codes (four old codes "overlaid" with four new ones), and every phone number is 10 or 11 digits. Even if you're calling next door, you must dial the area code first. In Boston proper, the area codes are **617** and **857;** in the immediate suburbs, **781** and **339;** to the north and west, **978** and **351;** to the south and east, **508** and **774.**

Emergencies   Call ☎ **911** for fire, ambulance, or the police. This is a free call from pay phones.

Hospitals   Massachusetts General Hospital, 55 Fruit St. (☎ **617/726-2000**), and New England Medical Center, 750 Washington St. (☎ **617/636-5000**), are closest to downtown. At the Harvard Medical Area on the Boston–Brookline border are Beth Israel Deaconess Medical Center, 330 Brookline Ave. (☎ **617/667-7000**); Brigham and Women's Hospital, 75 Francis St. (☎ **617/732-5500**); and Children's Hospital, 300 Longwood Ave. (☎ **617/355-6000**). In Cambridge are Mount Auburn Hospital, 330 Mount Auburn St. (☎ **617/492-3500**), and Cambridge Hospital, 1493 Cambridge St. (☎ **617/498-1000**).

Internet Access   Your hotel may have a terminal for guests' use. The ubiquitous **Kinko's** charges 10¢ to 20¢ a minute. Locations include 2 Center Plaza, Government Center (☎ **617/973-9000**); 10 Post Office Sq., Financial District (☎ **617/482-4400**); 187 Dartmouth St., Back Bay (☎ **617/ 262-6188**); and 1 Mifflin Place, off Mount Auburn Street near Eliot Street, Harvard Square (☎ **617/497-0125**).

Liquor Laws   The legal drinking age is 21. In many bars, particularly near college campuses, you may be asked to show identification if you appear to be under 30 or so. At sporting events, everyone buying alcohol must show ID. Liquor stores and a few supermarkets and convenience stores sell alcohol. Liquor stores (and the liquor sections of other stores) are closed on Sundays, but restaurants and bars may serve alcohol. Most restaurants have full liquor licenses, but some are restricted to beer, wine, and cordials.

Newspapers/Magazines   The *Boston Globe* and *Boston Herald* are published daily. See "Publications" under "Visitor Information," above, for more information.

Pharmacies   Downtown Boston has no 24-hour pharmacy. The CVS/Pharmacy in the Porter Square Shopping Center, off Mass. Ave. in Cambridge (☎ **617/876-5519**), is open 24 hours, 7 days a week. The CVS/Pharmacy at 155–157 Charles St. in Boston (☎ **617/523-1028**), next to the Charles/MGH Red Line stop, is open until midnight. Some emergency rooms can fill your prescription at the hospital's pharmacy.

Police   Call ☎ **911** for emergencies.

Post Office   The main post office at 25 Dorchester Ave. (☎ **617/654-5326**), behind South Station, is open 24 hours, 7 days a week.

Rest Rooms   The visitor center at 15 State St. has a public rest room, as do most tourist attractions, hotels, department stores, and public buildings. The CambridgeSide Galleria, Copley Place, Prudential Center, and Quincy Market shopping areas and most branches of Starbucks have clean rest rooms.

Safety   On the whole, Boston is a safe city for walking. As in any large city, stay out of parks (including the Esplanade) at night unless you're in a crowd. In general, trust your instincts— a dark, deserted street is probably deserted for a reason. Specific areas to avoid at night include Boylston Street between Tremont and Washington streets, and Tremont Street from Stuart to Boylston streets. Try not to walk alone late at night in the Theater District and around North Station. Public transportation in the areas you're likely to visit is busy and safe, but service stops between 12:30 and 1am. At any hour, be alert for pickpockets, especially during the holiday shopping season.

Taxes   The 5% sales tax does not apply to prescription drugs, newspapers, or clothing that costs less than $175. The meal tax, which also applies to takeout food, is 5%. The lodging tax in Boston and Cambridge is 12.45%.

Time Zone   Boston is in the eastern time zone. Daylight saving time begins on the first Sunday in April and ends on the last Sunday in October.

Transit Info   Call ☎ **617/222-3200** for the MBTA (subways, local buses, commuter rail) and ☎ **800/23-LOGAN** for the Massachusetts Port Authority (airport transportation).

Weather   Call ☎ **617/936-1234.**

3

Accommodations

*B*oston has one of the busiest hotel markets in the country, with some of the highest prices. Rooms are in short supply, occupancy rates are soaring, and renovations and new construction are going on all over the area. Almost every large property in town has undergone a significant refurbishment or renovation in the past 5 years. That doesn't mean you need to pay through the nose for comfort or stay in a windowless cell for affordability, but you do need to do some planning.

As you go through this chapter, keep Boston's relatively small size in mind, and check a map before you rule out a particular location. The listings in this chapter match the neighborhood descriptions in chapter 2, "Getting to Know Boston"; especially downtown, the areas are so small and close together that the borders are somewhat arbitrary. The division to consider is **downtown vs. the Back Bay vs. Cambridge,** and not, say, the Waterfront vs. the Financial District.

With enough notice and flexibility, you probably won't have much difficulty finding a suitable place to stay in or near the city, but it's always a good idea to make a reservation. Book ahead between April and November, when spring conventions, college graduations, summer vacation, foliage season, and fall conventions follow one after the other and overlap.

A **reservation service** can often be helpful if you're having trouble finding a room. These outfits usually work as consolidators, buying up or reserving rooms in bulk and dealing them out to customers at a profit. While these services do offer deals that range from 10% to 50% off, remember, the discounts apply to rack rates. You're probably better off dealing directly with a hotel, but if you don't like bargaining, this is certainly a viable option. Most offer online reservations, and as long as you're surfing around, it's worth checking more than one—prices can vary widely. Here are a few reputable providers: Citywide Reservation Services (☎ **800-HOTEL-93;** www.cityres.com);

Hotel Conxions (☎ **800-522-9991**; www.hotelconxions. com); Accommodations Express (☎ **800-906-4685**; www. accommodationsxpress.com); and hoteldiscount!com, also known as Hotel Reservations Network (☎ **800-964-6835**; www.180096hotel.com).

Online, try booking your hotel through **Arthur Frommer's Budget Travel** (www.frommers.com) and save up to 50% on the cost of your room. **Microsoft Expedia** (www.expedia.com) features a "Travel Agent" that can also direct you to affordable lodgings.

The **Hotel Hot Line** (☎ **800/777-6001**), a service of the **Greater Boston Convention and Visitors Bureau,** can help make reservations even during the busiest times. It's staffed weekdays until 8pm, weekends until 4pm.

The listings below give **rack rates**—the maximum price a hotel charges for a room—for a double room. Before you call the whole thing off, remember that hardly anybody pays those prices, and there are many ways around them. If you can land a weekend deal (easier than you might think at downtown business hotels), travel during a slow time (especially January through March), or just coax a reservations agent into telling you about a lower rate, you can cut your costs considerably. The rates given here do not include the **5.7% state hotel tax.** In Boston and Cambridge there's a **2.75% convention center tax** on top of the **4% city tax,** making the **total tax 12.45%.** Not all suburbs have a local tax, so some towns charge only the 5.7% state tax.

BED-AND-BREAKFASTS If a big hotel isn't for you, financially or philosophically, a **bed-and-breakfast** can be a good option. Reserve as soon as you start planning your trip, especially if you'll be visiting during foliage season. Expect to pay at least $65 a night for a double in the summer and fall, and more during special events. The room rate usually includes breakfast. Many lodgings require a minimum stay of at least 2 nights, and most offer winter specials—discounts or third-night-free deals.

The following organizations can help match you with a suitable B&B in Boston, Cambridge, or the Greater Boston area: **Bed and Breakfast Agency of Boston** (☎ **800/248-9262** or 617/ 720-3540; from the U.K., 0800/89-5128; fax 617/523-5761; www.boston-bnbagency.com); **Bed and Breakfast Associates Bay Colony Ltd.** (☎ **888/486-6018** or 781/449-5302; fax 781/ 449-5958; www.bnbboston.com); **Bed & Breakfast Reservations**

Where There's Smoke . . .

Accommodations reserved for nonsmokers—often in blocks as large as several floors—are so common that we no longer single out hotels that offer them. However, nonsmokers should not assume that they'll get a smoke-free room without specifically requesting one. As hotels squeeze smokers into fewer and fewer rooms, the ones they are allowed to use become saturated with the smell of smoke, even in lodgings that are otherwise antiseptic. To avoid this disagreeable situation, be sure that everyone who handles your reservation knows you need a smoke-free room.

North Shore/Greater Boston/Cape Cod (☎ 800/832-2632 outside Massachusetts, 978/281-9505, or 617/964-1606; fax 978/281-9426; www.bbreserve.com); **Host Homes of Boston** (☎ 800/600-1308 or 617/244-1308; fax 617/244-5156); or **New England Bed and Breakfast** (☎ 617/244-2112).

1 Downtown

THE WATERFRONT & FANEUIL HALL MARKETPLACE

At all hotels in these neighborhoods, **ask for a room on a high floor**—you'll want to be as far as possible from the noise and disarray of the Big Dig.

VERY EXPENSIVE

✪ **Boston Harbor Hotel.** 70 Rowes Wharf (entrance on Atlantic Ave.), Boston, MA 02110. ☎ **800/752-7077** or 617/439-7000. Fax 617/330-9450. www.bhh.com. 230 units. A/C MINIBAR TV TEL. $255–$510 double; from $365 suite. Extra person $50. Children under 18 free in parents' room. Weekend packages available. AE, CB, DC, DISC, MC, V. Valet parking $28 weekdays, $20 weekends; self-parking $24 weekdays, $15 weekends. T: Red Line to South Station (or Blue Line to Aquarium if it's open). Pets accepted.

The Boston Harbor Hotel is one of the finest in town, and certainly the prettiest, whether you approach its landmark arch from land or sea (the Airport Water Shuttle stops here). The 16-story brick building is within walking distance of downtown and the waterfront attractions, and it prides itself on offering top-notch service to travelers pursuing both business and pleasure.

The plush guest rooms, which were renovated in 1998 and 1999, look out on the harbor or the skyline (rooms with city views are less expensive). Each unit is a luxurious bedroom–living

Boston Accommodations

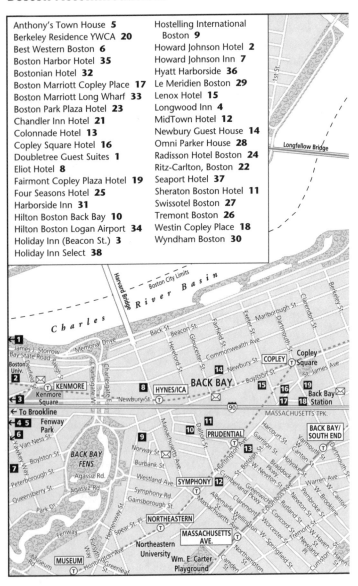

Anthony's Town House **5**
Berkeley Residence YWCA **20**
Best Western Boston **6**
Boston Harbor Hotel **35**
Bostonian Hotel **32**
Boston Marriott Copley Place **17**
Boston Marriott Long Wharf **33**
Boston Park Plaza Hotel **23**
Chandler Inn Hotel **21**
Colonnade Hotel **13**
Copley Square Hotel **16**
Doubletree Guest Suites **1**
Eliot Hotel **8**
Fairmont Copley Plaza Hotel **19**
Four Seasons Hotel **25**
Harborside Inn **31**
Hilton Boston Back Bay **10**
Hilton Boston Logan Airport **34**
Holiday Inn (Beacon St.) **3**
Holiday Inn Select **38**

Hostelling International
   Boston **9**
Howard Johnson Hotel **2**
Howard Johnson Inn **7**
Hyatt Harborside **36**
Le Meridien Boston **29**
Lenox Hotel **15**
Longwood Inn **4**
MidTown Hotel **12**
Newbury Guest House **14**
Omni Parker House **28**
Radisson Hotel Boston **24**
Ritz-Carlton, Boston **22**
Seaport Hotel **37**
Sheraton Boston Hotel **11**
Swissotel Boston **27**
Tremont Boston **26**
Westin Copley Place **18**
Wyndham Boston **30**

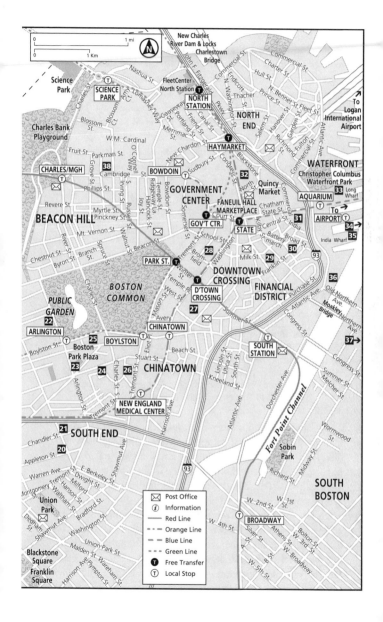

room combination, with mahogany furnishings that include an armoire, a desk, and comfortable chairs. Standard guest-room features include three telephones, data ports, hair dryers, robes, slippers, umbrellas, and windows that open. Some suites have private terraces. A museum-quality collection of paintings, drawings, prints, and nautical charts enhances the grand public spaces.

Dining/Diversions: The excellent **Rowes Wharf Restaurant** overlooks the harbor, as does **Intrigue,** the ground-floor cafe. The latter opens at 5:30am for breakfast (take-out or sit-down); serves lunch, dinner, and afternoon tea; and has seasonal outdoor seating. The **Rowes Wharf Bar** serves cocktails and light fare.

Amenities: Health club and spa with 60-foot lap pool; whirlpool; sauna, steam, and exercise rooms; salon for facials, massage, manicures, pedicures, and spa treatments. State-of-the-art business center with professional staff; conference rooms; concierge; 24-hour room service; dry cleaning and laundry; video rentals; newspaper delivery; in-room massage; twice-daily maid service; baby-sitting available; express checkout; valet parking; courtesy car; complimentary shoeshine. Rooms for travelers with disabilities are available.

✪ **Bostonian Hotel.** At Faneuil Hall Marketplace, 40 North St., Boston, MA 02109. ☎ **800/343-0922** or 617/523-3600. Fax 617/523-2454. www. millennium-hotels.com. 201 units. A/C MINIBAR TV TEL. $245–$420 double; $265–$450 deluxe double; $500–$775 suite. Extra person $20. Children under 18 free in parents' room. Weekend and other packages available. AE, DC, DISC, JCB, MC, V. Parking $30. T: Green or Blue Line to Government Center, or Orange Line to State.

The relatively small Bostonian offers excellent service and features that make it competitive with larger hotels. Although it doesn't offer wall-to-wall business features, its boutique feel makes it popular with travelers who want a break from more convention-oriented rivals. The recently redecorated, traditionally appointed guest rooms vary in size. All boast top-of-the-line furnishings and amenities, including on-command video, safes, terry robes, irons and ironing boards, and two-line phones with data ports. The bathrooms have hair dryers, heat lamps, and both overhead and European-style handheld shower sprays. Half of the units have French doors that open onto small private balconies, and some suites have working fireplaces or Jacuzzis.

Three brick 19th-century buildings make up the hotel; the 38 units in the new wing, added in 1999, include a suite and four rooms on the glass-enclosed top floor. Soundproofing throughout the hotel means you can watch the scene at Faneuil Hall Marketplace or Haymarket (or the Big Dig, from some rooms) without hearing all the noise.

Dining/Diversions: On the fourth-floor rooftop is the glass-enclosed **Seasons** restaurant. The **Atrium** lounge in the glass-walled lobby affords a great view of the scene at the marketplace.

Amenities: 24-hour room service, conference rooms, concierge, dry cleaning and laundry, newspaper delivery, in-room massage, twice-daily maid service, secretarial services available, express checkout, valet parking, complimentary morning limousine service. Complimentary health-club and swimming-pool privileges at the excellent Sky Club, 4 blocks away; small fitness room; in-room exercise equipment delivery on request. Rooms for travelers with disabilities; rooms with special amenities for female travelers.

Boston Marriott Long Wharf. 296 State St., Boston, MA 02109. ☎ **800/ 228-9290** or 617/227-0800. Fax 617/227-2867. www.marriott.com/marriott/ BOSLW. 400 units. A/C TV TEL. Apr–Nov $285–$375 double, Dec–Mar $199– $285 double; $450–$490 suite year-round. Weekend packages from $155 per night. AE, DC, DISC, JCB, MC, V. Parking $30. T: Blue or Orange Line to State (or Blue Line to Aquarium if it's open).

The terraced brick exterior of this seven-story hotel looks nothing like the ocean liner it supposedly resembles, but it is one of the most recognizable sights on the harbor. The chief appeal of this otherwise ordinary Marriott is its location, a stone's throw from the New England Aquarium, convenient to downtown and waterfront attractions, and just two subway stops from the airport.

Rooms are large and decor varies; each has either one king-size or two double beds, two phones, a coffeemaker, a hair dryer, and a table and chairs in front of the window. The Big Dig construction is directly under the windows of the rooms near the street. Ask to be as close to the water as possible, and you'll have good views of the wharves and waterfront without all the noise. The seventh floor is the Concierge Level, with complimentary continental breakfast, cocktails, and hors d'oeuvres served in a private lounge, and private exercise facilities.

Dining/Diversions: Oceana Restaurant, with a 180-degree expanse of glass wall fronting the harbor; cafe and lounge; bar and grill.

Amenities: Indoor pool with outdoor terrace, exercise room, whirlpools, saunas, game room. Business center, conference rooms, concierge, room service (until 2am), dry cleaning and laundry, newspaper delivery, twice-daily maid service, express checkout, valet parking, baby-sitting available.

MODERATE

✪ **Harborside Inn.** 185 State St. (between I-93 and the Custom House Tower), Boston, MA 02109. ☎ **617/723-7500.** Fax 617/670-2010. www. hagopianhotels.com. 54 units. A/C TV TEL. $170–$210 double; $210–$295 suite. Extra person $15. Rates include continental breakfast. Rates may be higher during special events. AE, DC, DISC, MC, V. Parking $24–$30 at nearby public garages. T: Blue or Orange Line to State (or Blue Line to Aquarium if it's open).

Under the same management as the Newbury Guest House in the Back Bay, the Harborside Inn offers a similar combination of value and location. The renovated 1858 warehouse is across the street from Faneuil Hall Marketplace and the harbor, a short walk from the Financial District, and near ground zero of the Big Dig. The nicely appointed guest rooms have queen-size beds, hair dryers, hardwood floors, Oriental rugs, and Victorian-style furniture. They surround a sky-lit atrium; those with city views are more expensive but noisier. Interior rooms have windows that open only to the atrium. Rooms on the top floors of the eight-story building have lower ceilings but better views. The hotel has some features you'd expect at pricier lodgings, including room service (until 10pm), free local phone calls, and voice mail. The hotel is wheelchair accessible, and accessories for hearing-impaired guests are available. On the ground floor are a small exercise room and the Mermaid Restaurant, which serves lunch and dinner.

FINANCIAL DISTRICT & DOWNTOWN CROSSING

Besides being great for corporate travelers, the hotels in this area can be even more convenient than those nearer the water—they're that much closer to the major shopping areas and the start of the Freedom Trail. Especially in the winter, all offer sensational weekend packages.

VERY EXPENSIVE

✪ **Le Meridien Boston.** 250 Franklin St. (at Post Office Sq.), Boston, MA 02110. ☎ **800/543-4300** or 617/451-1900. Fax 617/423-2844. www. lemeridienboston.com. 326 units. A/C MINIBAR TV TEL. $295–$415 double; $475–$1,330 suite. Extra person $30. Weekend rates from $209. AE, CB, DC,

DISC, MC, V. Valet parking $29, $13 Fri–Sat; self-parking $28, $8 Fri–Sat. T: Red Line to Downtown Crossing or South Station, or Blue or Orange Line to State. Small pets accepted.

This is the city's premier business hotel. If you don't need to leave the Financial District, you might not even need to leave the premises—ask for a Business Traveler room (with a fax machine, oversized desk, coffeemaker, and halogen lighting) and arrange a power lunch in the elegant Julien restaurant. Vacationing visitors are near the waterfront and downtown attractions but not all that close to public transportation. Whatever your purpose, you'll find the service by the multilingual staff superb.

Guest rooms have 153 configurations, including loft suites with two bathrooms. All rooms have two telephones (one in the bathroom) and hair dryers. The glass mansard roof surrounds the top three stories, where a number of rooms have large sloped windows and extraordinary views. The imposing nine-story building, designed by R. Clipston Sturgis in 1922 in the style of a 16th-century Roman palace, originally housed the Federal Reserve Bank. The bank's original grand marble staircase now leads to the dining areas, and two murals by N. C. Wyeth grace the walls of the bar.

Dining/Diversions: **Julien** serves lunch and dinner; the bar features live piano music 6 nights a week. The less formal **Café Fleuri** serves three meals daily, the Saturday "Chocolate Bar Buffet" (September through May), and Sunday jazz brunch. **La Terrasse** is the seasonal outdoor cafe.

Amenities: 40-foot indoor pool, well-equipped health club with whirlpool and sauna, staffed business center with library, conference rooms, concierge, 24-hour room service, dry cleaning and laundry, newspaper delivery, twice-daily maid service, express checkout, valet parking, weekend courtesy car to Newbury Street, daily weather report. Two rooms on each floor for travelers with disabilities.

Swissôtel Boston. 1 Avenue de Lafayette, Boston, MA 02111. ☎ **888/ 73-SWISS** or 617/451-2600. Fax 617/451-0054. www.swissotel.com. 501 units. A/C MINIBAR TV TEL. $329–$379 double; $399–$449 deluxe double; $499–$699 suite or Swiss Butler Executive Level; $2,500 Presidential Suite. Extra person $25. Children under 12 free in parents' room. Weekend packages from $139 per night. AE, CB, DC, DISC, JCB, MC, V. Valet parking $30; self-parking $26. T: Red Line to Downtown Crossing, or Green Line to Boylston. If you're driving, call for directions to avoid construction traffic. Small pets accepted.

This centrally located 22-story hotel lives two lives. It's a busy convention and business destination during the week, and the excellent weekend packages make it popular with sightseers. The plain exterior contrasts with the luxurious second-floor lobby, where elegant European style takes over. Guest rooms cluster around four atriums with semiprivate lobbies, creating the effect of several small hotels in one. Rooms have sitting areas with a desk and settee, and king or European twin beds. All rooms have three telephones with data ports, fax machines, and coffeemakers. On the Executive Level, a Swiss butler performs traditional valet functions, acts as a private concierge, and even runs errands.

Dining/Diversions: Café Suisse serves three meals daily and Sunday brunch. The lounge in the atrium offers cocktails, vintage wines by the glass, and light meals.

Amenities: 52-foot indoor pool, health club, exercise room, saunas, sun terrace, high-tech business center, conference rooms, 24-hour room service, dry cleaning, valet service, nightly turndown.

Wyndham Boston. 89 Broad St., Boston, MA 02110. ☎ **800/WYNDHAM** or 617/556-0006. Fax 617/556-0053. www.wyndham.com. 362 units. A/C MINIBAR TV TEL. $295–$535 double; $335–$560 suite. Children under 13 free in parents' room. Weekend, holiday, and other packages available. AE, CB, DC, DISC, JCB, MC, V. Valet parking $30 weekdays, $16 weekends. T: Blue or Orange Line to State, or Red Line to South Station.

Boston's newest luxury hotel is contemporary yet conservative—21st-century technology in an art deco package. The meticulously designed hotel (a complete rehab of the 1928 Batterymarch Building) opened in 1999. The 14-story building is near Faneuil Hall Marketplace and the Waterfront, but not all that close (by downtown standards) to the T. The spacious guest rooms have 9½-foot ceilings, high-speed Internet access, triple-glazed windows that open, individual climate control, hair dryers, coffeemakers, terry robes, umbrellas, irons, and ironing boards. Units on the upper floors have great views of the harbor and downtown, and soundproofing throughout makes the whole building—even the halls—exceptionally quiet. The Wyndham's closest competitor (literally and figuratively) is Le Meridien, which is less convenient to public transit but has a swimming pool.

Dining: Caliterra Bar & Grille serves California- and Italian-inspired cuisine at breakfast, lunch, and dinner.

Amenities: Concierge, 24-hour room service, business center (staffed 7am to 7pm), 24-hour fitness center, saunas; state-of-the-art conference rooms, dry cleaning and laundry, weekday newspaper delivery, baby-sitting, valet parking. Rooms with special amenities for female travelers and travelers with disabilities.

EXPENSIVE

✪ **Omni Parker House.** 60 School St., Boston, MA 02108. ☎ **800/ THE-OMNI** or 617/227-8600. Fax 617/742-5729. www.omnihotels.com. 552 units (some with shower only). A/C MINIBAR TV TEL. $189–$295 double; $249–$375 superior double; $279–$435 1-bedroom suite. Children under 18 free in parents' room. Weekend packages available. AE, CB, DC, DISC, MC, V. Valet parking $27; self-parking $20. T: Green or Blue Line to Government Center, or Red Line to Park St.

The Parker House offers a great combination of nearly 150 years of history and extensive renovations. It has operated continuously longer than any other hotel in America—since 1855—and a massive overhaul completed in 1998 upgraded it throughout and added a business center and an exercise facility. Guest rooms have two-line phones, modem hookups, hair dryers, and irons and ironing boards. They're not huge, but they are thoughtfully laid out and nicely appointed; many have views of Old City Hall or Government Center. The pattern on the bedspreads—so gaudy that it's elegant—is a reproduction of the original, and the lobby of the 14-story hotel boasts its original American oak paneling.

Dining/Diversions: **Parker's Restaurant** serves three meals daily. There are two bars: **The Last Hurrah,** off the lobby, is a hopping after-work destination; **Parker's Bar** has live piano music Monday through Saturday nights.

Amenities: Health club, staffed business center, conference rooms, concierge, 24-hour room service, dry cleaning and laundry, newspaper delivery, in-room massage, express checkout, valet parking. Rooms for travelers with disabilities are available.

2 Beacon Hill

EXPENSIVE

Holiday Inn Select Boston Government Center. 5 Blossom St., Boston, MA 02114. ☎ **800/HOLIDAY** or 617/742-7630. Fax 617/742-4192. www. bristolhotels.com. 303 units. A/C TV TEL. From $200 double. Extra person $20. Rollaway $20. Children under 18 free in parents' room. Weekend and corporate packages and 10% AARP discount available. AE, DC, DISC, JCB, MC, V. Parking $25. T: Red Line to Charles/MGH.

At the base of Beacon Hill, near Massachusetts General Hospital, this utilitarian hotel rises 15 stories above a retail plaza with a supermarket, shops, and restaurants. It's scheduled for renovations, so be sure to ask for a room that's away from the work area. This location was one of the chain's leaders in its battle for the business traveler—rooms, which are furnished in contemporary style, have fax machines, data ports, coffeemakers, hair dryers, and irons and ironing boards. Each unit has a picture-window view of the city or the State House (or the parking lot—ask to be as high up as possible). Executive rooms, on the 12th and 14th floors, have two phones, terry robes, turndown service, and minifridges; rates there include continental breakfast and access to a private lounge.

Dining: Foster's Bar & Grille serves three meals daily.

Amenities: Outdoor heated pool, small exercise room, sundeck, business center, conference rooms, coin laundry, concierge, room service until 11pm, dry cleaning and laundry, newspaper delivery, express checkout, currency exchange. Rooms for travelers with disabilities are available.

3 South Boston Waterfront (Seaport District)

VERY EXPENSIVE

Seaport Hotel. At the World Trade Center, 1 Seaport Lane, Boston, MA 02210. ☎ **877/SEAPORT** or 617/385-4000. Fax 617/385-5090. www.seaporthotel. com. 426 units. A/C MINIBAR TV TEL. $299 double; $329 concierge level; $349–$1,700 suite. Service charge $3 per room per night. Children under 17 free in parents' room. Weekend packages available. AE, CB, DC, DISC, JCB, MC, V. Valet parking $24; self-parking $20. T: Red Line to South Station, then take free shuttle bus (or walk 20 min.). Pets under 50 lbs. accepted.

The independent Seaport Hotel rises out of the Big Dig like the Emerald City, and it has an air of fantasy about it. The hotel was built with every feature the pampered, techno-savvy business traveler might dream of. It's across Northern Avenue from the World Trade Center, about the same distance from the airport as from the Financial District (10 minutes by cab), but a long walk from the subway.

The decent-sized rooms are exceptionally well appointed. They have high-speed Internet access, Logan Airport flight information (and Nintendo) on the TV, oversized towels, hair dryers, coffeemakers, individual climate control, safes, and three phones, including a speakerphone with Caller ID. Rooms have excellent views of the city or harbor, especially from the higher floors. T-1 lines throughout the building, shuttle service to downtown, and great weekend packages—among other appealing features—make it no surprise that the hotel has been busy since it opened in 1998.

Dining/Diversions: The lobby restaurant, **Aura** (☎ **617/ 385-4300**), serves three meals a day and Sunday brunch, often to nonguests drawn by chef Ed Doyle's growing reputation. There's a lounge and also a cafe that serves quick meals and snacks to eat in or take out.

Amenities: 24-hour business center with professional staff (7am to 8pm) and meeting space; conference rooms, 24-hour room service; concierge; excellent health club with 50-foot indoor pool, sauna, spa treatments; dry cleaning and laundry; newspaper delivery; twice-daily maid service; baby-sitting available; express check-in and checkout; valet parking; gift shop; florist; shuttle to downtown.

4 Chinatown/Theater District

EXPENSIVE

Radisson Hotel Boston. 200 Stuart St. (at Charles St. S.), Boston, MA 02116. ☎ 800/333-3333 or 617/482-1800. Fax 617/451-2750. www.radisson.com. 356 units. A/C TV TEL. $160–$359 double. Extra person $20. Cot $20. Cribs free. Children under 18 free in parents' room. Weekend, theater, and other packages available. AE, DC, DISC, JCB, MC, V. Parking $19. T: Green Line to Boylston, or Orange Line to New England Medical Center.

A top-to-bottom renovation completed in 1997 left the centrally located Radisson in great shape. The 24-story hotel was already quite agreeable, and a recent push to attract business travelers has made it even more so. The tastefully decorated guest rooms are among the largest in the city. Each has a private balcony (with great views from the higher floors), sitting area, king or two queen-size beds, hair dryer, coffeemaker, iron and ironing board, and two phones. Business-traveler rooms on the top four floors come with upgraded amenities and access to a private lounge.

Dining/Diversions: The 57 Steakhouse is a traditional à la carte restaurant; the **Theatre Café** is more casual. The **Stuart Street Playhouse** is an intimate venue that often books one-person shows.

Amenities: Heated indoor pool with sundeck and exercise room, staffed business center, conference rooms, concierge, room service until 11pm, dry cleaning and laundry, newspaper delivery, express checkout, valet parking.

The Tremont Boston. 275 Tremont St., Boston, MA 02116. ☎ **800/331-9998** or 617/426-1400. Fax 617/482-6730. www.wyndham.com. 322 units (most with shower only). A/C TV TEL. $159–$412 double; $399–$599 suite. Extra person $20. Children under 17 free in parents' room. Weekend packages and 10% AAA discount available. AE, DC, DISC, MC, V. Valet parking $24; self-parking $15 in nearby garage. T: Orange Line to New England Medical Center or Green Line to Boylston.

This hotel, a Wyndham Grand Heritage property, is as close to Boston's theaters as you can be without actually attending a show. It's also convenient to downtown and the Back Bay. The neighborhood is improving, and a recently completed $15 million renovation expanded some units and spruced up all of them. An overhaul of the public areas, which will gain a fitness facility and business center, was scheduled at press time. The good-size guest rooms have modern furnishings, coffeemakers, and hair dryers. The 15-story brick building captures the style that prevailed when the hotel was built in 1924. The original gold-leaf decorations and crafted ceilings in the huge lobby and ballrooms have been restored and the original marble walls and columns refurbished.

Dining/Diversions: Caprice restaurant serves food until 1am (for the post-theater crowd); the **Roxy** nightclub features dancing, live music, and occasional concerts.

Amenities: Conference rooms, secretarial services, dry cleaning and laundry, newspaper delivery, concierge, room service until 10pm, express checkout, valet parking. Rooms for travelers with disabilities are available.

5 The South End

Berkeley Street runs from the Back Bay across the Mass. Pike to the most convenient corner of the sprawling South End, where you'll find these two lodgings.

MODERATE

Chandler Inn Hotel. 26 Chandler St. (at Berkeley St.), Boston, MA 02116. ☎ **800/842-3450** or 617/482-3450. Fax 617/542-3428. www.chandlerinn. com. 56 units. A/C TV TEL. Apr–Dec $145–$155 double; Jan–Mar $125–$135 double. Rates include continental breakfast. Children under 12 free in parents' room. AE, CB, DC, DISC, MC, V. No parking available. T: Orange Line to Back Bay.

The Chandler Inn underwent a transformation in early 2000, with the completion of $1 million in renovations. Even with the

---

Planning Pointer

If your trip involves a cultural event—a big show at a museum, a performance of *The Nutcracker*—seek out a hotel package that includes tickets. Usually offered on weekends, these deals always save time and often save money.

---

accompanying price hike, the comfortable, unpretentious hotel is an excellent deal. The guest rooms, revamped from the walls out, have individual climate control and tasteful contemporary-style furniture, including desks, small wardrobes, and TV armoires. Each holds either a queen or double bed or two twin beds, without enough room to squeeze in a cot. Bathrooms are tiny but contain hair dryers. The one elevator in the eight-story inn can be slow. But the staff is friendly and helpful, and the Back Bay is 2 blocks away. This is a gay-friendly hotel—Fritz, the bar next to the lobby, is a neighborhood hangout—that often books up early. Plan ahead.

INEXPENSIVE

Berkeley Residence YWCA. 40 Berkeley St., Boston, MA 02116. ☎ **617/ 482-8850.** Fax 617/482-9692. www.ywcaboston.org. 200 units (none with bathroom). $60 single; $100 double; $120 triple. Rates include breakfast. Long-term rates available (5-week minimum). JCB, MC, V. Parking $16 in public lot 1 block away. T: Orange Line to Back Bay or Green Line to Arlington.

This pleasant, convenient hotel/residence for women offers a dining room, a patio garden, pianos, a library, and laundry facilities. The guest rooms are basic, containing little more than beds, but are well maintained and comfortable—definitely not luxurious, but not cells either. That description might not seem to justify the prices, but check around a little before you turn up your nose. The public areas were renovated in 1997. Guests have access to the pool and exercise room at the YWCA 3 blocks away.

6 Back Bay

BOSTON COMMON/PUBLIC GARDEN
VERY EXPENSIVE

The Ritz-Carlton, Boston, 15 Arlington St. (☎ **800/241-3333** or 617/536-5700; www.ritzcarlton.com), will close in mid-2001 for an 8-month overhaul. During the shutdown, the chain will direct prospective patrons to the nearby Ritz-Carlton Hotel & Towers, which was under construction at press time.

✪ **Four Seasons Hotel.** 200 Boylston St., Boston, MA 02116. ☎ **800/ 332-3442** or 617/338-4400. Fax 617/423-0154. www.fourseasons.com. 288 units. A/C MINIBAR TV TEL. $465–$695 double; $1,950 1-bedroom suite; $2,300 2-bedroom suite. Weekend packages available. AE, CB, DC, DISC, JCB, MC, V. Valet parking $27. T: Green Line to Arlington. Pets accepted.

Many hotels offer exquisite service, a beautiful location, elegant guest rooms and public areas, a terrific health club, and wonderful restaurants. No other hotel in Boston—indeed, in New England—combines every element of a luxury hotel as seamlessly as the Four Seasons. If I were traveling with someone else's credit cards, I'd head straight here.

Overlooking the Public Garden, the 16-story brick-and-glass building (the hotel occupies eight stories) incorporates the traditional and the contemporary. Each spacious room is elegantly appointed and has a striking view. All rooms have bay windows that open, climate control, three two-line phones with computer and fax capability, hair dryers, terry robes, and a safe. Children receive bedtime snacks and toys, and can ask at the concierge desk for duck food to take to the Public Garden. Small pets even enjoy a special menu and amenities. Larger accommodations range from Executive Suites, with enlarged alcove areas for meetings or entertaining, to luxurious one-, two-, and three-bedroom deluxe suites.

Dining/Diversions: Aujourd'hui, one of Boston's best restaurants, serves contemporary American cuisine. The **Bristol Lounge** is open for lunch, afternoon tea, dinner, and Sunday breakfast, and features live entertainment nightly.

Amenities: In general, if you want it, you'll get it. VCRs; free video rentals; indoor heated 51-foot pool and whirlpool with a view of the Public Garden; excellent spa with fitness equipment, private masseuse, Jacuzzi, and sauna (residents of the condominiums on the upper floors of the hotel share the pool and spa); excellent business center; conference rooms; concierge; 24-hour room service; dry cleaning and laundry; newspaper delivery; in-room massage; twice-daily maid service; baby-sitting available; express checkout; valet parking; complimentary shoeshine; complimentary limousine service to downtown Boston addresses. Rooms for travelers with disabilities are available.

EXPENSIVE

Boston Park Plaza Hotel. 64 Arlington St., Boston, MA 02116. ☎ **800/
225-2008** or 617/426-2000. Fax 617/423-1708. www.bostonparkplaza.com.
960 units (some with shower only). A/C TV TEL. $175–$265 double;
$375–$2,000 suite. Extra person $20. Children under 18 free in parents' room.
Senior discount and weekend and family packages available. AE, CB, DC, DISC,
MC, V. Valet parking $23; self-parking $19. T: Green Line to Arlington.

A Boston mainstay—it was built as the Statler Hilton in 1927—
the Park Plaza Hotel does a hopping convention and function
business. It's the antithesis of generic, with an old-fashioned
atmosphere and a cavernous, ornate lobby, yet it offers the full
range of modern comforts. Room size and decor vary greatly, and
some rooms are quite small. All have hair dryers, and many have
two phones and a coffeemaker. The lobby of the 15-story hotel
is a little commercial hub, with a travel agency, a currency
exchange, Amtrak and airline ticket offices, and a pharmacy.

Dining/Diversions: On the ground floor are two restaurants,
Finale and the **Arlington Street Grille,** and two lounges, **Swans
Court** and the cozy **Captain's Bar.**

Amenities: Health club, business center, conference rooms,
beauty salon, concierge, room service until 11pm, dry cleaning
and laundry, express checkout, valet parking.

COPLEY SQUARE/HYNES CONVENTION CENTER
VERY EXPENSIVE

The Colonnade Hotel. 120 Huntington Ave., Boston, MA 02116. ☎ **800/
962-3030** or 617/424-7000. Fax 617/424-1717. www.colonnadehotel.com.
285 units. A/C MINIBAR TV TEL. $315–$395 double; $450–$1,400 suite.
Children under 12 free in parents' room. Weekend packages available. AE, CB,
DC, DISC, MC, V. Parking $24. T: Green Line E to Prudential. Pets accepted.

The swimming pool and "rooftop resort" are probably this hotel's
best-known features, with excellent service a close runner-up.
Adjacent to Copley Place and the Prudential Center, the
independently owned Colonnade is a slice of Europe in the
all-American shopping mecca of the Back Bay. You might hear
a dozen languages spoken by the guests and employees of the
11-story concrete-and-glass hotel, whose friendly, professional
staff is known for personalized service.

The elegance of the quiet, high-ceilinged public spaces carries
over to the large guest rooms, which have contemporary oak
or mahogany furnishings, marble bathrooms, two phones (one
in the bathroom), robes, on-demand movies, hair dryers, and

windows that open. Suites have dining rooms and sitting areas, and the "author's suite" contains autographed copies of the work of celebrated (or at least published) literary guests.

Dining: The authentically sassy waitstaff at **Brasserie Jo** serves French-Alsatian cuisine until 1am.

Amenities: Seasonal "rooftop resort" with heated outdoor pool and sundeck, well-equipped fitness center, business center, conference rooms, concierge, 24-hour room service, dry cleaning and laundry, newspaper delivery, children's programs, baby-sitting available, express checkout, car-rental desk, currency exchange. Rooms for travelers with disabilities are available.

✪ **Eliot Hotel.** 370 Commonwealth Ave. (at Mass. Ave.), Boston, MA 02215. ☎ **800/44-ELIOT** or 617/267-1607. Fax 617/536-9114. www.eliothotel.com. 95 units. A/C MINIBAR TV TEL. $315–$415 1-bedroom suite for 2; $570–$740 2-bedroom suite. Extra person $20. Children under 18 free in parents' room. AE, DC, MC, V. Valet parking $24. T: Green Line B, C, or D to Hynes/ICA. Small pets accepted.

This exquisite hotel combines the flavor of Yankee Boston with European-style service and amenities. It feels more like a classy apartment building than a hotel, with features that attract tycoons as well as honeymooners. The spacious suites have antique furnishings, traditional English-style chintz fabrics, and authentic botanical prints. French doors separate the living rooms and bedrooms, and bathrooms are outfitted in Italian marble. Standard features include dual-line telephones with data ports, high-speed Internet access, a personal fax-copier-printer, and two TVs. Many suites also have a pantry with a microwave. The hotel is near Boston University and MIT (across the river), and the location on tree-lined Commonwealth Avenue contrasts pleasantly with the bustle of Newbury Street, a block away.

Dining: The elegant restaurant, **Clio,** serves breakfast. At dinner, Clio specializes in contemporary French and American cuisine.

Amenities: VCRs, safe-deposit boxes, concierge, room service until midnight, dry cleaning and laundry, newspaper delivery, twice-daily maid service, baby-sitting and secretarial services available, express checkout, valet parking. Rooms for travelers with disabilities are available.

✪ **The Fairmont Copley Plaza Hotel.** 138 St. James Ave., Boston, MA 02116. ☎ **800/527-4727** or 617/267-5300. Fax 617/247-6681. www. fairmont.com. 379 units. A/C MINIBAR TV TEL. From $249 double; from $429 suite. Extra person $30. Weekend and other packages available. AE, CB, DC, JCB, MC, V. Valet parking $30. T: Green Line to Copley, or Orange Line to Back Bay. Small pets accepted.

The Fairmont Hotel Group acquired the grande dame of Boston hotels in 1996 and upgraded it into a true "grand hotel," in line with the chain's most famous property, New York's Plaza. Extensive renovations, plush accommodations, and superb service indicate a job well done. Built in 1912, the six-story Renaissance-revival building faces Copley Square, with Trinity Church and the Boston Public Library on either side. The large guest rooms underwent renovation and restoration from 1996 to 1998. Furnished with reproduction Edwardian antiques, they reflect the elegance of the opulent public spaces. In-room features include oversized desks, climate control, coffeemakers, phones with data ports, and irons and ironing boards. Bathrooms have hair dryers, terry robes, and oversize towels.

Dining/Diversions: There are two restaurants—the **Oak Room,** a traditional steak house, and **Copley's Grand Café**—and two lounges, the clubby **Oak Bar** and **Copley's Bar.**

Amenities: Concierge, 24-hour room service, VCRs, fitness center, well-equipped business center, conference rooms, dry cleaning and laundry, newspaper delivery. In-room massage, twice-daily maid service, baby-sitting, express checkout, valet parking, currency exchange, complimentary shoeshine, beauty salon, gift shop. Guests have access to the nearby coed YWCA, which has a swimming pool. Rooms for travelers with disabilities are available.

✪ **The Lenox Hotel.** 710 Boylston St., Boston, MA 02116. ☎ **800/225-7676** or 617/536-5300. Fax 617/236-0351. www.lenoxhotel.com. 212 units. A/C TV TEL. From $308 double; $398 executive corner room with fireplace; $498 fireplace suit. Extra person $20. Cots $20. Cribs free. Children under 18 free in parents' room. Corporate and weekend packages available. AE, CB, DC, DISC, JCB, MC, V. Valet and self-parking $28. T: Green Line to Copley.

The Lenox was the latest thing when it opened in 1900, and in its second century, it echoes that *fin-de-siècle* splendor everywhere from the ornate lobby to the spacious, luxurious rooms. Building on its great location, the 11-story hotel courts business travelers with in-room fax machines, two-line speakerphones, data ports, function space, and an accommodating staff. The high-ceilinged guest rooms have sitting areas with custom-designed wood furnishings, marble bathrooms, terry robes, hair dryers, umbrellas, and irons and ironing boards. Twelve corner rooms have wood-burning fireplaces, and rooms on the top two floors have excellent views.

Dining: The excellent restaurant **Anago** serves dinner and Sunday brunch and provides the hotel's food services. **The Upstairs Grille** serves breakfast; the congenial **Samuel Adams Brew House** serves lunch and dinner and has a dozen brews on tap.

Amenities: Small exercise room, conference rooms, concierge, room service until midnight, dry cleaning and laundry, newspaper delivery, express checkout, nightly turndown, secretarial services available, barbershop, car-rental desk, valet parking. Children's TV channel, baby-sitting available. Rooms for travelers with disabilities and a wheelchair lift to the lobby are available.

✪ **The Westin Copley Place Boston.** 10 Huntington Ave., Boston, MA 02116. ☎ **800/WESTIN-1** or 617/262-9600. Fax 617/424-7483. www. westin.com. 800 units. A/C MINIBAR TV TEL. $229–$499 double; $269–$2,200 suite. Extra person $25; $40 junior suites and Executive Club Level; $20 Guest Office. Weekend packages available. AE, CB, DC, DISC, JCB, MC, V. Valet parking $28. T: Green Line to Copley, or Orange Line to Back Bay. Pets under 20 lbs. accepted.

Towering 36 stories above Copley Square, the Westin attracts conventiongoers, sightseers, and dedicated shoppers. Skybridges link the hotel to Copley Place and the Prudential Center complex, and Copley Square is across the street from the pedestrian entrance. The multilingual staff emphasizes quick check-in.

The spacious guest rooms—all on the eighth floor or higher—have traditional oak and mahogany furniture, coffeemakers, two phones, data ports, hair dryers, safes, and windows that open. They're scheduled to be spruced up and outfitted with even more comfortable beds by early 2001. You might not notice any of that at first, because you'll be captivated by the view. Qualms you might have had about choosing a huge chain hotel will fade as you survey downtown Boston, the airport and harbor, or the Charles River and Cambridge. Executive Club Level guests have private check-in and a lounge that serves complimentary continental breakfast and hors d'oeuvres.

Dining/Diversions: The Palm, a branch of the famous New York–based chain, serves lunch and dinner—steak, chops, and jumbo lobsters. The excellent seafood restaurant **Turner Fisheries** features live jazz Thursday through Saturday after 8pm. **Bar 10** serves drinks and Mediterranean food in a posh space off the lobby.

⊕ Family-Friendly Hotels

Almost every hotel in the Boston area regularly plays host to children, and many offer special family packages. Moderately priced chains have the most experience with young guests— you can't go wrong with a Howard Johnson's or a Holiday Inn—but their higher-end competitors put on a good show.

Units at the **Doubletree Guest Suites** (see p. 58) have two rooms in which to spread out, and they cost far less than adjoining rooms at any other hotel this nice. You can use the in-room coffeemaker and refrigerator to prepare your own breakfast, then splurge on lunch and dinner.

In the Back Bay, the **Colonnade Hotel** (see p. 49) offers a family weekend package that includes parking; breakfast for two adults; up to four passes (two adult, two children) to an attraction of your choice; and a fanny pack for younger guests that holds sunglasses, a pad and pen, a yo-yo, and a toy duck.

The **Seaport Hotel** (see p. 44), near Museum Wharf, offers excellent weekend deals, splendid views of the Big Dig and the airport, underwater music piped into the swimming pool, and even a grandparent-grandchild package.

In Cambridge, the **Royal Sonesta Hotel** (see p. 65) fills the vacation months with Summerfest, which includes complimentary use of bicycles, the health club and indoor/outdoor pool, free ice cream every day, and boat rides along the Charles River. And it's right around the corner from the Museum of Science.

Another riverfront hotel, the **Hyatt Regency Cambridge** (see p. 64), courts families with its pool, bicycle rentals, easy access to the banks of the Charles, and discounted rates (subject to availability) on a separate room for the kids.

At Cambridge's **Charles Hotel** (see p. 61), the adjoining WellBridge Health and Fitness Center sets aside time for family swimming. The Harvard Square scavenger hunt is fun, as is the room service menu, which includes pepperoni pizza. Phone the "Children's Storyline" to hear four bedtime tales for guests under 7.

Amenities: Indoor pool, health club with Nautilus equipment and saunas, concierge, 24-hour room service, business center with computer rentals and secretarial services, conference rooms, car-rental desk, tour desk, barbershop, dry cleaning and laundry, newspaper delivery, twice-daily maid service, express checkout, valet parking. Forty-eight guest rooms for travelers with disabilities adjoin standard rooms.

EXPENSIVE

Boston Marriott Copley Place. 110 Huntington Ave., Boston, MA 02116. ☎ **800/228-9290** or 617/236-5800. Fax 617/236-5885. www.marriott.com/marriott/BOSCO. 1,147 units. A/C TV TEL. $199–$344 double; $450–$1,050 suite. Children free in parents' room. Weekend and other packages available. AE, DC, DISC, JCB, MC, V. Valet parking $24; self-parking $22. T: Orange Line to Back Bay, or Green Line E to Prudential.

Yes, 1,147 units. This 38-story tower feels generic, but it does offer something for everyone—namely, complete business facilities and easy access to Boston's shopping wonderland. The guest rooms have Queen Anne–style mahogany furniture and are large enough to hold a desk and table and either two armchairs or an armchair and an ottoman. Other features include hair dryers, coffeemakers, full-length mirrors, irons, ironing boards, and phones with data ports. Ultrasuites feature individual whirlpool bathtubs. The Concierge Level has a private lounge that serves complimentary continental breakfast, cocktails, and hors d'oeuvres. This is New England's biggest convention hotel (the Sheraton is larger but attracts more vacationers), so if you're not part of a group, you may feel a bit lost.

Dining/Diversions: The sports bar **Champions** is a fun place to watch TV and eat bar food and burgers. There are two restaurants, a sushi bar, and a lounge that offers live entertainment 5 nights a week.

Amenities: Heated indoor pool; well-equipped health club with exercise room, whirlpools, saunas; full-service business center; conference rooms with Internet access; car-rental desk; tour desk; concierge; 24-hour room service; dry cleaning and laundry; valet parking. Rooms for travelers with disabilities are available.

Copley Square Hotel. 47 Huntington Ave., Boston, MA 02116. ☎ **800/225-7062** or 617/536-9000. Fax 617/236-0351. www.copleysquarehotel.com. 143 units. A/C TV TEL. $225–$285 double; $385 suite. Children under 17 free in parents' room. Packages and senior discounts available. AE, CB, DC, DISC, JCB, MC, V. Parking in adjacent garage $25. T: Green Line to Copley, or Orange Line to Back Bay.

The Copley Square Hotel offers a great location along with the advantages and drawbacks of its relatively small size. Built in 1891, the seven-story hotel extends attentive service that's hard to find at the nearby megahotels, without those giants' abundant amenities. If you don't need to engineer a corporate takeover from your room, it's a fine choice, but a larger competitor might offer more features for the same price. Each attractively decorated unit has a queen- or king-size bed or two double beds; some rooms are on the small side. All have hair dryers, coffeemakers, safes, and phones with modem hookups and guest voice mail.

Dining/Diversions: Afternoon tea is served in the lobby. **Speeder & Earl's** serves breakfast. **Café Budapest** (Hungarian and Continental cuisine) and the **Original Sports Saloon** (barbecue) serve lunch and dinner.

Amenities: Concierge, room service until 11pm, dry cleaning, 24-hour currency exchange.

Hilton Boston Back Bay. 40 Dalton St., Boston, MA 02115. ☎ **800/ 874-0663**, 800/HILTONS, or 617/236-1100. Fax 617/867-6104. www. bostonbackbay.hilton.com. 385 units (some with shower only). A/C TV TEL. $179–$295 double; $450 minisuite; $650 1-bedroom suite; $850 2-bedroom suite. Packages and AAA discount available. Extra person $20. Rollaway $20. Children free in parents' room. AE, CB, DC, DISC, MC, V. Valet parking $24; self-parking $17. T: Green Line B, C, or D to Hynes/ICA. Small pets accepted.

Across the street from the Prudential Center complex, this 26-story tower is primarily a business hotel, but vacationing families also find it convenient and comfortable. Rooms are large and soundproofed; 44 are executive units added in 1998. All have modern furnishings, with either one king-size or two double beds, windows that open, coffeemakers, hair dryers, irons, and ironing boards. Rates for executive rooms include continental breakfast and upgraded amenities.

Dining/Diversions: Boodles Restaurant draws businesspeople for grilled steaks and seafood, and **Boodles Bar** offers nearly 100 American microbrews. There is a lounge and a nightclub, **Club Nicole,** which attracts a young crowd.

Amenities: Heated indoor pool, sundeck, well-equipped 24-hour fitness center, business center, conference rooms, concierge, room service until 1am, dry cleaning and laundry, newspaper delivery, express checkout, currency exchange. Rooms for travelers with disabilities are available.

✪ **Sheraton Boston Hotel.** 39 Dalton St., Boston, MA 02199. ☎ **800/ 325-3535** or 617/236-2000. Fax 617/236-1702. www.sheraton.com. 1,181 units. A/C TV TEL. $149–$369 double; suites from $400. Children under 17 free in parents' room. Weekend packages available. 25% discount for students, faculty, and retired persons with ID, depending on availability. AE, CB,

DC, DISC, JCB, MC, V. Valet or self-parking $28. T: Green Line E to Prudential, or B, C, or D to Hynes/ICA. Small pets accepted.

Its central location, range of accommodations, lavish convention facilities, and huge pool make this 29-story hotel one of the most popular in the city. It offers direct access to the Hynes Convention Center and the Prudential Center complex, and recent and ongoing renovations have left it in remarkably good shape.

A $73 million overhaul upgraded the bathrooms, installed individual climate control and new windows, and reconfigured the convention space and lobby. The fairly large guest rooms are being redecorated in sleek contemporary style and outfitted with "pillow top" beds. They also boast coffeemakers, hair dryers, irons, and ironing boards. Many suites have a wet bar and a refrigerator. Club Level guests get free local calls, no access charges on long-distance calls, personal printer-fax-copiers, safes, and admission to a lounge that serves complimentary continental breakfast and hors d'oeuvres.

Dining/Diversions: The lobby restaurant, **Apropos,** serves three meals daily; the **Turning Point Lounge** offers picture-window views of the neighborhood. The clubby **Punch Bar** serves after-dinner drinks, cordials, and a breathtaking selection of cigars.

Amenities: Heated indoor/outdoor pool with retractable dome, pavilion, Jacuzzi, and sauna; large, well-equipped health club; recently expanded and reconfigured conference and function space. Concierge, 24-hour room service, dry cleaning and laundry, car-rental desk, newspaper delivery, in-room massage, express checkout, valet parking, courtesy car. Rooms for travelers with disabilities are available.

MODERATE

The MidTown Hotel. 220 Huntington Ave., Boston, MA 02115. ☎ **800/ 343-1177** or 617/262-1000. Fax 617/262-8739. www.midtownhotel. com. 159 units. A/C TV TEL. Apr–Aug $149–$209 double; Sept to mid-Dec $189–$249 double; mid-Dec to Mar $99–$169 double. Extra person $15. Children under 18 free in parents' room. 10% AARP discount available; government employees' discount, subject to availability. AE, CB, DC, DISC, MC, V. Free parking. T: Green Line E to Prudential, or Orange Line to Mass. Ave.

Even without free parking and a pool (open seasonally), this centrally located two-story hotel would be a good deal for families and budget-conscious businesspeople. It's on a busy street within easy walking distance of Symphony Hall, the Museum of Fine Arts, and the Back Bay attractions. The recently renovated rooms are large, bright, and attractively outfitted, although bathrooms are on the small side. All units have coffeemakers and hair dryers, and some have connecting doors that allow families to spread out. For business travelers, many rooms have two-line phones; photo-copying and fax services are available at the front desk. Dry clean-ing and video rentals are available, and baby-sitting can be arranged. The heated outdoor pool is open from Memorial Day through Labor Day. The on-premises restaurant serves breakfast from 7 to 11am.

✪ **Newbury Guest House.** 261 Newbury St. (between Fairfield and Gloucester sts.), Boston, MA 02116. ☎ **617/437-7666.** Fax 617/262-4243. www.hagopianhotels.com. 32 units (some with shower only). A/C TV TEL. $140–$190 double; winter discounts available. Extra person $15. Rates include continental breakfast. Rates may be higher during special events. Minimum 2 nights on weekends. AE, CB, DC, DISC, MC, V. Parking $15 (reservation required). T: Green Line B, C, or D to Hynes/ICA.

After just a little shopping in the Back Bay, you'll appreciate what a find this cozy inn is—a bargain on Newbury Street. It's a pair of brick town houses built in the 1880s and combined into a refined guesthouse. It offers comfortable furnishings, a pleasant staff, nifty architectural details, and—*such* a deal—a buffet break-fast served in the ground-level dining room, which adjoins a brick patio. Rooms are modest in size but nicely appointed and well maintained. The Hagopian family opened the B&B in 1991, and it operates near capacity all year, drawing business travelers dur-ing the week and sightseers on weekends. A room for travelers with disabilities is available. At these prices in this location, there's only one caveat: Reserve early.

INEXPENSIVE

Hostelling International–Boston. 12 Hemenway St., Boston, MA 02115. ☎ **888/HOST222** or 617/536-9455. Fax 617/424-6558. www.bostonhostel. org. 205 beds. Members $24 per bed; nonmembers $27 per bed. JCB, MC, V. T: Green Line B, C, or D to Hynes/ICA.

This hostel near the Berklee College of Music and Symphony Hall caters to students, youth groups, and other travelers in search of comfortable, no-frills lodging. It has two full dine-in kitchens, 19 bathrooms, a coin laundry, and a large common room. The recently remodeled public areas contain meeting and workshop space. Accommodations are dorm-style, with three to six beds per room.

The hostel provides a "sheet sleeping sack," or you can bring your own; sleeping bags are not permitted. The enthusiastic staff organizes free and inexpensive cultural, educational, and recreational programs on the premises and throughout the Boston area. The first-floor rooms and bathrooms are wheelchair accessible, and there's a wheelchair lift at the entrance to the building.

Note: To get a bed during the summer, you must be a member of Hostelling International–American Youth Hostels. For information and an application, contact HI–AYH, P.O. Box 37613, Washington, DC 20013 (☎ **202/783-6161;** www.hiayh.org). If you are not a U.S. citizen, apply to your home country's hostelling association.

7 Outskirts & Brookline

What Bostonians consider "outskirts" would be centrally located in many larger cities. Lodgings in this area are close to Fenway Park, the hospitals at the Longwood Medical Area, and several colleges and museums. Brookline starts about 3 blocks beyond Boston's Kenmore Square.

EXPENSIVE

✪ **Doubletree Guest Suites.** 400 Soldiers Field Rd., Boston, MA 02134. ☎ **800/222-TREE** or 617/783-0090. Fax 617/783-0897. www. doubletreehotels.com. 308 units. A/C MINIBAR TV TEL. $139–$259 double. Extra person $20. Children under 18 free in parents' room. Weekend packages $154–$264. AARP and AAA discounts available. AE, CB, DC, DISC, JCB, MC, V. Parking $15–$18.

This hotel is one of the best deals in town—every unit is a two-room suite with a living room, bedroom, and bathroom. Business travelers can entertain in their rooms, and families can spread out, making this a good choice for both. Overlooking the Charles River at the Allston/Cambridge exit of the Mass. Pike, the hotel is near Cambridge and the bike and jogging path that runs along the river, although not in an actual neighborhood. There's complimentary van service to and from attractions and business areas in Boston and Cambridge, making the somewhat inconvenient location easier to handle.

The suites surround a 15-story atrium. Rooms are large and attractively furnished, and most bedrooms have king-size beds and a writing desk. Each living room contains a full-size sofa bed, a dining table, and a good-size refrigerator. Each suite has a coffeemaker, two TVs, and three telephones (one in the bathroom).

Dining/Diversions: Scullers Grille and **Scullers Lounge** serve meals from 6:30am to 11pm. The celebrated **Scullers Jazz Club** schedules two nightly shows.

Amenities: Heated indoor pool, exercise room, whirlpool, sauna, 24-hour room service, 24-hour business center, conference rooms, concierge, newspaper delivery, express checkout. Dry cleaning and laundry, laundry room, game room, baby-sitting available, car-rental desk, van service. Suites for travelers with disabilities on each floor.

MODERATE

Best Western Boston/The Inn at Longwood Medical. 342 Longwood Ave., Boston, MA 02115. ☎ **800/528-1234** or 617/731-4700. TDD 617/731-9088. Fax 617/731-6273. E-mail: innlwm@erols.com. 158 units (14 with kitchenette). A/C TV TEL. $139–$209 double; $219–$259 suite. Extra person $15. Children under 18 free in parents' room. AE, CB, DC, DISC, MC, V. Parking $14. T: Green Line D or E to Longwood.

Next to Children's Hospital in the Longwood Medical Area (Beth Israel Deaconess and Brigham and Women's hospitals, the Dana–Farber Cancer Institute, and the Joslin Diabetes Center are nearby), this eight-story hotel is a good base for those with business at the hospitals. Near museums, colleges, and Fenway Park, it's about 15 minutes from downtown Boston by public transportation.

Guest rooms are quite large and equipped with hair dryers, irons, and ironing boards. There's room service until 11pm. Hotel facilities include a restaurant, a lounge, meeting rooms, dry-cleaning and laundry service, and a laundry room. Rooms for travelers with disabilities are available. The hotel abuts the Longwood Galleria business complex, which has a food court, retail stores, and a fitness center that's available to hotel guests for $8 to $10 a day.

Holiday Inn Boston Brookline. 1200 Beacon St., Brookline, MA 02446. ☎ **800/HOLIDAY** or 617/277-1200. Fax 617/734-6991. www.holiday-inn.com/brookline. 225 units (some with shower only). A/C TV TEL. $139–$199 double; $199–$300 suite. Extra person $10. Children under 18 free in parents' room. AE, DC, DISC, JCB, MC, V. Parking $10. T: Green Line C to St. Paul St.

Just 15 minutes from downtown on the subway, this sparkling hotel is more than just another Holiday Inn. It offers recently redecorated rooms that are large and well appointed, with coffeemakers, hair dryers, and irons and ironing boards. The lobby surrounds a colorful atrium with a small indoor pool, whirlpool, and exercise room. Dry cleaning is available. Ten rooms are equipped for guests with disabilities. The six-story hotel has a restaurant, lounge, and coffee shop. The bustling Coolidge Corner neighborhood is a 10-minute walk away.

Howard Johnson Hotel Kenmore. 575 Commonwealth Ave., Boston, MA 02215. ☎ **800/654-2000** or 617/267-3100. Fax 617/424-1045. www.hojo. com. 179 units. A/C TV TEL. $125–$225 double. Extra person $10. Children under 18 free in parents' room. Senior and AAA discounts available. AE, CB, DC, DISC, JCB, MC, V. Free parking. T: Green Line B to Blandford St. Pets accepted.

If the location doesn't get you, the pool and free parking might. The Boston University campus surrounds this eight-story hotel, with the T to downtown out front and Kenmore Square and Fenway Park nearby. The recently refurbished rooms are standard-issue Howard Johnson's—comfortable, but still nothing fancy—and some are small. The hotel has a glass-enclosed elevator, which runs to the rooftop lounge and provides a good view of the area. The indoor swimming pool and skylit sundeck on the roof are open year-round from 11am to 9pm.

Howard Johnson Inn. 1271 Boylston St., Boston, MA 02215. ☎ **800/654-2000** or 617/267-8300. Fax 617/267-2763. www.hojo.com. 94 units. A/C TV TEL. $115–$185 double. Extra person $10. Children under 18 free in parents' room. Family packages and senior and AAA discounts available. AE, CB, DC, DISC, JCB, MC, V. Free parking. T: Green Line B, C, or D to Kenmore; 10-min. walk. Pets accepted.

This is as close to Fenway Park as you can get without buying a ticket. The outdoor pool and free parking make the motel particularly attractive to vacationing families. If you're not visiting during baseball season, the busy street in a commercial-residential neighborhood is convenient to the Back Bay, the Museum of Fine Arts, and the Isabella Stewart Gardner Museum. When the Red Sox are playing, guests contend with crowded sidewalks and raucous fans who flood the area. The decent-sized rooms contain coffeemakers, and some have microwaves and refrigerators. Laundry service is available. There's an outdoor pool, open from 9am to 7pm in the summer. On the premises are a steak house and a popular lounge that has live jazz entertainment.

INEXPENSIVE

Anthony's Town House. 1085 Beacon St., Brookline, MA 02446. ☎ **617/566-3972.** Fax 617/232-1085. 12 units (none with private bathroom). A/C TV. $65–$95 double. Extra person $10. Weekly rates and winter discounts available. No credit cards. Free parking. T: Green Line C to Hawes St.

The Anthony family has operated this four-story brownstone guesthouse since 1944, and a stay here is very much like tagging along with a friend who's spending the night at Grandma's place. Each floor has three high-ceilinged rooms furnished in rather ornate Queen Anne or Victorian style, and a shared bathroom with enclosed shower. Smaller rooms (one per floor) have twin beds, and the large front rooms have bay windows. Guests have the use of two refrigerators. The guesthouse is 1 mile from Boston's Kenmore Square, about 15 minutes from downtown by subway, and 2 blocks from a busy commercial strip. The turn-of-the-20th-century building is listed on the National Register of Historic Places.

Longwood Inn. 123 Longwood Ave., Brookline, MA 02446. ☎ **617/ 566-8615.** Fax 617/738-1070. http://go.boston.com/longwoodinn. 22 units, 17 with bathroom (some with shower only). A/C TEL. Apr–Nov $79–$109 double, Dec–Mar $65–$89 double; 1-bedroom apt (sleeps 4-plus) $89–$119. Weekly rates available. No credit cards. Free parking. T: Green Line D to Longwood, or C to Coolidge Corner.

In a residential area 3 blocks from the Boston–Brookline border, this three-story Victorian guesthouse offers comfortable accommodations at modest rates. Guests have the use of a fully equipped kitchen and common dining room, coin laundry, and TV lounge. The apartment has a private bathroom, kitchen, and balcony. Tennis courts, a running track, and a playground at the school next door are open to the public. Public transportation is easily accessible, and the Longwood Medical Area and busy Coolidge Corner neighborhood are within walking distance.

8 Cambridge

Just across the Charles River from Boston, Cambridge has its own attractions and excellent hotels. College graduation season (May and early June) is especially busy, but campus events can cause high demand at unexpected times, so plan ahead.

VERY EXPENSIVE

✪ **The Charles Hotel.** 1 Bennett St., Cambridge, MA 02138. ☎ **800/ 882-1818** outside Mass., or 617/864-1200. Fax 617/864-5715. www. charleshotel.com. 293 units. A/C MINIBAR TV TEL. $349–$429 double; $489–$3,000 suite. Extra person $20. Children under 18 free in parents' room. Weekend packages available. AE, CB, DC, JCB, MC, V. Valet and self-parking $18. T: Red Line to Harvard. Pets accepted.

The Charles Hotel is a phenomenon—an instant classic. The nine-story brick hotel a block from Harvard Square has been *the* place for business and leisure travelers to Cambridge since it opened in 1985. Much of its fame derives from its excellent restaurants, jazz bar, and day spa, and the service is, if anything,

Cambridge Accommodations & Dining

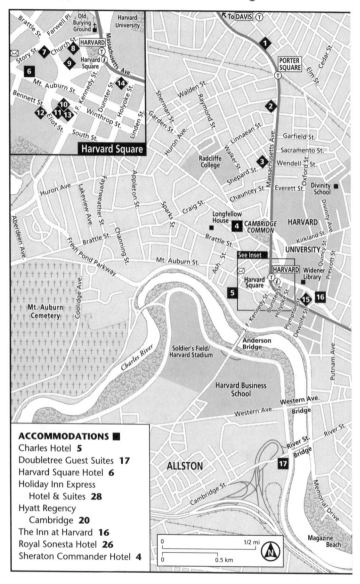

ACCOMMODATIONS ■
Charles Hotel **5**
Doubletree Guest Suites **17**
Harvard Square Hotel **6**
Holiday Inn Express
  Hotel & Suites **28**
Hyatt Regency
  Cambridge **20**
The Inn at Harvard **16**
Royal Sonesta Hotel **26**
Sheraton Commander Hotel **4**

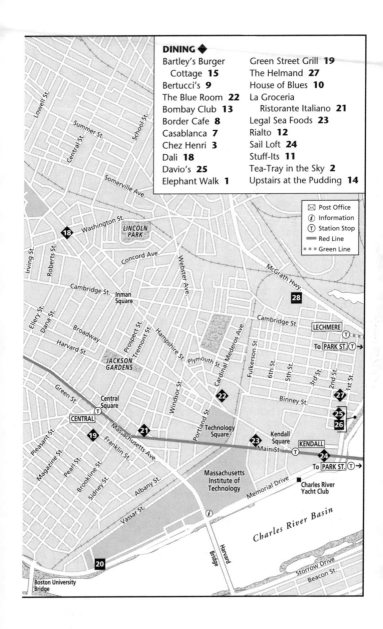

DINING ◆

Bartley's Burger Cottage **15**
Bertucci's **9**
The Blue Room **22**
Bombay Club **13**
Border Cafe **8**
Casablanca **7**
Chez Henri **3**
Dali **18**
Davio's **25**
Elephant Walk **1**
Green Street Grill **19**
The Helmand **27**
House of Blues **10**
La Groceria Ristorante Italiano **21**
Legal Sea Foods **23**
Rialto **12**
Sail Loft **24**
Stuff-Its **11**
Tea-Tray in the Sky **2**
Upstairs at the Pudding **14**

⊠ Post Office
ⓘ Information
Ⓣ Station Stop
— Red Line
▪▪▪ Green Line

equally exalted. In the posh guest rooms, the style is contemporary country, with custom-designed adaptations of Early American Shaker furniture and down quilts. Bathrooms have telephones, TVs, hair dryers, and scales. All rooms have large windows that open, three phones, data ports, and state-of-the-art Bose Wave radios. And it wouldn't be Cambridge if your intellectual needs went unfulfilled—you can order books over the phone, and a Charles staffer will pick them up at WordsWorth Books and bill your room.

Dining/Diversions: Rialto, one of the best restaurants in Greater Boston, serves Mediterranean cuisine by award-winning chef Jody Adams. **Henrietta's Table** offers New England country cooking. The renowned **Regattabar** features live jazz Tuesday through Saturday nights, and the **Tini Bar** specializes in martinis.

Amenities: Concierge, 24-hour room service, dry cleaning and laundry, newspaper delivery, in-room massage, twice-daily maid service. Baby-sitting and secretarial services available, express checkout, video rentals, valet parking, newly expanded conference rooms, facilities for teleconferencing, car-rental desk. Glass-enclosed pool, Jacuzzi, and exercise room at the adjacent WellBridge Health and Fitness Center; beauty treatments available at the European-style Le Pli Spa and Salon. Rooms for travelers with disabilities; rooms with special amenities for female travelers.

The Hyatt Regency Cambridge. 575 Memorial Dr., Cambridge, MA 02139. ☎ **800/233-1234** or 617/492-1234. Fax 617/491-6906. www.cambridge. hyatt.com. 469 units. A/C TV TEL. $239–$399 double weekdays, $149–$234 weekend; $265–$394 Regency Club; $450–$750 suite. Extra person $25. Children under 18 free in parents' room. Weekend packages available. AE, DC, DISC, JCB, MC, V. Valet parking $17; self-parking $15.

This dramatic brick hotel, a prominent feature of the Cambridge skyline, makes up for its not-exactly-central location with its appointments and architecture. Across the street from the Charles River and not far from the Allston/Brighton exit of the turnpike, it encloses a 16-story atrium with glass elevators, fountains, trees, and balconies. The spacious guest rooms were renovated in 1997. All have coffeemakers and hair dryers, and some have breathtaking views of Boston and the river. Families are especially welcome, with special two-room rates (subject to availability), and bicycles for rent. The hotel is about 10 minutes from downtown Boston by car and convenient for those visiting colleges—it's between Harvard and MIT and across the bridge from Boston University.

Dining/Diversions: On the rooftop, the revolving, glass-enclosed **Spinnaker Italia** restaurant serves dinner and Sunday brunch, and it has a lounge where there's dancing on Friday and Saturday nights. A new restaurant and lounge, overlooking the river, serves three meals daily and specializes in wood-grilled cuisine.

Amenities: 75-foot indoor lap pool; health club with whirlpool, sauna, and steam room; sundeck; business center; conference rooms; car-rental desk; concierge; room service until late evening; dry cleaning and laundry; baby-sitting referrals; valet parking; ATM and currency exchange. Complimentary scheduled shuttle service to Cambridge and Boston destinations. Twenty-four rooms for travelers with disabilities.

✪ **Royal Sonesta Hotel.** 5 Cambridge Pkwy., Cambridge, MA 02142. ☎ **800/SONESTA** or 617/806-4200. Fax 617/806-4232. www.sonesta.com. 400 units. A/C MINIBAR TV TEL. $239–$279 standard double, $259–$299 superior double, $279–$319 deluxe double; $329–$950 suite. Extra person $25. Children under 18 free in parents' room. Weekend and other packages available. AE, CB, DC, DISC, JCB, MC, V. Parking $16. T: Green Line to Lechmere; 10-min. walk.

This luxurious hotel is in a curious location—it's close to only a few things but convenient to everything, making it a good choice for both businesspeople and families. The CambridgeSide Galleria mall is across the street, and the Museum of Science is around the corner on the bridge to Boston, which is closer than Harvard Square. In the other direction, MIT is a 10-minute walk. Most of the spacious rooms have a lovely view of the river or the city (higher prices are for better views), and all have two phones plus hair dryers. Everything is custom designed and renovated regularly—every unit has been completely revamped in the past 4 years. Original contemporary artwork, including pieces by Andy Warhol and Frank Stella, hangs throughout the public spaces and guest rooms.

Dining/Diversions: Davio's, a branch of the Newbury Street favorite, serves three meals daily and has an outdoor patio overlooking the Charles River. The casual **Gallery Café** also has a patio. Both restaurants offer live music on summer evenings (schedules vary).

Amenities: Heated indoor/outdoor pool with retractable roof; well-equipped health club; Jacuzzi; sauna; spa services, including massage. Business center, conference rooms, concierge, room service until 1am (2am on weekends), dry cleaning and laundry, baby-sitting available, express checkout, valet parking.

Eleven wheelchair-accessible rooms, 16 for those with hearing impairments; staff trained in disability awareness.

Sheraton Commander Hotel. 16 Garden St., Cambridge, MA 02138. ☎ **800/325-3535** or 617/547-4800. Fax 617/868-8322. www. sheratoncommander.com. 175 units. A/C TV TEL. $195–$345 double; $330–$550 suite. Extra person $20. Children under 18 free in parents' room. Weekend packages and AAA and AARP discounts available. AE, CB, DC, DISC, JCB, MC, V. Free parking. T: Red Line to Harvard.

This six-story hotel in the heart of Cambridge's historic district opened in 1927, and it's exactly what you'd expect of a traditional hostelry within sight of the Harvard campus. It doesn't have the cachet of the Charles, but free parking in Harvard Square is worth a barrel of cachet. The Colonial-style decor begins in the elegant lobby and extends to the decent-sized guest rooms, which are attractively furnished and well maintained. Rooms have two phones with data ports, coffeemakers, hair dryers, irons and iron-ing boards, and nightlights. The Club Level offers additional amenities, including in-room fax machines, free local phone calls, and a private lounge that serves complimentary continental break-fast and afternoon hors d'oeuvres on weekdays. Suites have two TVs, and some have wet bars, refrigerators, and whirlpools.

Dining: The restaurant serves three meals daily and Sunday brunch. The cafe serves lighter fare in the afternoon and evening.

Amenities: Small fitness center, sundeck, conference rooms, laundry room, concierge, room service until 11pm, dry cleaning and laundry, newspaper delivery, baby-sitting available, express checkout, valet parking.

EXPENSIVE

The Inn at Harvard. 1201 Mass. Ave. (at Quincy St.), Cambridge, MA 02138. ☎ **800/458-5886** or 617/491-2222. Fax 617/491-6520. www. theinnatharvard.com. 109 units (some with shower only). A/C TV TEL. $169–$309 double; $500 presidential suite. Extra person $10. Children under 19 free in parents' room. Packages and senior, AAA, and AARP discounts available. AE, CB, DC, DISC, MC, V. Valet parking $25. T: Red Line to Harvard.

At first glance, the red-brick Inn at Harvard looks almost like a college dorm—it's adjacent to Harvard Yard, and its Georgian-style architecture would fit nicely on campus. Inside, there's no mistaking it for anything other than an elegant hotel, popular with business travelers and university visitors. The four-story skylit atrium holds the "living room," a well-appointed guest lounge. The elegantly decorated guest rooms have cherry furniture, and each has a lounge chair or two armchairs around a table, a work area, windows that open, and an original painting from the Fogg Art Museum. Each room has two phones, one with a modem hookup. Some rooms have dormer windows and window seats.

Dining: The Atrium Dining Room serves seasonal New England fare at breakfast, lunch, dinner, and afternoon tea. Guests have dining privileges at the Harvard Faculty Club, a half-block away.

Amenities: Conference rooms, safe-deposit boxes, room service, dry cleaning and laundry, newspaper delivery, secretarial services available, express checkout, valet parking. Six wheelchair-accessible rooms.

MODERATE

The **Holiday Inn Express Hotel and Suites,** 250 Msgr. O'Brien Hwy., Cambridge, MA 02141 (☎ **888/887-7690** or 617/577-7600; fax 617/354-1313; www.bristolhotels.com), is a limited-services lodging on a busy street a 5-minute walk from Lechmere station on the Green Line. The neighborhood is busy and noisy, but the hotel is convenient. Rates for a standard double run $119 to $199.

Harvard Square Hotel. 110 Mount Auburn St., Cambridge, MA 02138. ☎ **800/458-5886** or 617/864-5200. Fax 617/864-2409. www.doubletreehotels.com. 73 units. A/C TV TEL. $129–$209 double. Extra person $10. Children under 17 free in parents' room. Corporate rates and AAA and AARP discounts available. AE, DC, DISC, MC, V. Parking $20. T: Red Line to Harvard.

Smack in the middle of Harvard Square, this six-story brick hotel is a favorite with visiting parents and budget-conscious business travelers. The unpretentious guest rooms were renovated in early 2000 and outfitted with new furniture and carpeting. They're relatively small, but comfortable and neatly decorated in contemporary style. All have data ports, voice mail, hair dryers, irons, and ironing boards; some overlook Harvard Square. The front desk handles fax and copy services and distributes complimentary newspapers (weekdays only). Dry-cleaning and laundry service are available. There are four wheelchair-accessible rooms. Guests have dining privileges at the Inn at Harvard and the Harvard Faculty Club.

9 At the Airport

✪ **Hilton Boston Logan Airport.** 85 Terminal Rd., Logan International Airport, Boston, MA 02128. ☎ **800/HILTONS** or 617/568-6700. Fax 617/568-6800. www.bostonloganairport.hilton.com. 599 units. A/C MINIBAR TV TEL. $149–$259 double; from $500 suite. Children under 19 free in parents' room. Weekend and other packages from $159 per night. AE, CB, DC, DISC, MC, V. Valet parking $25; self-parking $18. T: Blue Line to Airport, then take shuttle bus.

This spanking-new hotel in the middle of the airport draws most of its guests from meetings, conventions, and recently canceled flights. Opened in 1999, it's accessible through walkways from Terminals A (close) and E (distant), and by shuttle bus from all over the airport. It's convenient and well equipped for business travelers, and an excellent fall-back for vacationers in search of a deal. Guest rooms are large and tastefully furnished; they have two two-line speakerphones, wireless Internet access through the TV, coffeemakers, hair dryers, irons, and ironing boards. There's high-speed Internet access throughout the 10-story building and great views from the higher floors. Guests on the concierge level (10th floor) have access to a staffed private lounge that serves continental breakfast, snacks, and hors d'oeuvres.

The big concern with a hotel this close to the runways is noise, but the picture-window views of approaching aircraft—and some lingering construction—look like TV with the sound off. The Hyatt Harborside is the closest competition (see below); it's at the edge of the airport, on the water, which means less commotion outside but less convenient access to the T.

Dining/Diversions: Off the lobby, **Berkshire's** serves breakfast (continental, buffet, and à la carte), lunch, and dinner; **Kitty O'Shea's Irish Pub** (lunch and dinner) is open until 1:30am. There's a gourmet coffee counter in the lobby.

Amenities: Health club with large exercise room, indoor lap pool, whirlpool, saunas, massage, and tanning bed; well-equipped business center; conference rooms with Internet access; 24-hour room service; dry-cleaning and laundry service; weekday newspaper delivery; gift shop; 24-hour shuttle bus service to airport destinations, including car-rental offices and ferry dock; on-bus electronic check-in.

Hyatt Harborside. 101 Harborside Dr., Boston, MA 02128. ☎ **800/233-1234** or 617/568-1234. Fax 617/567-8856. www.boston.hyatt.com. 270 units. A/C TV TEL. From $169 double. Children under 12 free in parents' room.

AE, CB, DC, DISC, JCB, MC, V. Parking $15. T: Blue Line to Airport, then take shuttle bus. By car, follow signs to Logan Airport and take Harborside Dr. past car-rental area and tunnel entrance.

This striking 14-story waterfront hotel offers unobstructed views of the harbor and city skyline. It caters to the convention and business trade; sightseers whose budget for transportation doesn't include a fair amount of time (on the shuttle bus and subway) or money (on ferries, parking, or cabs) will be better off closer to downtown. Water shuttles to the waterfront leave from the hotel's rear entrance.

The good-sized guest rooms have all the features you'd expect at a deluxe hotel, plus such extras as hair dryers, coffeemakers, irons and ironing boards, luxury bathrooms, and fine wood furnishings. Particularly from the higher floors, the views are dramatic. And there's an interesting architectural quirk: The building's tower is a lighthouse (the airport control tower manages the beacon so that it doesn't interfere with runway lights).

Dining/Diversions: The restaurant serves three meals daily and has floor-to-ceiling windows that offer spectacular views. The lounge offers live music on Friday and Saturday nights.

Amenities: Indoor heated pool, health club with sauna and whirlpool, business center, room service until midnight, conference rooms, concierge, dry cleaning and laundry, express checkout, valet parking, 24-hour airport shuttle service. Ferries to Rowes Wharf and Long Wharf dock outside. Rooms for travelers with disabilities are available.

4

Dining

A friend once laughed and said, "From 1940 to 1970, you could
have used the same dining guide every year—now you could
probably do a new one every 6 months or so." Boston's restaurant
scene is one of the most dynamic in the country, and likely to
remain that way for as long as the economy can support it. Hot
spots open and former hot spots close almost as often as block-
buster movies, and top chefs and their protégés turn up everywhere.

Seafood is a specialty in Boston, where you'll find it on the
menu at almost every restaurant—trendy or classic, expensive or
cheap, typical American (whatever that is) or ethnic. Ipswich and
Essex clams, Atlantic lobsters, Wellfleet oysters, mussels, and all
kinds of fish are available in every imaginable form. Chowder
fans who have never had fresh clams are in for a treat.

Almost every menu in every price range includes vegetarian
offerings. Like the rest of the country, Boston has embraced the
return of meat (not that it ever really went away). Another trend
is the rise of hotel restaurants, which have shed their colorless reputation; some of the most imaginative dining rooms in the area
are in hotels. Female chefs and co-owners are now so common as
to be almost unremarkable. And as in any college community,
many little restaurants serve ethnic cuisine from around the
world.

The guiding thought for this chapter, without regard to price,
was, "If this were your only meal in Boston, would you be
delighted with it?" At the restaurants in this chapter, the answer,
for one reason or another, is yes.

1 The Waterfront

VERY EXPENSIVE

Rowes Wharf Restaurant. In the Boston Harbor Hotel, 70 Rowes Wharf
(entrance on Atlantic Ave.). ☎ **617/439-3995.** www.bhh.com. Reservations
recommended. Main courses $11.25–$18.50 at lunch, $28–$38 at dinner;
wine pairing menu varies; breakfast $9–$14.50; Sun buffet brunch $47. AE, CB,

Time Is Money

Lunch is an excellent, economical way to check out a fancy restaurant without breaking the bank. At restaurants that take reservations, it's always a good idea to make them, particularly for dinner. Boston restaurants are far less busy early in the week than they are from Thursday through Sunday. If you're flexible about when you indulge in fine cuisine and when you go for pizza and a movie, choose the low-budget option on the weekend and pamper yourself on a weeknight.

DC, DISC, MC, V. Mon–Fri 6:30–11am and 11:30am–2:30pm, Sun brunch 10:30am–2pm; daily 5:30–10pm. Valet parking available. T: Red Line to South Station or Blue or Orange Line to State (or Blue Line to Aquarium if it's open). NEW ENGLAND.

Tucked away on the second floor of the Boston Harbor Hotel, the wood-paneled Rowes Wharf Restaurant feels almost like a private club—one with breathtaking picture-window views of the water. It's not a trendy destination, but regularly appears on lists of the city's best restaurants because the food and wine are consistently excellent. Chef Daniel Bruce uses local ingredients prepared in deceptively simple ways that accent natural flavors without overwhelming them.

The signature appetizer is luscious Maine lobster meat seasoned and formed into a sausage, grilled, sliced, and served in a light cream sauce with lobster claw meat and lemon pasta. Or try polenta topped with flavorful wild mushrooms. Entrees might include herb- and mustard-rubbed grilled filet mignon, lobster with chorizo and sweet corn pudding, and pan-seared turbot over couscous with carrot-lime sauce. Desserts vary with the inspiration of the chef—there's usually an excellent sorbet sampler. Symbols on the menu indicate items low in fat, sodium, and calories.

EXPENSIVE

Legal Sea Foods (see "Back Bay," below) has a branch at 255 State St. (☎ **617/227-3115**) opposite the New England Aquarium.

MODERATE

Billy Tse Restaurant. 240 Commercial St. ☎ **617/227-9990**. Reservations recommended at dinner on weekends. Main courses $5–$20; lunch specials $5.50–$7.50. AE, DC, DISC, MC, V. Mon–Thurs 11:30am–11:30pm; Fri–Sat 11:30am–midnight; Sun 11:30am–11pm. T: Green or Orange Line to Haymarket. CHINESE/PAN-ASIAN/SUSHI.

Boston Dining

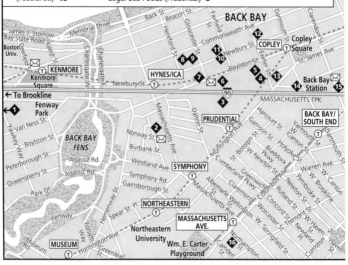

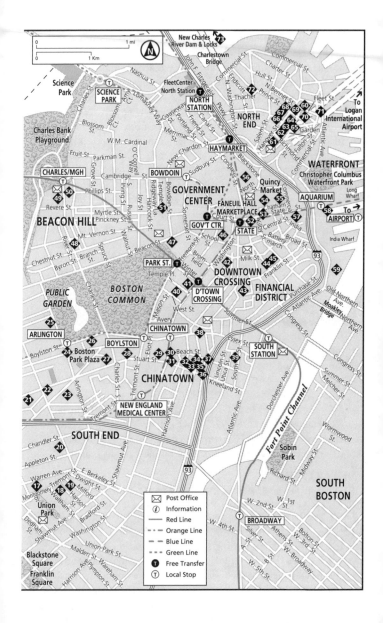

A pan-Asian restaurant on the edge of the Italian North End might seem incongruous, but this casual, economical spot is no ordinary Chinese restaurant. It serves excellent renditions of the usual dishes, and the kitchen also has a flair for fresh seafood. The pan-Asian selections and sushi are just as enjoyable. Start with wonderful soup, sinfully good crab rangoon, or fried calamari with garlic and pepper. Main dishes range from seven kinds of fried rice to scallops with garlic sauce to the house special fried noodles, topped with shrimp, calamari, and scallops in a scrumptious sauce.

Be sure to ask about the daily specials—bitter Chinese broccoli, when it's available, is deftly prepared. Lunch specials, served until 4pm, include vegetable fried rice or vegetable lo mein. You can eat in the comfortable main dining room or near the bar, which has French doors that open to the street. Although it's opposite a trolley stop, Billy Tse doesn't have an especially touristy clientele—the neighborhood patrons obviously welcome a break from pizza and pasta.

2 The North End

Boston's Italian-American enclave has dozens of restaurants; many are tiny and don't serve dessert and coffee. Hit the *caffès* for coffee and fresh pastry in an atmosphere where lingering is welcome—as is smoking. Favorites include **Caffè dello Sport,** 308 Hanover St. (☎ 617/523-5063), **Caffè Graffiti,** 307 Hanover St. (☎ 617/367-3016), and **Caffè Vittoria,** 296 Hanover St. (☎ 617/227-7606). There's also table service at **Mike's Pastry,** 300 Hanover St. (☎ 617/742-3050), a bakery that's famous for its bustling take-out business and its cannoli.

VERY EXPENSIVE

✪ **Mamma Maria.** 3 North Sq. ☎ 617/523-0077. www.mammamaria. com. Reservations recommended. Main courses $19–$35. AE, DC, DISC, MC, V. Sun–Thurs 5–9:30pm; Fri–Sat 5–10:30pm. Closed 1 week in Jan. Valet parking available. T: Green or Orange Line to Haymarket. REGIONAL ITALIAN.

In a townhouse overlooking North Square and the Paul Revere House, this traditional-looking restaurant offers innovative cuisine and a level of sophistication far removed from the North End's familiar "Hey, whaddaya want?" service. The menu changes seasonally; you can usually start with excellent *pasta e fagioli* (bean-and-pasta soup) or risotto, and the daily pasta special is always a great choice. The excellent entrees are unlike anything else in this neighborhood, except in size—portions are more than generous. The fork-tender osso buco is almost enough for two, but you'll want it all for yourself. You can't go wrong with any of the pastas on the menu either, and the fresh seafood specials are uniformly marvelous. The pasta, bread, and desserts are home-made, and the shadowy, whitewashed rooms make this a popular spot for getting engaged—we have to assume the kitchen staff regularly fields offers.

EXPENSIVE

Giacomo's. 355 Hanover St. ☎ **617/523-9026.** Reservations not accepted. Main courses $15–$25. No credit cards. Mon–Thurs 5–10pm; Fri–Sat 5–10:30pm; Sun 4–10pm. T: Green or Orange Line to Haymarket. ITALIAN/SEAFOOD.

Fans of Giacomo's seem to have adopted the Postal Service's motto: They brave snow, sleet, rain, and gloom of night. The line forms early, especially on weekends. No reservations, cash only, a tiny dining room with an open kitchen—what's the secret? Well, the food is terrific, there's plenty of it, and the we're-all-in-this-together atmosphere certainly helps.

The fried calamari appetizer, served with marinara sauce, is light and crisp. You can take the chef's advice or put together your own main dish from the list of daily ingredients on a board on the wall. Salmon in pesto cream sauce with fettuccine is a keeper, as is any dish with shrimp. Nonseafood offerings such as butternut squash ravioli in mascarpone cheese sauce are equally memorable. Service is friendly but incredibly swift, and lingering is not encouraged—but unless you have a heart of stone, you won't want to take up a table when people are standing outside in 90° heat or an ice storm waiting for your seat.

MODERATE

Artú. 6 Prince St. ☎ **617/742-4336.** Reservations not accepted. Main courses $9–$18; sandwiches $5.50–$9. MC, V. Daily 11am–10pm. T: Green or Orange Line to Haymarket. ITALIAN.

Plates of roasted vegetables draw your eye to the front window at Artú, and the accompanying aromas will draw the rest of you. Don't resist—this is a neighborhood favorite for a reason. The best appetizer consists of those gorgeous veggies. Trust the chef to choose for you, or ask to have something included (excellent carrots) or left out (licorice-tasting fennel isn't for everyone). The helpful waitstaff can offer advice. Move on to superb roasted meats or bounteous home-style pasta dishes. Roast lamb, ziti with sausage and broccoli rabe, and chicken stuffed with ham and cheese are all terrific. The *panini* (sandwiches) are big in size and flavor—prosciutto, mozzarella, and tomato is sublime, and chicken parmigiana is tender and filling. This isn't a great place for quiet conversation, especially during dinner in the noisy main room, but do you really want to talk with your mouth full?

There's another Artú on **Beacon Hill** at 89 Charles St. (☎ **617/227-9023**). It opens at 4pm on Sunday and Monday and stays open nightly until 11.

✪ **Daily Catch.** 323 Hanover St.☎ **617/523-8567.** Reservations not accepted. Main courses $10–$18. No credit cards. Sun–Thurs 11:30am– 10:30pm; Fri–Sat 11:30am–11pm. T: Green or Orange Line to Haymarket. SOUTHERN ITALIAN/SEAFOOD.

Look for the awning that says "Calamari Café," or just follow your nose to the source of all that garlic. The Daily Catch is a tiny storefront, and the line for a table can be long, but the food is terrific. The menu includes Sicilian-style calamari (squid stuffed with bread crumbs, raisins, pine nuts, parsley, and tons of garlic), freshly shucked clams, mussels in garlic-flavored sauce, broiled and fried fish, and shellfish. Calamari comes at least eight ways— even the garlic-and-oil pasta sauce has ground-up squid in it. Fried calamari makes an excellent appetizer. Squid ink pasta puttanesca is unusual and delicious. All food is prepared to order, and some dishes are served in the frying pans in which they were cooked.

La Summa. 30 Fleet St. ☎ **617/523-9503.** Reservations recommended. Main courses $11–$17. AE, CB, DC, DISC, MC, V. Daily 4:30–10:30pm. T: Green or Orange Line to Haymarket. ITALIAN.

Because La Summa isn't on the restaurant rows of Hanover and Salem streets, it maintains a cozy neighborhood atmosphere. Unlike some neighborhood places, it's friendly to outsiders— you'll feel welcome even if you're not greeted by name. La Summa is worth seeking out just for the wonderful homemade pasta and desserts, and most of the more elaborate entrees are scrumptious, too. You might start with ravioli or superb soup (our waitress one night didn't know exactly what was in the butternut-squash soup because, and I quote, "My mother made it"). Or stick to the salad that's included with each meal, and save room for sweets.

Try any seafood special, lobster ravioli, *pappardelle e melanzane* (strips of eggplant tossed with ethereal fresh pasta in light mari- nara sauce), or the aptly named "house special"—veal, chicken,

sausage, shrimp, artichokes, pepperoncini, olives, and mushrooms in white-wine sauce. Desserts, especially tiramisú, are
terrific.

Piccola Venezia. 263 Hanover St. ☎ **617/523-3888.** Reservations recom-
mended at dinner. Main courses $10–$20; lunch specialties $5–$8. AE, DISC,
MC, V. Daily 11am–10pm; lunch menu Mon–Fri 11am–4pm. T: Green or
Orange Line to Haymarket. ITALIAN.

The glass front wall of Piccola Venezia ("little Venice") shows off
the exposed-brick dining room, decorated with prints and photos
and filled with happy patrons. Portions are large, and the homey
food tends to be heavy on red sauce, although more sophisticated
dishes are available. The delicious sautéed mushroom appetizer is
solidly in the latter category; a more traditional starter is the tasty
pasta e fagioli (bean-and-pasta soup). Then dig into spaghetti and
meatballs, chicken parmigiana, eggplant rolatini, or pasta puttanesca. This is a good place to try traditional Italian-American
favorites such as polenta (home-style, not the yuppie croutons
available at so many other places), *baccala* (reconstituted salt cod),
or the house specialty, tripe.

INEXPENSIVE

Galleria Umberto. 289 Hanover St. ☎ **617/227-5709.** All items less than
$3. No credit cards. Mon–Sat 11am–2pm. Closed 3 weeks in July. T: Green or
Orange Line to Haymarket. ITALIAN.

The long, fast-moving line of businesspeople and tourists tips you
off to the fact that this cafeteria-style spot is a real bargain. The
food is good, too. You can fill up on a couple of slices of pizza,
but if you're feeling adventurous, try *arancini* (a rice ball filled
with ground beef, peas, and cheese). The calzones—ham and
cheese, spinach, spinach and cheese, or spinach and sausage—and
potato croquettes are tasty, too. Study the cases while you wait
and be ready to order at once when you reach the head of the line.
Have a quick lunch and get on with your sightseeing.

✪ **Pizzeria Regina.** 10½ Thacher St. ☎ **617/227-0765.** www.pizzeriaregina.
com. Reservations not accepted. Pizza $9–$16. No credit cards. Mon–Thurs
11am–11:30pm; Fri–Sat 11am–midnight; Sun noon–11pm. T: Green or Orange
Line to Haymarket. PIZZA.

Regina's looks almost like a movie set, but look a little closer—
this is the place the movie sets are trying to re-create. Busy waitresses who call everyone "dear" weave through the boisterous
dining room—sorry, no slices here—delivering peerless pizza
steaming hot out of the brick oven. Let it cool a little before you

dig in. Nouveau ingredients like sun-dried tomatoes appear on the list of toppings, but that's not authentic. House-made sausage, maybe some pepperoni, and a couple of beers—now, *that's* authentic.

3　Faneuil Hall Marketplace & Financial District

VERY EXPENSIVE

✪ **The Bay Tower.** 60 State St. ☎ **617/723-1666.** www.baytower.com. Reservations recommended. Jacket requested for men in dining room. Main courses $22–$36. AE, CB, DC, JCB, MC, V. Mon–Thurs 5:30–10pm; Fri 5:30–11pm; Sat 5–11pm. Validated parking available. T: Blue or Orange Line to State or Green Line to Government Center. CREATIVE AMERICAN.

Let's cut to the chase: Would you pay this much at a restaurant with a view of a brick wall or a street corner? Of course not. Is it worth it? Absolutely. One of the most beautiful dining rooms in Boston, the 33rd-floor Bay Tower has enormous glass walls facing a glorious panorama of Faneuil Hall Marketplace, the harbor, and the airport. The terraced table area is arranged so that every seat has a view, and the shiny (polished, not mirrored) surfaces lend a casinolike air to the romantic, candlelit room.

The menu, an intriguing variety of traditional and contemporary dishes, changes seasonally. You might start with lobster bisque, shrimp cocktail, or beef carpaccio. Entrees include the usual meat, chicken, and seafood, often with a twist. Roast chicken is served with herb risotto, smoked-shrimp mousse, and red-pepper cream; for more traditional palates, Dover sole is filleted at the table. There's always at least one vegetarian entree. Many people come just for sweets, drinks, and dancing in the lounge, so desserts are wonderful, with an emphasis on chocolate.

Julien. In Le Meridien Boston, 250 Franklin St. ☎ **617/451-1900.** Reservations recommended. Main courses $14.50–$18.75 at lunch, $29–$34 at dinner; business lunch $28. AE, CB, DC, MC, V. Tues–Fri noon–2pm; Mon–Thurs 6–10pm; Fri–Sat 6–10:30pm. T: Blue or Orange Line to State or Red Line to Downtown Crossing. FRENCH/MEDITERRANEAN.

Julien is in one of the most beautiful rooms in the city, under a vaulted, gilt-edged ceiling and five crystal chandeliers. Listen closely and you can almost hear the business deals going down, especially at lunch. The seasonal menus emphasize fresh regional products. Specialty starters include terrine of fresh homemade foie gras with truffles, and Maine lobster salad on a bed of diced vegetables. Sautéed tuna steak with brochette of asparagus and wild mushrooms is an excellent choice, as is rack of lamb with artichoke ragout and fresh asparagus. The desserts are among the best in town. The wine list offers selections from top French, American, German, and Italian wineries. The business lunch includes a soup or salad, a choice of entrees, and coffee or tea.

Café Fleuri, Le Meridien's atrium-style informal dining room, serves lunch on weekdays and Sunday brunch ($39 to $49 adult, $16.50 child) at 11 and 11:30am and 1 and 1:30pm. On Saturday afternoons from September through May, the "Chocolate Bar Buffet" takes over.

✪ **Maison Robert.** 45 School St. ☎ **617/227-3370.** www.maisonrobert. com. Reservations recommended. Main courses $12–$24 at lunch, $19–$32 at dinner. Le Café fixed-price menu $18 or $25; à la carte main courses $13–$28. AE, CB, DC, MC, V. Mon–Fri 11:30am–2:30pm; Mon–Sat 5:30–10pm. Valet parking available at dinner. T: Red Line to Park Street or Green Line to Government Center. CLASSIC AND INNOVATIVE FRENCH.

This world-class French restaurant has been a legend in Boston since it opened in Old City Hall in 1971. Like many excellent restaurants, it's family-owned and -operated —proprietors Lucien and Ann Robert are executive chef Andrée Robert's parents, and nephew Jacky Robert took over in the kitchen in 1996 after many years as a top chef in San Francisco (including 10 years at Ernie's).

The formal dining room is spectacular, with majestic crystal chandeliers and tall windows. The food equals the setting, classic but dramatic, with unexpected but welcome twists. You might start with a tender, airy cheese soufflé or smoked lobster cream soup. Entrees include options you would expect and pleasant surprises—filet mignon is a meat-lover's delight, Dover sole is served *à la meunière*, and ostrich fillet is marinated in pomegranate juice. The impressive desserts range from excellent soufflés to heart-stopping chocolate concoctions to upside-down apple tart, served warm with cinnamon sabayon.

The ground-floor **Café** is more casual and less expensive than the upstairs room, but also thoroughly French. In the summer, cafe seating spills onto the lovely terrace next to the landmark statue of Benjamin Franklin.

EXPENSIVE

✪ **Les Zygomates.** 129 South St. ☎ **617/542-5108.** www.winebar.com. Reservations recommended. Main courses $15–$25; prix-fixe $11 at lunch, $19 at dinner (Mon–Thurs). AE, CB, DC, DISC, MC, V. Mon–Fri 11:30am–1am (lunch until 2pm, dinner until 10:30pm); Sat 6pm–1am (dinner until 11:30pm). Valet parking available at dinner. T: Red Line to South Station. FRENCH/ECLECTIC.

You have to negotiate the construction wasteland near South Station to reach this delightful bistro and wine bar, but it's worth the trouble. The bar in the high-ceilinged, brick-walled space serves a great selection of wine, available by the bottle, the glass, and the 2-ounce "taste."

The efficient staff will guide you to a good accompaniment for chef and co-owner Ian Just's delicious food. Salads are excellent, lightly dressed and garden-fresh, and main courses are hearty and filling but not heavy. Roasted salmon fillet with French lentils and celery-root purée is toothsome, and meat-lovers will find flank steak with garlic mashed potatoes and sautéed vegetables succulent. For dessert, try not to fight over the lemon mousse, a cloud of citrus and air. Tuesday through Saturday night, you can linger over a glass of wine and listen to live jazz.

Ye Olde Union Oyster House. 41 Union St. (between North and Hanover sts.). ☎ **617/227-2750.** www.unionoysterhouse.com. Reservations recommended. Main courses $9.50–$20 at lunch, $15–$31 at dinner; children's menu $5–$10. AE, CB, DC, DISC, MC, V. Sun–Thurs 11am–9:30pm (lunch menu until 5pm); Fri–Sat 11am–10pm (lunch until 6pm). Union Bar daily 11am–midnight (lunch until 3pm, late-supper fare until 11pm). Closed Thanksgiving, Dec 25. Valet and validated parking available. T: Green or Orange Line to Haymarket. NEW ENGLAND/SEAFOOD.

America's oldest restaurant in continuous service, the Union Oyster House opened in 1826, and the booths and oyster bar haven't moved since. The food is tasty, traditional New England fare, popular with tourists on the adjacent Freedom Trail (the subject of a new mural by folk artist Thomas Lynch) and savvy locals. At the crescent-shaped bar on the lower level of the cramped, low-ceilinged building, "where Daniel Webster drank many a toddy in his day," try the cold seafood sampler of oysters, clams, and shrimp to start. Follow with a broiled or grilled dish such as scrod or salmon, or perhaps shrimp scampi, fried seafood, or grilled pork loin. A "shore dinner" of chowder, steamers or mussels, lobster, corn, potatoes, and dessert is an excellent introduction to local favorites. For dessert, try gingerbread with whipped cream. Ask to be seated at John F. Kennedy's favorite booth (no. 18), which is marked with a plaque.

MODERATE

✪ **Durgin-Park.** 340 Faneuil Hall Marketplace. ☎ **617/227-2038.** Reservations not accepted. Main courses $5–$18; specials $16–$25. AE, DC, DISC, MC, V. Daily 11:30am–2:30pm; Mon–Thurs 2:30–10pm, Fri–Sat 2:30–10:30pm,

Sun 2:30–9pm. T: Green or Blue Line to Government Center or Orange Line to Haymarket. NEW ENGLAND.

For huge portions of delicious food, a rowdy atmosphere where CEOs share tables with students, and famously cranky waitresses who can't seem to bear the sight of any of it, people have poured into Durgin-Park since 1827. It's everything it's cracked up to be—a tourist magnet that attracts hordes of locals, where everyone's disappointed when the waitresses are nice (they often are). Approximately 2,000 people a day find their way to the line that stretches down a flight of stairs to the first floor of Faneuil Hall Marketplace's North Market building. The queue moves quickly, and you'll probably wind up seated at a long table with other people (smaller tables are available).

The food is wonderful, and there's plenty of it—prime rib the size of a hubcap, giant lamb chops, piles of fried seafood, roast turkey that might fill you up till Thanksgiving. Steaks and chops are broiled on an open fire over wood charcoal. Fresh seafood arrives twice daily, and fish dinners are broiled to order. Vegetables come à la carte; if you want to try Boston baked beans, now's the time. For dessert, the strawberry shortcake is justly celebrated, and molasses lovers (this is not a dish for dabblers) will want to try Indian pudding: molasses and cornmeal baked for hours and served with ice cream.

Tatsukichi-Boston. 189 State St. ☎ **617/720-2468.** Reservations recommended at dinner. Main courses $11–$22; sushi $2.50–$7.50 per order; lunch specials from $6.75. AE, DC, DISC, JCB, MC, V. Mon–Fri 11:30am–2:30pm; Sun–Thurs 5–10pm, Fri–Sat 5–11pm. Validated parking available. T: Blue or Orange Line to State. JAPANESE/SUSHI.

A block from Faneuil Hall Marketplace, this award-winning restaurant with an excellent sushi bar is a favorite with the Japanese community and other fans of the cuisine. At half of the tables, patrons sit on chairs; at the rest, they kneel on an elevated platform. Non-sushi offerings include an extensive array of authentic Japanese dishes, such as *shabu shabu* (beef and vegetables cooked in seasoned boiling water) and *kushiage* (meat, seafood, and vegetables on skewers, lightly battered and fried, served with dipping sauces). At lunch, the *unagi-don* (grilled eel) is as tasty as it is scary-sounding.

Downstairs is the more casual, less expensive **Goemon** (☎ **617/367-8670**). It serves all kinds of noodles—excellent for a quick lunch—and Japanese tapas (how's that for multicultural?).

The little plates ($3.50 to $7.25), available at dinner only, are great for a group that wants some culinary adventure. They range from endive salad with Japanese plum vinaigrette to soy-flavored duck confit.

INEXPENSIVE

✪ **Cosí Sandwich Bar.** 53 State St. (at Congress St.). ☎ **617/723-4447.** Sandwiches $5.75–$8.25; soups and salads $2.95–$6.50. AE, DC, MC, V. Mon–Thurs 7am–6pm; Fri 7am–5pm. T: Orange or Blue Line to State. ITALIAN/ ECLECTIC.

Flavorful fillings on delectable bread make Cosí the newest lunch hot spot downtown—times three. This location, right on the Freedom Trail, makes a fantastic refueling stop. Italian flatbread baked fresh all day—so tasty that it's even good plain—gets split open and filled with your choice of meat, fish, vegetables, cheese, and spreads. The more fillings you choose, the more you pay. Tandoori chicken with caramelized onions is sensational, as is smoked salmon with spinach-artichoke spread. The lunch crowds are more manageable in the summer, when seating extends outdoors. Other branches are at 14 Milk St. (☎ **617/426-7565**), near Downtown Crossing, and at 133 Federal St. (☎ **617/292-2674**).

4 Downtown Crossing

VERY EXPENSIVE

Locke-Ober. 3–4 Winter Place. ☎ **617/542-1340.** Reservations required. Main courses $8–$24.50 at lunch, $17–$40 at dinner. AE, CB, DC, DISC, MC, V. Mon–Fri 11:30am–2:30pm; Mon–Fri 5:30–10pm, Sat 5:30–10:30pm. Valet parking available after 6pm. T: Red or Orange Line to Downtown Crossing. AMERICAN/CONTINENTAL.

"Locke's" is *the* traditional Boston restaurant, a power-broker favorite since 1875. At press time, rumors about a change of ownership were swirling, but the old-time atmosphere was unruffled. In a tiny alley off the Winter Street pedestrian mall, the dark, wood-paneled restaurant feels like a men's club, with exquisite service, stained-glass windows, and crystal chandeliers. The long, mirrored downstairs bar dates from 1880. Women won't feel unwelcome, but this is definitely not a "girls' night out" place; for one thing, anyone on a diet will be sorely tempted.

The food is definitely old-fashioned—famous Jonah crab cakes or steak tartare to start, then superb grilled salmon with horseradish sauce, Wiener schnitzel à la Holstein, or excellent veal chop. The signature dish is lobster Savannah, a sinful concoction that calls for the meat of a 3-pound lobster diced with pepper and mushrooms, bound with cheese and sherry sauce, stuffed into the shell, and baked. The dessert menu lists about 2 dozen items, and as you might expect, the chocolate mousse is a dish for the ages.

INEXPENSIVE

Fajitas & 'Ritas. 25 West St. (between Washington and Tremont sts.). ☎ **617/426-1222.** Most dishes under $9. AE, DC, DISC, MC, V. Mon–Tues 11:30am–9pm; Wed–Thurs 11:30am–10pm; Fri–Sat 11:30am–11pm. T: Red or Green Line to Park St. or Orange Line to Downtown Crossing. TEX-MEX.

This entertaining restaurant isn't the most authentic in town, but it's one of the most fun. You order by filling out a slip, checking off your choices of fillings and garnishes to go with your nachos, quesadillas, burritos, or, of course, fajitas. There's nothing exotic, just the usual beef, chicken, shrimp, beans, and so forth. You can also try barbecue items, such as smoked brisket or pulled pork. A member of the somewhat harried staff relays your order to the kitchen and returns with big portions of fresh food—this place is too busy for anything to be sitting around for very long. As the name indicates, 'ritas (margaritas, ordered from a list of about a dozen options using the same check-off system as the food) are a house specialty.

5 Beacon Hill

VERY EXPENSIVE

No. 9 Park. 9 Park St. ☎ **617/742-9991.** Reservations recommended. Main courses $21–$35. AE, DC, MC, V. Mon–Fri 11:30am–2:30pm; Mon–Sat 5:30–10:30pm. Valet parking available at dinner. T: Green or Red Line to Park St. CREATIVE NEW ENGLAND.

One of Boston's most acclaimed new restaurants sits in the shadow of the State House, an area better known for politicians' pubs than for fine dining. No. 9 Park is fine indeed, thanks to chef-owner Barbara Lynch's flair for strong flavors and superb pasta. To start, try beet salad—an upright cylinder of shredded vegetables atop blue cheese, surrounded by greens—or oysters on the half shell with unusually tasty cocktail sauce. Move on to succulent roast chicken served with outrageously buttery mashed potatoes, retro but luscious beef Wellington, braised lamb shank with baby flageolet beans, or a sampler of those famous pastas. For dessert, the profiteroles (a chocolate version served with coconut ice cream) are worth every calorie. One caveat: The austere but comfortable space can get a bit too loud.

MODERATE

Artú (see "The North End," above) has a branch at 89 Charles St. (☎ **617/227-9023**).

Istanbul Café. 37 Bowdoin St. ☎ **617/227-3434.** Main courses $7–$16.50; sandwiches $5–$6.50. MC, V. Mon–Wed 11am–10pm; Thurs–Sat 11am–11pm; Sun noon–10pm. T: Red or Green Line to Park St. or Blue Line to Bowdoin. TURKISH.

Hidden away behind the State House, the Istanbul Café is worth seeking out. It's a small, crowded room, four steps down from the street, where the scent of Middle Eastern spices hits you as soon as you open the door. This is a great place to go if you want to linger, because the always-helpful service sometimes grinds to a halt. But that's not a complaint—I go there to catch up with friends and tarry over the food, which ranges from familiar and unusually good to just unusual (and also good).

The appetizer sampler makes a great introduction to the cuisine. *Adana kebab* appears several times in main dishes; the elongated meatballs of spiced ground lamb, threaded onto skewers and grilled, are a must if you like lamb. Cheese lovers at the table will monopolize the plainest version of Turkish pizza, an odd but delicious dish. But unless you can't get enough okra, steer clear of the *etli bamya,* which is more vegetable than meat. The baklava is a lovely rendition of the traditional dessert, crunchy and not too sweet, perfect with a Turkish coffee.

6 Charlestown

VERY EXPENSIVE

✪ **Olives.** 10 City Sq. ☎ **617/242-1999.** Reservations accepted only for parties of 6 or more. Main courses $19–$32. AE, DC, MC, V. Mon–Fri 5:30–10pm; Sat 5–10:30pm. Valet parking available. T: Orange or Green Line to North Station; 15-min. walk. ECLECTIC.

This informal bistro near the Charlestown Navy Yard just keeps getting more popular. Patrons often line up shortly after 5pm—befriending five strangers and calling for a reservation won't sound so crazy after a couple of hours waiting for a table. If you don't arrive by 5:45pm, expect to spend at least 2 hours, at the bar if there's room. Once you're seated, perhaps on a cushy banquette, you'll find the noise level high (thanks partly to the open kitchen), the service uneven, and the ravenous customers festive.

Happily, the food is worth the wait. Celebrity chef Todd English, co-owner with his wife, Olivia, is a culinary genius. The regularly changing menu includes "Olives Classics"—perhaps a delicious tart of olives, caramelized onions, and anchovies, or spit-roasted chicken flavored with herbs and garlic, oozing succulent juices into old-fashioned mashed potatoes. Grilling is a favorite technique, and with reason—yellowfin tuna, atop parsley mashed potatoes and accented with perfect mussels, holds up beautifully, and any lamb dish is sure to please. When you order your entree, you'll be asked if you want falling chocolate cake for dessert. Say yes.

7 Chinatown/Theater District

The most entertaining and delicious introduction to Chinatown's cuisine is **dim sum,** the traditional midday meal featuring a variety of appetizer-style dishes. Waitresses wheel carts laden with tempting morsels to your table, and you order by pointing (unless you know Chinese). The waitress then stamps your check with the symbol of the dish, adding about $1 to $3 to your tab. Unless you're ravenous or you order à la carte items from the regular menu, the total usually won't be more than about $10 to $12 per person. This is a great group activity, especially on weekends. My favorite place for dim sum is **Empire Garden Restaurant,** also known as Emperor's Garden, 690–698 Washington St., 2nd floor (☎ 617/482-8898). Other popular destinations are the **Golden Palace Restaurant,** 14 Tyler St. (☎ 617/423-4565), **China Pearl,** 9 Tyler St., 2nd floor (☎ 617/426-4338), and **Chau Chow City,** 83 Essex St. (☎ 617/338-8158).

EXPENSIVE

There's a branch of **Legal Sea Foods** (see "Back Bay," later in this chapter) at 36 Park Sq., between Columbus Avenue and Stuart Street (☎ 617/426-4444).

Ginza Japanese Restaurant. 14 Hudson St. ☎ **617/338-2261.** Reservations accepted only for parties of 6 or more. Sushi from $3.50; main courses $11–$20. AE, DC, MC, V. Mon–Fri 11:30am–2:30pm, Sat–Sun 11:30am–4pm; Sun–Mon 5pm–2am, Tues–Sat 5pm–4am. T: Orange Line to New England Medical Center. SUSHI/JAPANESE.

Tucked away on a side street in Chinatown, you'll find one of the city's best Japanese restaurants. Track down the nondescript entrance, settle into one of the two rooms (in a booth if you're lucky), and watch as kimono-clad waitresses glide past, bearing sushi boats the size of small children. Ginza is a magnet for Japanese expatriates, sushi-lovers, and, in the wee hours, club-hoppers. It's not the only place in town where expert chefs work wonders with ocean-fresh ingredients, but it is the only place that serves "spider maki"—a soft-shelled crab fried and tucked into a *nori* (seaweed) wrapper with avocado, cucumber, and flying-fish roe. An excellent starter is the suddenly fashionable *edamame*—addictive boiled and salted soybeans served in the pod (you pull the beans out with your teeth). Then let your imagination run wild, or trust the chefs to assemble something dazzling. Green tea ice cream makes an unusually satisfying dessert, but nobody will blame you for finishing up with another round of California maki.

MODERATE

✪ **East Ocean City.** 25–29 Beach St. ☎ **617/542-2504.** Reservations accepted only for parties of 6 or more. Main courses $5–$22. AE, MC, V. Sun–Thurs 11am–3am; Fri–Sat 11am–4am. T: Orange Line to Chinatown. CANTONESE/SEAFOOD.

Don't get too attached to the inhabitants of the fish tanks here— they might turn up on your plate. Tanks make up one wall of the high-ceilinged space, decorated with lots of glass and other hard surfaces that make it rather noisy. The encyclopedic menu offers a huge range of dishes, but as the name indicates, seafood is the focus. It's fresh, delicious, and carefully prepared. One specialty is clams in black-bean sauce, a spicy rendering of a messy, delectable dish. Just about anything that swims can be ordered steamed with ginger and scallions; for variety, check out the chow foon section of the menu.

Grand Chau Chow. 45 Beach St. ☎ **617/292-5166.** Reservations accepted only for parties of 10 or more. Main courses $6–$24. AE, DC, DISC, MC, V. Sun–Thurs 10am–3am; Fri–Sat 10am–4am. T: Orange Line to China-town. CANTONESE.

This is one of the best and busiest restaurants in Chinatown, with niceties the smaller restaurants don't offer, such as tablecloths and tuxedoed waiters. In the large fish tanks, both salt- and freshwater, you can watch your dinner swimming around (if you have the heart). Clams with black-bean sauce is a signature dish, as is gray sole with fried fins and bones. Stick to seafood and you can't go wrong. Lunch specials are a great deal, but skip the chow fun, which quickly turns gelatinous. If you're in town during Chinese New Year celebrations, phone ahead and ask that a banquet be prepared for your group. For about $25 a person, you'll get so many courses that you'll lose track. It's a great way to start any year.

Across the street, **Chau Chow,** 52 Beach St. (☎ **617/ 426-6266**), is Grand Chau Chow's bare-bones sibling. It's downright ugly, doesn't accept credit cards, and packs them in for the excellent food and reasonable prices, not the unyielding red plastic benches. The salt-and-pepper shrimp is the best around.

Jacob Wirth Company. 33–37 Stuart St. ☎ **617/338-8586.** www. jacobwirthrestaurant.com. Reservations recommended at dinner. Main courses $7–$17. AE, DC, DISC, MC, V. Mon 11:30am–8pm; Tues–Thurs 11:30am–11pm; Fri–Sat 11:30am–midnight; Sun noon–8pm. Validated parking available. T: Green Line to Boylston or Orange Line to New England Medical Center. GERMAN/AMERICAN.

In the heart of the Theater District, "Jake's" has been serving Bostonians since 1868—even before there were theaters here. The wood floor and brass accents give the room the feeling of a saloon, or perhaps a beer garden. The hearty German specialties include Wiener schnitzel, sauerbraten, mixed grills, bratwurst, and knockwurst. Daily blue-plate specials, a large selection of sandwiches and brews on tap, and contemporary American fare—often including excellent prime rib—round out the menu. Service at lunchtime is snappy, but if you want to be on time for the theater, the suspense might be greater in the restaurant than at the show.

INEXPENSIVE

Buddha's Delight. 5 Beach St., 2nd floor. ☎ **617/451-2395.** Main courses $6–$12. MC, V. Sun–Thurs 11am–9:30pm; Fri–Sat 11am–10:30pm. T: Orange Line to Chinatown. VEGETARIAN/VIETNAMESE.

Fresh and healthful intersect with cheap and filling at this busy restaurant. The grim stairwell is off-putting, but the glass-walled dining room and cheerful service are worth the climb. The menu lists "chicken," "shrimp," "pork," and even "lobster"—all in quotes because the kitchen doesn't use meat, poultry, fish, or dairy (some beverages have condensed milk). The chefs fry and barbecue tofu and gluten into more-than-reasonable facsimiles using techniques owner Cuong Van Tran learned from Buddhist monks in a temple outside Los Angeles. Between trying to figure out how they do it and savoring the strong, clear flavors characteristic of Vietnamese cuisine, you might not miss your usual protein. To start, try delectable spring rolls, fried or "fresh" (in paper-thin mung-bean wrappers with mint leaves peeking through). Move on to "shrimp" or "pork" with rice noodles, any of the combination dishes, or excellent chow fun.

8 The South End

VERY EXPENSIVE

Hamersley's Bistro. 553 Tremont St. ☎ **617/423-2700.** www.hamersleysbistro.com. Reservations recommended. Main courses $23–$38. Menu dégustation varies. AE, DISC, MC, V. Mon–Fri 6–10pm; Sat 5:30–10pm; Sun 5:30–9:30pm. Closed 2 weeks in Jan. Valet parking available. T: Orange Line to Back Bay. ECLECTIC.

This is the place that put the South End on Boston's culinary map, a pioneering restaurant that's both classic and contemporary. The husband-and-wife team of Gordon and Fiona Hamersley presides over a long dining room with lots of soft surfaces that absorb sound, so you can see but not quite hear what's going on at the tables around you. That means you'll have to quiz one of the courteous servers about the dish that just passed by—perhaps an appetizer of tuna carpaccio over white-bean salad, or grilled mushrooms and garlic on country bread.

The menu changes seasonally and offers about a dozen carefully considered entrees (always including vegetarian dishes) noted for their emphasis on taste and texture. The signature dish is roast chicken, flavored with garlic, lemon, and parsley and served with roast potato, roast onions, and whole cloves of sweet baked garlic. Salmon au poivre with sorrel, leeks, and fingerling potatoes is delicious, as is grilled port-glazed fillet of beef. The wine list is excellent.

✪ **Icarus.** 3 Appleton St. ☎ **617/426-1790.** Reservations recommended. Main courses $19.50–$32.50. AE, CB, DC, DISC, MC, V. Mon–Thurs 6–10pm; Fri 6–10:30pm; Sat 5:30–10:30pm; Sun 5:30–10pm. Closed Sun July–Aug. Valet parking available. T: Green Line to Arlington or Orange Line to Back Bay. ECLECTIC.

This shamelessly romantic subterranean restaurant offers every element of a great dining experience. It's perfect for everything from helping a friend heal a broken heart to celebrating a milestone anniversary. Marble accents and dark-wood trim lend an elegant air to the two-level dining room, and the service is efficient but not formal. Chef-owner Christopher Douglass uses choice local seafood, poultry, meats, and produce to create imaginative dishes that seem more like alchemy than cooking. The menu changes regularly—you might start with braised exotic mushrooms atop polenta, or the daily "pasta whim." Move on to soft-shell crabs on a black-rice cake, or lemony grilled chicken with garlic mashed potatoes so good you'll want to ask for a plate of them. Don't. Instead, save room for one of the unbelievable desserts. The trio of fruit sorbets is one of the best nonchocolate desserts I've ever run across.

MODERATE

Addis Red Sea. 544 Tremont St. ☎ **617/426-8727.** Main courses $9–$17. AE, MC, V. Mon–Fri 5–10:30pm; Sat noon–11pm; Sun noon–10pm. T: Orange Line to Back Bay. ETHIOPIAN.

If you're in the mood to experiment, Addis Red Sea is a good place to start. Colorful carpets and wall hangings decorate the dimly lit, subterranean space, and you sit on stools at *mesobs,* traditional Ethiopian tables. Wash your hands! Ethiopian food is served family-style on a platter, without utensils. The waitress covers the platter with a layer of *injera,* a spongy, tangy bread, and spoons the food on top of it. Tear off a piece of injera, scoop up a mouthful of food, and dig in. Ask for more injera if you need it to finish off the stewlike main courses. Many are vegetarian, and the vegetable combination makes a good introduction to this cuisine, with a choice of dishes that might include lentils, split peas, cracked wheat, onions, potatoes, beans, carrots, and greens. The spice level varies, but even the mildest dishes are flavorful and filling. There are also tasty meat dishes—*doro wat* is lemon-marinated chicken, *yebez wat* is lamb with red pepper, and *kifto* is the Ethiopian version of steak tartare.

Bob the Chef's Jazz Cafe. 604 Columbus Ave. ☎ **617/536-6204.** Main courses $9–$15; sandwiches $5–$8. AE, DC, MC, V. Tues–Wed 11:30am–10pm; Thurs–Sat 11:30am–midnight; Sun 11am–9pm (brunch until 3pm). Self-parking ($5) across the street. T: Orange Line to Mass. Ave.; 5-min. walk. SOUTHERN/ CAJUN.

Bob the Chef's resembles a yuppie fern bar, but it serves generous portions of Southern specialties against a backdrop of jazz. The music is live Thursday through Saturday nights and at Sunday brunch. You'll find dishes such as fried chicken, served alone or with barbecued ribs; meat loaf; "soul fish" (in cornmeal batter); and Creole specialties like jambalaya and shrimp étoufée. Dinners come with a corn muffin and your choice of two side dishes— including black-eyed peas, macaroni and cheese, collard greens, and candied yams. Frying is done in vegetable oil, not the customary lard, and everywhere you'd expect bacon for flavoring, smoked turkey is used instead. For dessert, try the sweet-potato pie, which makes pumpkin pie seem like vanilla pudding.

Grillfish. 162 Columbus Ave. ☎ **617/357-1620.** www.grillfish.com. Reservations accepted only for parties of 6 or more. Main courses $10–$21. AE, DISC, MC, V. Sun–Mon 5:30–10pm; Tues–Thurs 5:30–11pm; Fri–Sat 5:30–midnight. SEAFOOD.

A splash of Florida style in conservative Boston, this sassy interloper specializes in reasonably priced seafood. It's part of a small chain that's also in the Miami and Washington areas. An open-fire grill and a PG-13–rated mural over the bar dominate the high-ceilinged dining room. Grilled shrimp scampi (an unusual version, with tomatoes in the sauce) is available as an appetizer or main course. The grilled fish selections—a regular roster augmented with specials—come with your choice of sweet onion or garlic-tomato sauce. Sautéed dishes have marsala or piccata sauce, and several types of shellfish are available over pasta. Diners shout to be heard over the loud music; ask for a table near the windows or on the small patio (open seasonally) if you prefer a quieter atmosphere.

INEXPENSIVE

Le Gamin Café. 550 Tremont St. ☎ **617/654-8969.** www.legamin.com. Main courses $5–$11.50; crêpes $3–$9.50. MC, V. Daily 8am–midnight. T: Orange Line to Back Bay. FRENCH.

The waiter has a heavy French accent. The posters on the walls do, too. It's freezing out, but the salad is right-from-the-garden fresh. The signature sandwiches—with three fillings mixed and matched from a list of more than a dozen—are splendid. The crêpes are perfect, and the homemade caramel sauce on the orange-filled one is swooningly good. The tuna in the salade Niçoise is a tad dry and the room a bit noisy, but everything else is just so. This is a perfect spot for lingering over morning coffee or a mid-afternoon glass of wine. It's a recent addition to a small chain that originated in Manhattan. Oh, shoot—another thing New York got right first.

9 Back Bay

VERY EXPENSIVE

Celebrity chef Stan Frankenthaler planned to move his celebrated **Salamander** (☎ **617/451-2150;** www.salamander-restaurant.com) here from Cambridge in late 2000. Besides elaborate

Asian-influenced creations, the new Salamander will have a satay bar. It's in a new residential building, Trinity Place, 25 Huntington Ave. (T: Green Line to Copley or Orange Line to Back Bay).

The Ritz-Carlton Dining Room, 15 Arlington St. (☎ 617/536-5700; T: Green Line to Arlington), is scheduled to close while the hotel undergoes renovations for eight months beginning in mid-2001. It makes a splendid setting for a special occasion, and chef Mark Allen's California-inspired contemporary French cuisine is out of this world. Dinner Tuesday through Sunday (prix-fixe menus from $61 per person) and Sunday brunch ($52); reservations required.

✪ **Anago.** In the Lenox Hotel, 65 Exeter St. ☎ **617/266-6222.** Reservations recommended. Main courses $18–$35. AE, DC, MC, V. Mon–Thurs 5:30–10pm; Fri–Sat 5:30–10:30pm; Sun 5–9pm; Sun brunch 11am–2:30pm. Valet parking available. T: Green Line to Copley. CREATIVE AMERICAN.

Anago opened in Boston in 1997 with a reputation for bold, inventive food (gained during its days as Anago Bistro in Cambridge) and quickly established itself as one of the city's top restaurants. You can schedule a business meeting, romantic rendezvous, or family brunch here with equal confidence. Chef Bob Calderone, co-owner with his wife, Susan Finegold, makes good use of fresh regional produce, seafood, and meats.

To start, winter-squash soup garnished with a risotto cake is impressive, as is the house antipasto (roast pear, prosciutto, mozzarella, and vegetables). Main dishes might include oven-roasted bass with warm potato salad, grilled corn, and heirloom tomato salad, and toothsome grilled sirloin with red-wine sauce and porcini baked potato. Desserts are fanciful—try "chocolate, chocolate, chocolate," when it's available, and be ready to swoon. Service is friendly but polite. Even with an open kitchen, the tall, wide room is surprisingly quiet, thanks to the soundproofed ceiling, plush upholstery, and well-spaced tables and banquettes.

✪ **Aujourd'hui.** In the Four Seasons Hotel, 200 Boylston St. ☎ **617/451-2071.** Reservations recommended (required on holidays). Main courses $19–$23.50 at lunch, $32–$45 at dinner; Sun buffet brunch $55 adult, $26 child. AE, CB, DC, DISC, MC, V. Mon–Fri 6:30–11am, Sat–Sun 7–11am; Mon–Fri 11:30am–2:30pm, Sun brunch 11:30am–2:30pm; Mon–Sat 5:30–10:30pm, Sun 6–10:30pm. Valet parking available. T: Green Line to Arlington. CONTEMPORARY AMERICAN.

On the second floor of the city's premier luxury hotel, the most beautiful restaurant in town has floor-to-ceiling windows overlooking the Public Garden. Even if it were under a pup tent, the incredible service and food would make Aujourd'hui a hit with its special-occasion and expense-account clientele. Yes, the cost is astronomical, but how often is it true that you get what you pay for? Here, you do.

The regularly changing menu encompasses basic offerings you'd expect in a hotel dining room and creations that characterize an inventive kitchen. Executive chef Edward Gannon uses regional products and the freshest ingredients available, and the wine list is excellent. To start, you might try a perfectly balanced seasonal soup or a huge salad. Entrees include rack of lamb served with eggplant galette, black-olive tapenade, and flageolet ragout; roasted lobster comes with pineapple compote and crabmeat wontons. "Alternative Cuisine" offerings slash calories, cholesterol, sodium, and fat, but not flavor. The dessert menu also changes but always includes picture-perfect soufflés and homemade sorbets.

✪ **Grill 23 & Bar.** 161 Berkeley St. ☎ **617/542-2255.** www.grill23.com. Reservations recommended. Main courses $20–$36. AE, CB, DC, DISC, MC, V. Mon–Thurs 5:30–10:30pm; Fri–Sat 5:30–11pm; Sun 5:30–10pm. Valet parking available. T: Green Line to Arlington. AMERICAN.

Grill 23, a wood-paneled, glass-walled room with a businesslike air, is more than just a steak house. A briefcase-toting crowd comes here for traditional slabs of beef and chops as well as bolder, more creative options. Steak au poivre and lamb chops are perfectly grilled, crusty, juicy, and tender. The inventively updated meat loaf incorporates sirloin and chorizo under tomato coulis. And if the fish dishes aren't quite as memorable as the meat offerings—hey, it's a steak house. The bountiful à la carte side dishes include creamed spinach, roasted portabellos, and out-of-this-world garlic mashed potatoes. Desserts, especially crème brûlée, are toothsome, but (this is *not* your father's steak house) they don't always include cheesecake. The service is exactly right for the setting, helpful but not familiar.

A couple of caveats: The wine list is pricey, and the noise grows louder as the evening progresses. Still, you probably won't realize you're shouting until you're outside yelling about what a good meal you had.

✪ **L'Espalier.** 30 Gloucester St. ☎ **617/262-3023.** www.lespalier.com. Reservations required. Prix-fixe (4 courses) $65; menu dégustation (7 courses; whole tables only) $82. AE, DISC, MC, V. Mon–Sat 6–10pm. Valet parking available. T: Green Line B, C, or D to Hynes/ICA. NEW ENGLAND/FRENCH.

Dinner at L'Espalier is a unique experience, very much like spending the evening at the home of a dear friend who has only your pleasure in mind—and has a dozen helpers in the kitchen. Owners Frank and Catherine McClelland (he's the chef) preside over three dining rooms on the second floor of an 1886 townhouse. The space is formal yet inviting, and the service is beyond excellent, in that eerie realm where it seems possible that the waiter just read your mind. The food, an exploration of the freshest and most interesting ingredients available, is magnificent.

A first course of foie gras strudel arrives with rhubarb and dried-cherry compote, and perfectly balanced fresh Cabernet grape vinaigrette dresses a salad of greens with wild rice, herbed polenta, and white asparagus. Main courses usually include a game offering, perhaps rack of venison with caramelized endive, wild-rice salad, and gooseberry *jus;* salmon in a sesame crust over noodles in a ginger-and-sesame broth is equally impressive. The breads, sorbets, ice creams, and alarmingly good desserts (many adapted from the family's heirloom cookbooks) are made on the premises. Even if you have one of the superb soufflés, which are ordered with dinner, ask to see the beautiful desserts. Or order the celebrated cheese tray, which always includes two local cheeses.

✪ **Top of the Hub.** In the Prudential Center, 800 Boylston St. ☎ **617/ 536-1775.** Reservations recommended. Jacket advised for men. Main courses $7–$16 at lunch, $18–$32 at dinner; tasting menus $55 (5 courses), $75 (7 courses); Sun brunch $34. AE, DC, DISC, MC, V. Mon–Sat 11:30am–2:30pm, Sun brunch 10am–2:30pm; Mon–Thurs 5:30–10pm, Fri 5:30–11pm, Sat 5–11pm, Sun 5–10pm. Discounted parking available in Prudential Center garage after 4pm Mon–Fri, all day Sat–Sun. T: Green Line B, C, or D to Hynes/ICA; or E to Prudential. CREATIVE AMERICAN.

For many years, the answer to the question "How's the food at Top of the Hub?" was "The view is spectacular." The cuisine has improved dramatically—not to the point where it's a match for the 52nd-floor panorama, but that would be nearly impossible. Still, if you can't reserve a table by the window, don't bother with the restaurant; you can always have a drink in the lounge. Check the weather forecast and aim to eat here when it's clear out, taking the best advantage of the space's three glass-walled sides. And consider coming before sunset and lingering until dark for a true spectacle.

The menu emphasizes the seafood that the tourist-intensive clientele expects, with the customary simple preparations and some that show off the kitchen's creative side—soy-glazed yellowfin tuna roasted and served with quinoa salad, for example. Grilled sirloin is another good choice at dinner. Lunch offerings include pizzas and half a dozen tasty sandwiches. At either meal, the clam chowder is a standout, with more broth than cream. Salads are large and varied, but if you don't like vegetables drowning in dressing, ask for it on the side.

EXPENSIVE

Tapéo, 266 Newbury St. (☎ 617/267-4799), has the same owners as **Dalí** (see "Outside Harvard Square," in the "Cambridge" section, below).

Casa Romero. 30 Gloucester St., side entrance. ☎ **617/536-4341.** Reservations recommended. Main courses $12.50–$24. DISC, MC, V. Sun–Thurs 5–10pm; Fri–Sat 5–11pm. T: Green Line B, C, or D to Hynes/ICA. MEXICAN.

There's something about restaurants in alleys. They feel like secret clubs or speakeasies, and if they're really worth seeking out, so much the better. Casa Romero is just such a place. The tiled floor, heavy wood furnishings, dim lighting, and clay pots lend a real Mexican feel—you're definitely not at the local Tex-Mex counter. The food is excellent, both authentic and accessible, with generous portions of spicy-hot and milder dishes; the friendly staff will help you negotiate the menu. If the soup of the day is garlic, don't miss it. Main-dish specialties include several kinds of enchiladas, excellent stuffed squid in tomato-and-chipotle sauce, chicken breast in mole poblano sauce (a spicy concoction with a hint of chocolate), and terrific pork tenderloin marinated with oranges and smoked peppers. In the summer, reserve a table in the walled garden.

Davio's. 269 Newbury St. ☎ **617/262-4810.** www.davios.com. Reservations recommended downstairs. Main courses $10–$25; pizzas $7–$8.50. AE, CB, DC, DISC, MC, V. Daily 11:30am–1am (lunch until 5pm, dinner until 11pm). Valet parking available. T: Green Line to Copley. CREATIVE NORTHERN ITALIAN.

While the rest of the Boston-area culinary community plays musical chefs, owner-chef Steve DiFillippo has buckled down and turned Davio's into a local favorite. The restaurant's excellent reputation rests on its top-notch kitchen, dedicated staff, and pleasant atmosphere. In a Back Bay brownstone, you wouldn't expect to find typical Italian fare, and you won't. Start with excellent minestrone, beautifully balanced salad, or the day's homemade ravioli selection (also available as a main course).

Move on to grilled veal chop in port wine sauce, salmon grilled to pink perfection, or any dish that involves homemade sausage. There are usually three special entrees daily, plus a house pâté. Desserts change regularly; try the ethereal tiramisú if it's available. Davio's has a well-edited wine selection, including some rare and expensive Italian vintages. The upstairs cafe (open 11:30am to 3pm and 5 to 11pm) offers terrace seating in good weather.

The **Cambridge** branch, at the Royal Sonesta Hotel, 5 Cambridge Pkwy. (☎ **617/661-4810**), keeps the same hours, except dinner service ends at 10pm nightly.

✪ **Legal Sea Foods.** In the Prudential Center, 800 Boylston St. ☎ **617/ 266-6800.** www.legalseafoods.com. Reservations recommended at lunch, not accepted at dinner. Main courses $7–$13 at lunch, $14–$27 at dinner; lobster priced daily. AE, CB, DC, DISC, MC, V. Mon–Thurs 11am–10:30pm; Fri–Sat 11am–11:30pm; Sun noon–10pm. T: Green Line B, C, or D to Hynes/ICA or E to Prudential. SEAFOOD.

The food at Legal Sea Foods ("Legal's" in Bostonian parlance) isn't the fanciest, the cheapest, or the trendiest. It's the freshest, and management's commitment to that policy has produced a thriving chain. The family-owned business has an international reputation for serving only top-quality fish and shellfish, prepared in every imaginable way. The menu includes regular selections (scrod, haddock, bluefish, salmon, shrimp, calamari, and lobster, among others) plus whatever looked good at the market that morning, and it's all splendid. The clam chowder is great, the fish chowder lighter but equally good, the smoked bluefish pâté rich and creamy. Entrees run the gamut from grilled fish served plain or with Cajun spices (try the Arctic char), to seafood fra'diavolo on fresh linguine, to salmon baked in parchment with vegetables and white wine. Or go the luxurious route and order the biggest lobster you can afford. The classic dessert is ice-cream bonbons, but a recent addition, Boston cream pie, is so good that you may come back just for that.

I suggest the Prudential Center branch because it takes reservations (at lunch only), a deviation from a long tradition. Equally annoying but equally traditional is the policy of serving each dish when it's ready, instead of one table at a time. Other locations include the first waterfront branch, at 255 State St. (☎ **617/ 227-3115**); 36 Park Sq., between Columbus Avenue and Stuart Street, opposite the Boston Park Plaza Hotel (☎ **617/426-4444**); on the second level of Copley Place (☎ **617/266-7775**); and in Kendall Square, 5 Cambridge Center (☎ **617/864-3400**).

Turner Fisheries of Boston. In the Westin Copley Place Boston, 10 Hunt-ington Ave. ☎ **617/424-7425.** Reservations recommended. Main courses $9–$15 at lunch, $17–$28 at dinner. AE, CB, DC, DISC, MC, V. Mon–Sat 11am–10:30pm (lunch until 2pm Mon–Fri, until 3pm Sat); Sun 11am–3pm (brunch) and 5–10:30pm. Valet parking available. T: Orange Line to Back Bay, or Green Line to Copley. SEAFOOD.

This restaurant is best known for winning the Boston Harborfest Chowderfest contest so many times that its superb clam chowder was elevated to the Hall of Fame. It's also known as a place to go when you can't get into Legal Sea Foods, which does it a disservice—it also serves some of the freshest fish in town, in a calmer atmosphere than you'll usually find at Legal's. Packed with businesspeople at lunch and out-of-towners (and savvy locals who appreciate the more placid setting) at dinner, Turner Fisheries is obviously doing something right.

The menu features each day's special catch and suggested preparations—pan-fried, broiled, grilled, baked, steamed, or "spicy bronzed." Specials are more inventive, from the signature bouilla-baisse to pan-seared scallops in miso broth to excellent pastas (with and without seafood). The raw bar is also a draw, and there are always a few nonseafood options. Ask for a booth if you want privacy, or a table if you want to enjoy the atriumlike ambience.

MODERATE

Bangkok Cuisine. 177A Mass. Ave. ☎ **617/262-5377.** Reservations not accepted. Main courses $5–$8 at lunch, $8–$15 at dinner. AE, DISC, MC, V. Daily 11:30am–10:30pm. T: Green Line B, C, or D to Hynes/ICA. THAI.

Extremely popular with patrons of nearby Symphony Hall and the students who dominate this neighborhood, Bangkok Cuisine is a classic. The first Thai restaurant in Boston, it opened in 1979 and set (and has maintained) high standards for the many others that followed. For the unadventurous, it serves fantastic pad Thai. The rest of the menu runs the gamut from excellent basil chicken to all sorts of curry offerings, pan-fried or deep-fried whole fish, noodle soups, and hot-and-sour salads. Green curry in coconut milk and vegetables prepared with strong green Thai chili pepper are the most incendiary dishes. In this long, narrow room, there are no secrets—if the person at the next table is eating something appealing, ask what it is.

INEXPENSIVE

Café Jaffa. 48 Gloucester St. ☎ **617/536-0230.** Main courses $4.75–$12.95. AE, DC, DISC, MC, V. Mon–Thurs 11am–10:30pm; Fri–Sat 11am–11pm; Sun 1–10pm. T: Green Line B, C, or D to Hynes/ICA. MIDDLE EASTERN.

A brick-walled room with a glass front, Café Jaffa looks more like a snazzy pizza place than the excellent Middle Eastern restaurant it is. The reasonable prices, high quality, and large portions draw hordes of young people for traditional offerings such as falafel, baba ghanoush, and hummus, as well as burgers and steak tips. Lamb, beef, and chicken kabobs come with Greek salad, rice pilaf, and pita bread. For dessert, try the baklava if it's fresh (give it a pass if not). There is a short list of beer and wine and, somewhat incongruously, many fancy coffee offerings.

10 Kenmore Square

MODERATE

The Elephant Walk. 900 Beacon St. ☎ **617/247-1500.** Reservations recommended at dinner Sun–Thurs, not accepted Fri–Sat. Main courses $6–$18.50 at lunch, $9.50–$23.95 at dinner. AE, DC, DISC, MC, V. Mon–Sat 11:30am–2:30pm; Mon–Thurs 5–10pm, Fri 5–11pm, Sat 4:30–11pm, Sun 4:30–10pm. Valet parking available at dinner. T: Green Line C to St. Mary's St. FRENCH/CAMBODIAN.

France meets Cambodia on the menu at the Elephant Walk, 4 blocks from Kenmore Square on the Boston–Brookline border and decorated with lots of little pachyderms. This madly popular spot has a two-part menu (French on one side, Cambodian on the other), but the boundary is quite porous. Many Cambodian dishes have part-French names, such as *poulet dhomrei* (chicken with Asian basil, bamboo shoots, fresh pineapple, and kaffir lime leaves) and *curry de crevettes* (shrimp curry with picture-perfect vegetables). My mouth is still burning from *loc lac,* fork-tender beef cubes in addictively spicy sauce. On the French side, you'll find pan-seared filet mignon with *pommes frites,* and pan-seared tuna with three-peppercorn crust. Many dishes are available with tofu substituted for animal protein. The pleasant staff members will help out if you need guidance. Ask to be seated in the plant-filled front room, which is less noisy than the main dining room and has a view of the street.

11 Cambridge

See map p. 62

HARVARD SQUARE & VICINITY
VERY EXPENSIVE

✪ **Rialto.** In the Charles Hotel, 1 Bennett St. ☎ **617/661-5050.** Reservations recommended. Main courses $20–$33. AE, CB, DC, MC, V. Sun–Thurs 5:30–10pm;

⊕ Family-Friendly Restaurants

Like chocolate and champagne, well-behaved children are welcome almost everywhere. Most Boston-area restaurants can accommodate families, and many youngsters can be stunned into tranquillity if a place is fancy enough. If your kids can't or won't sign a good-conduct pledge, here are some suggestions.

The ✪ **Bertucci's** chain of pizzerias appeals to children and adults equally, with wood-fired brick ovens that are visible from many tables, great rolls made from pizza dough, and pizzas and pastas that range from basic to sophisticated. There are convenient branches at Faneuil Hall Marketplace (☎ **617/227-7889**); in the Back Bay at 43 Stanhope St. (☎ **617/247-6161**), around the corner from the Hard Rock Cafe; and in Cambridge at 21 Brattle St., Harvard Square (☎ **617/864-4748**).

The **Hard Rock Cafe,** 131 Clarendon St. (☎ **617/424-ROCK**), and ✪ **House of Blues,** 96 Winthrop St., Cambridge (☎ **617/491-2583**), serve up music with their food—and your kids will think you're *so* cool.

The nonstop activity and smart-mouthed service at ✪ **Durgin-Park,** 340 Faneuil Hall Marketplace (☎ **617/227-2038**), will entrance any child, and parents of picky eaters will appreciate the straightforward New England fare.

Another chain, **TGI Friday's,** 26 Exeter St., at Newbury Street (☎ **617/266-9040**), made its reputation by catering to singles. All that pairing off apparently led to children, who are courted as well. They receive a kids' package with balloons, crayons, a coloring book, peanut butter and crackers, and surprises wrapped in the chain's signature red-and-white stripes.

California Pizza Kitchen (yes, another chain) has two Boston locations, 137 Stuart St., in the Theater District (☎ **617/720-0999**), and the Prudential Center, near the Huntington Avenue entrance (☎ **617/247-0888**).

The **Bristol Lounge,** in the Four Seasons Hotel, 200 Boylston St. (☎ **617/351-2053**), looks almost too nice to have a kids' menu (with appetizers, plain main courses, desserts, and beverages). The staff is unflappable and accommodating, and high chairs and sticker fun books are available.

Fri–Sat 5:30–11pm. Bar Sun–Thurs 4:30pm–midnight; Fri–Sat 5pm–1am. Valet and validated parking available. T: Red Line to Harvard. MEDITERRANEAN.

If Rialto isn't the best restaurant in the Boston area, it's close. It attracts a chic crowd, but it's not a "scene" in the sense that out-of-towners will feel left behind. Every element is carefully thought out, from the architecture to the service to chef Jody Adams's extraordinary food. It's a dramatic but comfortable room, with floor-to-ceiling windows overlooking Harvard Square, cushy banquettes, and standing lamps that cast a golden glow.

The menu changes regularly. You might start with grilled mussels with andouille sausage and garlic bread, or Provençal fisherman's soup with rouille, gruyère, and basil oil, the very essence of seafood. Main courses are so good that you might as well close your eyes and point. Seared duck breast with foie gras, squash raviolis, and quince is wonderful, and any fish is a guaranteed winner—say, seared tuna in mustard seeds with wild rice and olive vinaigrette. A plate of creamy potato slices and mushrooms is so juicy it's almost like eating meat. For dessert, seasonal sorbets are a great choice, alone or in a combination such as tarte Tatin with mulled-cider sorbet.

✪ **Upstairs at the Pudding.** 10 Holyoke St. ☎ **617/864-1933.** Reservations recommended. Main courses $9–$14 at lunch, $20–$38 at dinner, $9–$15 at brunch; tasting menu (dinner) $45. AE, CB, DC, MC, V. Mon–Sat 11:30am–2:30pm, Sun brunch 11am–2:30pm; daily 6–11pm. Validated parking available. T: Red Line to Harvard. CONTINENTAL/NORTHERN ITALIAN.

An oasis of calm above the tumult of Harvard Square, Upstairs at the Pudding is a special-occasion spot with food so good you'll want to make up a reason (and save up some money) to go there. At the top of the Hasty Pudding Club's creaky stairs, it's a high-ceilinged room with soft, romantic lighting. The menu changes daily and always features hand-rolled pasta.

To start, you might try fettuccine with truffle cream, or pizzetta with tomato confit, olives, garlic, chèvre, and Parmesan. Entrees include at least one pasta dish and a small but choice selection of meat and fish. If mashed potatoes are on the menu, you can't go wrong by ordering any main course that comes with them—perhaps peppered beef tenderloin with blue cheese and charred tomato coulis. Rack of lamb might be offered with braised artichokes, roasted onions, creamer potatoes, and rosemary-mustard *jus*. Portions are large, but try to save room for dessert—anything with chocolate is a good choice. There are a lovely terrace and herb garden off the dining room for seasonal alfresco dining.

EXPENSIVE

Casablanca. 40 Brattle St. ☎ **617/876-0999.** Reservations recommended at dinner. Main courses $7–$12 at lunch, $14–$23 at dinner. AE, MC, V. Daily 11:30am–3pm; Sun–Thurs 5:30–10pm; Fri–Sat 5:30–11pm. T: Red Line to Harvard. MEDITERRANEAN.

This old-time Harvard Square favorite has long been known more for its hopping bar scene than for its food. These days the dining room is the place where you're sure to get lucky— Casablanca remains true to its reputation for serving tasty Mediterranean cuisine. Service is erratic (it's better at lunch than at dinner), but there's plenty to look at while you wait. The walls of the long, skylit dining room and crowded, noisy bar sport murals of scenes from the movie. Humphrey Bogart looks as though he might lean down to ask for a taste of your crispy mascarpone chicken or juicy pork tenderloin over spaetzle (tell him no—you'll want them all to yourself). Appetizers—North African flatbread with bean puree and spicy eggplant spreads; hot goat cheese with garlic toast and carrot salad; Provençal chickpea fries—are so good you might want to assemble them into a meal. Just be sure to leave room for dessert. The plate of cookies is a good choice, as is gingerbread.

Chez Henri. 1 Shepard St. (at Mass. Ave.). ☎ **617/354-8980.** Reservations accepted only for parties of 6 or more. Main courses $17–$24; bar food $5–$8. AE, DC, MC, V. Mon–Thurs 6–10pm; Fri–Sat 5:30–11pm; Sun 5:30–9pm; Sun brunch 11am–2pm. Bar food Mon–Sat until midnight, Sun until 10pm. T: Red Line to Harvard. FRENCH/CUBAN.

In a dark, elegant space off Mass. Ave. near Harvard Law School, Chez Henri is an example of how good fusion cuisine can be. Academic types and foodies flock here for French bistro-style food with Cuban accents. The menu changes regularly; to start, try coconut shrimp with black-bean salad, or brioche-crusted frog's legs. (This is one of the only places in the area where you can try frog's legs—no, really, they're good.) Entrees include generous portions of meat, fish, and vegetables. You might find a wood-grilled pork chop served with roasted pears and mashed potatoes, traditional Cuban paella, or layered eggplant torte. The dessert menu is a bit short on chocolate options, but I swear you won't mind—the crème brûlée is magnificent. The food at the bar is Cuban, as are the strong specialty drinks.

MODERATE

Bombay Club. In the Galleria Mall, 57 John F. Kennedy St. ☎ **617/661-8100.**
Lunch buffet $7 Mon–Fri, $9–$12 Sat–Sun; main courses $5–$9 at lunch, $9–$18
at dinner. AE, CB, DC, MC, V. Daily 11:30am–11pm. T: Red Line to Harvard.
INDIAN.

This third-floor spot overlooking Harvard Square gained fame
through its lunch buffet, a generous assortment of some of the
best items on the menu. The buffet's reasonable price and the
lively daytime scene make midday the best time to dine here. At
all times, the food—a wide-ranging selection of typical dishes
from across the subcontinent—is fresh and flavorful. The breads,
baked to perfection in a traditional charcoal-fired clay oven, and
the lamb offerings are especially tasty. The "chef's recommenda-
tions" platters of assorted meat or vegetarian dishes make good
samplers if you're new to the cuisine (or indecisive). If grazing
isn't your thing, *rogan josh* (lamb in garlicky tomato sauce) and
fiery chicken vindaloo merit ordering full portions.

Border Café. 32 Church St. ☎ **617/864-6100.** Reservations not accepted.
Main courses $7–$15. AE, MC, V. Mon–Thurs 11am–1am; Fri–Sat 11am–2am;
Sun noon–11pm. T: Red Line to Harvard. TEX-MEX/CAJUN.

When you first see this restaurant, your thoughts might turn to,
of all people, baseball Hall of Famer Yogi Berra. He supposedly
said, "Nobody goes there anymore; it's too crowded." He was
talking about a New York club, but people have been saying it
about this Harvard Square hangout for over 15 years. Patrons
loiter at the bar for hours, enhancing the festival atmosphere.
Many are waiting to be seated for generous portions of tasty, if
not completely authentic, food. The menu features Tex-Mex,
Cajun, and some Caribbean specialties, and the beleaguered staff
keeps the chips and salsa coming. When you shout your order
over the roar of the crowd, try the excellent chorizo appetizer,
enchiladas (seafood are particularly delectable), any kind of tacos,
or popcorn shrimp. Fajitas for one or two, sizzling noisily in a
large iron frying pan, are also a popular choice. Set aside a couple
of hours, be in a party mood, and ask to be seated downstairs if
you want to be able to hear your companions.

INEXPENSIVE

✪ **Bartley's Burger Cottage.** 1246 Mass. Ave. ☎ **617/354-6559.** Most
items under $7. No credit cards. Mon–Wed, Sat 11am–9pm; Thurs–Fri
11am–10pm. T: Red Line to Harvard. AMERICAN.

Great burgers and the best onion rings in the world make Bartley's a perennial favorite with a cross section of Cambridge, from

Harvard students to regular folks. It's not a cottage, but a high-ceilinged, crowded room plastered with signs and posters (there's also a small outdoor seating area), where the waitresses might call you "honey." Burgers bear the names of local and national celebrities; the names change, but the ingredients stay the same.

Anything you can think of to put on ground beef is available, from American cheese to béarnaise sauce. There are also some good dishes that don't involve meat, notably veggie burgers and creamy, garlicky hummus. Bartley's is one of the only places in the area where you can still get a real raspberry lime rickey (raspberry syrup, lime juice, lime wedges, and club soda—the taste of summer even in the winter).

Tea-Tray in the Sky. 1796 Mass. Ave. ☎ **617/492-8327.** Reservations not accepted. Main courses $5–$12.75. AE, DISC, MC, V. Tues–Fri 10am–10pm; Sat 10am–11pm; Sun 10am–7pm. Closed Sun in summer. T: Red Line to Porter. AMERICAN/TEAROOM.

This cozy little storefront is a perfect stop for a meal or snack on a shopping expedition north of Harvard Square. Lavishly decorated with tea-related accessories and original art (much of it for sale), the room seats just 20. The encyclopedic tea menu encompasses the familiar and the exotic (white tea, several kinds of *chai*) and accompanies an extensive food menu. The baked goods, all made in-house, are as fresh as can be—arrive early enough and you might have to wait for your sandwich until the bread cools off. Salads, soups, and sandwiches served on focaccia (including a superb tuna melt) are so delectable that you might forget to save room for the cakes, tarts, scones, and other pastries. Try anything involving chocolate, and be prepared to share. Oh, and the name? It's a tribute to *Alice's Adventures in Wonderland*— check out the mural at the front of the room.

OUTSIDE HARVARD SQUARE
EXPENSIVE

There's a **Legal Sea Foods** (see "Back Bay," earlier in this chapter) at 5 Cambridge Center, Kendall Square (☎ **617/864-3400**).

✪ **The Blue Room.** 1 Kendall Sq. ☎ **617/494-9034.** www.blueroom.net. Reservations recommended. Main courses $16–$22. AE, DC, DISC, MC, V. Sun–Thurs 5:30–10pm; Fri–Sat 5:30–11pm; Sun brunch 11am–2:30pm. Validated parking available. T: Red Line to Kendall/MIT; 10-min. walk. ECLECTIC.

The Blue Room sits just below plaza level in an office-retail complex, a slice of foodie paradise in high-tech heaven. Its out-of-the-way location means it doesn't get as much publicity as it deserves, but it's one of the best restaurants in the Boston area. The cuisine is a rousing combination of top-notch ingredients and layers of aggressive flavors, the service is excellent, and the crowded dining room is not as noisy as you might fear when you first spy it through the glass front wall. Upholstered banquettes, carpeting, and draperies help soften the din, but this is still not a place for cooing lovers—it's a place for food lovers, who savor co-owner Steve Johnson's regularly changing menu.

Appetizers range from salad with an assertive vinaigrette to seared scallops with hoisin and sesame to summer vegetables served with a lemony aïoli. Entrees tend to be roasted, grilled, or braised, with at least two vegetarian choices. The roast chicken, served with garlic mashed potatoes, is world class. Grilled tuna appears often, and pork loin with cider glaze will make you think twice the next time you skip over pork on a menu to get to the steak. In warm weather, there's seating on the brick patio.

✪ **Dalí.** 415 Washington St., Somerville. ☎ **617/661-3254.** www. DaliRestaurant.com. Reservations not accepted. Tapas $3.50–$7.50; main courses $17–$22. AE, DC, MC, V. Daily winter 5:30–11pm; summer 6–11pm. T: Red Line to Harvard; follow Kirkland St. to intersection of Washington and Beacon sts. (20 min.). SPANISH.

Dalí casts an irresistible spell—it's noisy and crowded, it doesn't take reservations, it's not all that close to Harvard Square (but it's a short cab ride), and it still fills with people cheerfully waiting an hour or more for a table. The bar offers plenty to look at while you wait, including a clothesline festooned with lingerie. The payoff is authentic Spanish food, notably tapas, little plates of hot or cold creations that burst with flavor.

Entrees include excellent paella, but most people come in a group and cut a swath through the delectable tapas offerings—32 on the menu and 9 monthly specials, all perfect for sharing. They include *patatas ali-oli* (garlic potatoes), *albóndigas de salmón* (salmon balls with not-too-salty caper sauce), *setas al ajillo* (sautéed mushrooms), and *lomito al cabrales* (pork tenderloin with blue goat cheese and mushrooms). The helpful staff sometimes seems rushed but never fails to supply bread for sopping up juices and sangria for washing it all down. If you want to experiment and order in stages, that's fine. Finish up with excellent flan, or try the super-rich *tarta de chocolates* (order your own if you like chocolate).

The owners of Dalí also run **Tapéo** at 266 Newbury St. (☎ **617/267-4799**), between Fairfield and Dartmouth streets in Boston's **Back Bay.** It offers the same menu and similarly wacky decor in a more sedate two-level setting.

MODERATE

✪ **Green Street Grill.** 280 Green St. ☎ **617/876-1655.** www.2nite.com/greenstreet. Reservations not accepted. Main courses $14–$19. AE, MC, V. Daily 6–10pm. T: Red Line to Central Sq. CARIBBEAN/SEAFOOD.

Out-of-towners lean in close and ask conspiratorially, "Where do people who live around here *really* go?" If the no-frills atmosphere won't put them off, I whisper this name. It's basically a bar (and not a very promising-looking one, either) where the food is among the tastiest and hottest in town. If you can take the heat, you'll be in heaven; if not, you might feel like a cartoon character with flames licking out of your ears. Some dishes have as many as five kinds of peppers. Red-wine and squid-ink fettuccine with shrimp, scallops, and squid will clear that head cold right up, and I'd walk a mile for the yellowfin tuna. Not everything is completely incendiary—the helpful staff can steer you in the right direction. Grilled seafood is also done well, and there's a wide variety of beers to help put out the fire.

✪ **The Helmand.** 143 First St. ☎ **617/492-4646.** Reservations recommended. Main courses $9–$16. AE, MC, V. Sun–Thurs 5–10pm; Fri–Sat 5–11pm. T: Green Line to Lechmere. AFGHAN.

Even in cosmopolitan Cambridge, Afghan food is a novelty, and if any competitors are setting their sights on the Helmand, they're contemplating a daunting task. The elegant setting belies the reasonable prices at this spacious spot near the CambridgeSide Galleria mall. The courteous staff patiently answers questions about the unusual cuisine, which is distinctly Middle Eastern with Indian and Pakistani influences. Many dishes are vegetarian, and meat is often one element of a dish rather than the centerpiece. Every meal comes with delectable bread made while you watch in a wood-fired brick oven.

To start, you might try the slightly sweet baked pumpkin topped with a spicy ground meat sauce—a great contrast of flavors and textures—or *aushak,* pasta pockets filled with leeks or potatoes and buried under a sauce of split peas and carrots. Aushak, also available as a main course, can be prepared with meat sauce as well. Other entrees include several versions of what Americans would call stew, including *deygee kabob,* an excellent mélange of lamb, yellow split peas, onion, and red peppers. For dessert, don't miss the Afghan version of baklava.

The Great Outdoors: Picnic Food

With its acres of waterfront property, Boston is the perfect place for a meal or snack. For a classic experience, pick up takeout from the Colonnade food court at **Faneuil Hall Marketplace** and cross the street under the Expressway. Walk past the Marriott to the end of Long Wharf and eat on the plaza as you watch the boats and planes, or walk around to the left of the hotel and eat in Christopher Columbus Park overlooking the marina.

In the **Financial District,** the **Milk Street Café** operates a kiosk (☎ **617/350-7275**) in the park at Zero Post Office Square. Its strictly kosher offerings include salads, meat sandwiches (on bread and rolled up in pita), fish dishes, fruit, and pastries. Eat in the park, or head to the harbor.

On the Cambridge side of the river, **Harvard Square** is close enough to the water to allow a riverside repast. For many years before wraps were trendy, **Stuff-Its,** 8½ Eliot St. (☎ **617/ 497-2220**), was serving delectable sandwiches rolled up in pita. (Watch out for the incredibly strong onions.) Take yours to John F. Kennedy Park, on Memorial Drive and Kennedy Street, or right to the riverbank.

On the way to a concert or movie on the Esplanade (also along the river, on the Boston side), stop at the foot of **Beacon Hill** for provisions. **Savenor's Supermarket,** 160 Charles St. (☎ **617/723-6328**), carries all you need for a do-it-yourself feast. Or call ahead to **Figs,** 42 Charles St. (☎ **617/742-3447**), a minuscule pizzeria that's an offshoot of the celebrated Olives. The upscale fare isn't cheap, but avoiding that long line is worth the price—as is the delectable pizza.

La Groceria Ristorante Italiano. 853 Main St., Central Sq. ☎ **617/ 497-4214.** Reservations recommended at dinner. Main courses $6–$10 at lunch; $11–$18 at dinner. Pizzas $6.25–$10. Children's menu $7. AE, CB, DC, DISC, MC, V. Mon–Fri 11:30am–4pm; Mon–Thurs 4–10pm, Fri–Sat 4–11pm; Sun 1–10pm. Valet parking available on weekends. T: Red Line to Central Sq. ITALIAN.

The Mastromauro family has dished up large portions of delicious Italian food at this colorful, welcoming restaurant since 1972. You'll see business meetings at lunch, family outings at dinner, and students and bargain-hunters at all times. Cheery voices bounce off the stucco walls and tile floors, but it seldom gets terribly noisy, probably because everyone's mouth is full. You might start with the house garlic bread, lavished with chopped tomato, red onion, fennel seed, and olive oil. The antipasto platter overflows with the chef's choice of meats, cheeses, and roasted vegetables. Main dishes might include homemade pasta from the machine you see as you enter—the daily specials are always good bets. Lasagna (a vegetarian version) is an excellent choice, as are lobster ravioli and savory chicken marsala. Chicken also comes roasted, and 10 varieties of brick-oven pizza are available in individual and large sizes.

12 Afternoon Tea

In Boston, the only city that has a whole tea party named after it, the tradition of afternoon tea at a plush hotel is alive and well. Make a reservation at the first two well in advance, especially on Saturdays and during the holidays.

The Ritz-Carlton, Boston, 15 Arlington St. (☎ **617/536-5700**), will close for renovations for 8 months starting in mid-2001. If you're in town while it's open, head to the elegant Lounge for the city's most celebrated tea ($22). Harp music plays as you're served pastries, breads, delectable scones, and finger sandwiches. Seatings are daily at 3 and 4:30pm.

Across the Public Garden, the **Bristol Lounge** at the Four Seasons Hotel, 200 Boylston St. (☎ **617/351-2053**), offers a sensational view and wonderful scones, tea sandwiches, pastries, and nut bread ($21.50, or $28.50 with a kir royale) every day from 3 to 4:30pm.

A player piano serenades tea partyers at **Swans Court,** in the lobby of the Boston Park Plaza Hotel, 64 Arlington St. (☎ **617/426-2000**), daily from 3 to 5pm. There's no view, and the finger sandwiches, strawberries and cream, and petit fours ($10.50) aren't quite as elegant as at the other hotels, but it's still fun—and a great deal.

5

Exploring Boston

*B*oston offers something for everyone, and plenty of it. Throw out your preconceptions of the city as some sort of open-air history museum—although that's certainly one of the guises it can assume—and allow your interests to dictate where you go. It's possible but not advisable to take in most major attractions in 2 or 3 days if you don't linger anywhere too long. For a more enjoyable and less rushed visit, plan fewer activities and spend more time on them.

1 The Top Attractions

✪ **Faneuil Hall Marketplace.** Between North, Congress, and State sts. and I-93. ☎ **617/338-2323.** Marketplace Mon–Sat 10am–9pm; Sun noon–6pm. Colonnade food court opens earlier; some restaurants open early and close at 2am daily. T: Green Line to Government Center, Orange or Blue Line to State, or Orange Line to Haymarket.

It's impossible to overstate the effect of Faneuil Hall Marketplace on Boston's economy and reputation. A daring idea when it opened in 1976, the "festival market" has been widely imitated, and each new complex of shops, food stands, restaurants, bars, and public spaces in urban centers around the country reflects its city. Faneuil Hall Marketplace, brimming with Boston flavor and regional goods and souvenirs, is no exception. Its success with tourists and suburbanites is so great, in fact, that you could be forgiven for thinking that the only Bostonians in the crowd are employees.

The marketplace includes five buildings—the central three-building complex is on the National Register of Historic Places—set on brick and stone plazas that teem with crowds shopping, eating, performing, watching performers, and just people-watching. **Quincy Market** (you'll hear the whole complex called by that name as well) is the central three-level Greek revival–style building. It reopened after extensive renovations on August 26, 1976, 150 years of hard use after Mayor Josiah Quincy opened

Boston Attractions

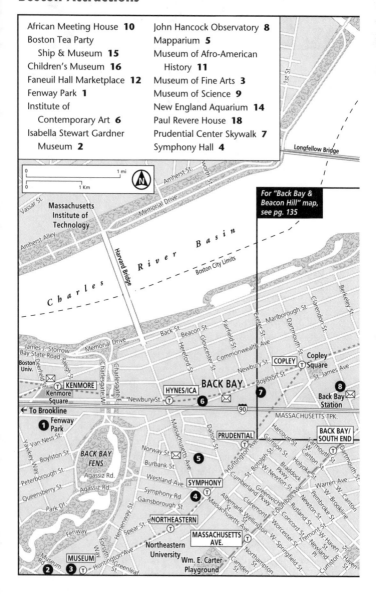

African Meeting House **10**

Boston Tea Party
  Ship & Museum **15**

Children's Museum **16**

Faneuil Hall Marketplace **12**

Fenway Park **1**

Institute of
  Contemporary Art **6**

Isabella Stewart Gardner
  Museum **2**

John Hancock Observatory **8**

Mapparium **5**

Museum of Afro-American
  History **11**

Museum of Fine Arts **3**

Museum of Science **9**

New England Aquarium **14**

Paul Revere House **18**

Prudential Center Skywalk **7**

Symphony Hall **4**

For "Back Bay & Beacon Hill" map, see pg. 135

Longfellow Bridge

Massachusetts
Institute of
Technology

Memorial Drive

Amherst St.

Worth St.

1st St.

Vassar St.

Amherst Alley

Harvard Bridge

Charles   River   Basin

Boston City Limits

Berkeley St.

Clarendon St.

Dartmouth St.

Exeter St.

Fairfield St.

Gloucester St.

Hereford St.

Back St.

Beacon St.

Commonwealth Ave.

Marlborough St.

James J. Storrow
Memorial Drive

Bay State Road

Deerfield St.

Raleigh St.

Charlesgate W.

Charlesgate E.

Newbury St.

Boylston St.

St. James Ave.

COPLEY ⓣ Copley
Square

Boston
Univ.

☒ ⓣ **KENMORE**
Kenmore
Square

← To Brookline

HYNES/ICA
ⓣ "Newbury St." ⓣ ☒ **6**

BACK BAY

☒ **7**

90

MASSACHUSETTS TPK.

8 ☒
Back Bay
Station

❶ Fenway
Park

Yawkey Way

Van Ness St.

Boylston St.

Peterborough St.

Queensberry St.

Park Dr.

**BACK BAY
FENS**

Agassiz Rd.

Agassiz Rd.

Westland Ave.

Norway St. ☒ **5**
PRUDENTIAL ⓣ

Burbank St.

Massachusetts Ave.

Dalton St.

Hemenway St.

Huntington Ave.

Forsyth St.

Symphony Rd.

Gainsborough St.

SYMPHONY
ⓣ **4**

Spear St.

❶NORTHEASTERN
ⓣ

Northeastern
University

Museum Rd.

Fenway

Way

Greenleaf

MUSEUM
ⓣ

❷ **❸** ⓣ

**MASSACHUSETTS
AVE.**
ⓣ

Wm. E. Carter
Playground

Harcourt St.

Garrison St.

Huntington Ave.

Cumberland Ave.

Botolph St.

Blackwood St.

Braddock Pkwy.

Greenwich St.

Claremont Pkwy.

Wellington St.

W. Concord St.

Albemarle St.

W. Newton St.

W. Rutland St.

Worcester St.

W. Springfield St.

Northampton St.

Camden St.

St. Botolph St.

Holyoke St.

Cumberland St.

Concord St.

W. Canton St.

Warren Ave.

Pembroke St.

W. Brookline St.

W. Newton St.

W. Haven St.

Haven St.

Cumston St.

Tremont St.

Columbus Ave.

Montgomery St.

Clarendon St.

Yarmouth St.

Dartmouth St.

W. Canton St.

Canton St.

**BACK BAY/
SOUTH END**
ⓣ

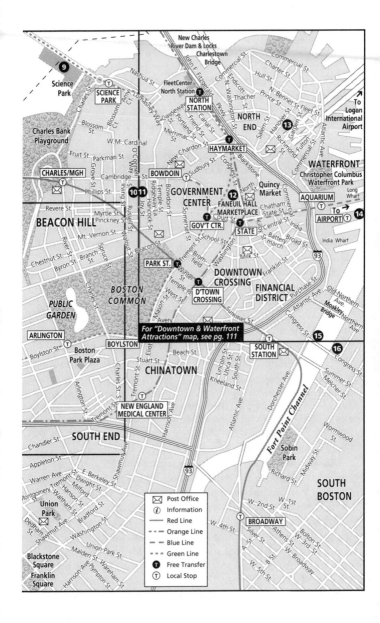

For "Downtown & Waterfront Attractions" map, see pg. 111

Post Office ⊠
Information ⓘ
Red Line ——
Orange Line - - -
Blue Line – – –
Green Line - - -
Free Transfer ⬤
Local Stop Ⓣ

the original market. The **South Market building** reopened on August 26, 1977, the **North Market building** on August 26, 1978.

The central corridor of Quincy Market, known as the **Colonnade,** is the food court, where you can find anything from a bagel to a full Greek dinner, a fruit smoothie to a hunk of fudge. On either side, under the glass canopies, pushcarts hold everything from crafts created by New England artisans to hokey souvenirs. In the plaza between the **South Canopy** and the South Market building is an **information kiosk,** and throughout the complex you'll find an enticing mix of chain stores and unique shops (see chapter 6). On summer evenings, the tables that spill outdoors from the restaurants and bars fill with people. One constant since the year after the market—the *original* market—opened is **Durgin-Park,** a traditional New England restaurant with traditionally crabby waitresses (see chapter 4).

✪ **Faneuil Hall** itself sometimes gets overlooked, but it's well worth a visit. Known as the "Cradle of Liberty" for its role as a center of inspirational (some might say inflammatory) speech in the years leading to the Revolutionary War, the building opened in 1742 and was expanded using a Charles Bulfinch design in 1805. National Park Service rangers give **free 20-minute talks** every half hour from 9am to 5pm in the second-floor auditorium.

✪ **Isabella Stewart Gardner Museum.** 280 The Fenway. ☎ **617/ 566-1401.** www.boston.com/gardner. Admission $11 adults weekends, $10 adults weekdays; $7 seniors, $5 college students with valid ID, $3 college students on Wed, free for children under 18. Tues–Sun, some Mon holidays 11am–5pm. T: Green Line E to Museum.

Isabella Stewart Gardner (1840–1924) was an incorrigible individualist long before such behavior was acceptable for a woman in polite Boston society, and her iconoclasm has paid off for art lovers. "Mrs. Jack" designed her exquisite home in the style of a 15th-century Venetian palace and filled it with European, American, and Asian painting and sculpture, much chosen with the help of her friend and protégé Bernard Berenson. You'll see works by Titian, Botticelli, Raphael, Rembrandt, Matisse, and Mrs. Gardner's friends James McNeill Whistler and John Singer Sargent. Titian's magnificent *Europa,* which many scholars consider his finest work, is one of the most important Renaissance paintings in the United States.

The building, which opened to the public after Mrs. Gardner's death, holds a hodgepodge of furniture and architectural details

Downtown & Waterfront Attractions

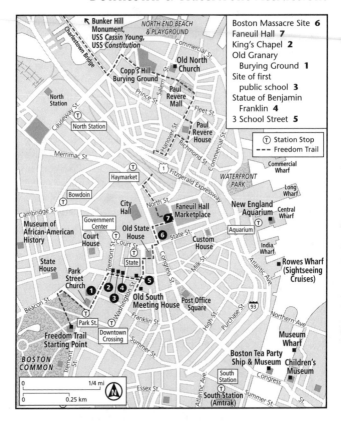

Boston Massacre Site **6**
Faneuil Hall **7**
King's Chapel **2**
Old Granary
   Burying Ground **1**
Site of first
   public school **3**
Statue of Benjamin
   Franklin **4**
3 School Street **5**

Ⓣ Station Stop
- - - Freedom Trail

imported from European churches and palaces. The pièce de résistance is the magnificent skylit courtyard, filled year-round with fresh flowers from the museum greenhouse. Although the terms of Mrs. Gardner's will forbid changing the arrangement of the museum's content, there has been some evolution: A special exhibition gallery features two or three changing shows a year, often by contemporary artists in residence.

✪ **John F. Kennedy Library and Museum.** Columbia Point. ☎ **617/ 929-4523.** www.cs.umb.edu/jfklibrary. Admission $8 adults, $6 seniors and students with ID, $4 youths 13–17, free for children under 13. Daily 9am–5pm (last film begins at 3:55pm). T: Red Line to JFK/UMass, then take free shuttle bus, which runs every 20 min. By car, take Southeast Expwy. (I-93/Rte. 3) south to Exit 15 (Morrissey Blvd./JFK Library), turn left onto Columbia Rd., and follow signs to free parking lot.

The Kennedy era springs to life at this dramatic library, museum, and educational research complex overlooking Dorchester Bay. It captures the 35th president's accomplishments and legacy in sound and video recordings and fascinating displays of memorabilia and photos. Far from being a static experience, it changes regularly, with temporary shows and reinterpreted displays that highlight and complement the permanent exhibits.

Your visit begins with a 17-minute film narrated by John F. Kennedy—a detail that seems eerie for a moment, then perfectly natural. Through skillfully edited audio clips, he discusses his childhood, education, war experience, and early political career. Then you enter the museum to spend as much time as you like on each exhibit. Starting with the 1960 presidential campaign, you're immersed in the era. The connected galleries hold campaign souvenirs, a film of Kennedy debating Richard Nixon and delivering his inaugural address, a replica of the Oval Office, gifts from foreign dignitaries, letters, documents, and keepsakes. There's a film about the Cuban Missile Crisis, and displays on the civil rights movement, the Peace Corps, the space program, and the Kennedy family. Expanded exhibits focus on First Lady Jacqueline Bouvier Kennedy and Attorney General Robert F. Kennedy. As the tour winds down, you pass through a darkened chamber where news reports of John Kennedy's assassination and funeral play.

From the final room, the soaring glass-enclosed pavilion that is the heart of the I. M. Pei design, there's a glorious view of the water and the Boston skyline. In the summer, JFK's boyhood sailboat, *Victura*, sits on a strip of dune grass between the library and the harbor.

✪ **Museum of Fine Arts.** 465 Huntington Ave. ☎ **617/267-9300.** www.mfa.org. Adults $12 when entire museum is open, $10 when only West Wing is open. Students and seniors $10 when entire museum is open, $9 when only West Wing is open. Children 7–17 $5 on school days before 3pm, otherwise free. Voluntary contribution Wed 4–9:45pm. Surcharges may apply for special exhibitions. No admission fee to visit only the Museum Shop, library, restaurants, or auditoriums. Entire museum Mon–Tues 10am–4:45pm, Wed 10am–9:45pm, Thurs–Fri 10am–5pm, Sat–Sun 10am–5:45pm; West Wing only, Thurs–Fri 5–9:45pm. T: Green Line E to Museum, or Orange Line to Ruggles.

Not content with the MFA's reputation as the second-best art museum in the country (after New York's Metropolitan Museum of Art), the management team works nonstop to make the collections more accessible and interesting. Recent moves to raise the museum's profile have included mounting even more top-notch exhibitions, expanding educational programs, and opening new permanent galleries for the art of Africa, Oceania, and the ancient Americas.

The museum's not-so-secret weapon in its quest is a powerful one: its magnificent collections. Every installation reflects a curatorial attitude that makes even those who go in with a sense of obligation leave with a sense of discovery and wonder. The MFA is especially noted for its Impressionist paintings (including 43 Monets—the largest collection outside Paris), Asian and Old Kingdom Egyptian collections, classical art, Buddhist temple, and medieval sculpture and tapestries. It's also expanding its modern and contemporary art collections.

The works you might find more familiar are paintings and sculpture by Americans and Europeans. Some favorites: Renoir's *Dance at Bougival,* Van Gogh's *Postman Joseph Roulin,* Childe Hassam's *Boston Common at Twilight,* Gilbert Stuart's 1796 portrait of George Washington, John Singleton Copley's 1768 portrait of Paul Revere, a bronze casting of Edgar Degas's sculpture *Little Dancer,* John Singer Sargent's *The Daughters of Edward Darley Boit,* and Fitz Hugh Lane's Luminist masterpieces. There are also magnificent print and photography collections, and that's not even touching on the furnishings and decorative arts, including the finest collection of Paul Revere silver in the world.

I. M. Pei designed the West Wing (1981), the latest addition to the original 1909 structure. It contains the main entrance, an auditorium, and an atrium with a tree-lined "sidewalk" cafe. The excellent Museum Shop carries the full range of souvenirs and a huge selection of art books. The museum has two restaurants: the cafe and a cafeteria. Pick up a floor plan at the information desk, or take a free guided tour (weekdays except Monday holidays at 10:30am and 1:30pm, Wednesday at 6:15pm, Saturday at 10:30am and 1pm).

✪ **Museum of Science.** Science Park. ☎ **617/723-2500.** www.mos.org. Admission to exhibit halls $10 adults, $7 seniors and children 3–11, free for children under 3. To Mugar Omni Theater, Hayden Planetarium, or laser shows $7.50 adults, $5.50 seniors and children 3–11, free for children under 3. Discounted tickets to 2 or 3 parts of the complex available. July 5–Labor Day Sat–Thurs 9am–7pm; Fri 9am–9pm. Day after Labor Day to July 4 Sat–Thurs 9am–5pm; Fri 9am–9pm. T: Green Line to Science Park. Or commuter rail to North Station, then 10-min. walk.

For the ultimate pain-free educational experience, head to the Museum of Science. The demonstrations, experiments, and interactive displays introduce facts and concepts so effortlessly that everyone winds up learning something. Take a couple of hours or a whole day to explore the permanent and temporary exhibits, which are dedicated to improving "science literacy."

Among the more than 600 exhibits, you might meet an iguana or a dinosaur, find out how much you'd weigh on the moon, or climb into a space module. Visitors to the activity center **Investigate!** learn to think like scientists, formulating questions, finding evidence, and drawing conclusions through activities such as strapping on a skin sensor to measure reactions to stimuli or sifting through an archaeological dig. In the **Seeing Is Deceiving** section, auditory and visual illusions challenge your belief in what is "real." The **Science in the Park** exhibit introduces the concepts of Newtonian physics—through familiar recreational tools such as playground equipment and skateboards. You can also visit the theater of electricity to see lightning manufactured indoors. And there's a **Discovery Center** especially for preschoolers.

In 1999 the museum joined forces with the **Computer Museum** and acquired the latter's fascinating interactive exhibits. The first to find a home here, the **Virtual FishTank**, uses 3-D computer graphics and character-animation software to allow visitors to program their own fish and watch as they relate to other people's creations.

The separate-admission **theaters** are worth planning for. Even if you're skipping the exhibits, try to see a show. If you're making a day of it, buy all your tickets at once, not only because it's cheaper but also because shows sometimes sell out. Tickets for daytime shows must be purchased in person. Evening show tickets can be ordered over the phone using a credit card; there's a service charge for doing so.

The **Mugar Omni Theater**, which shows IMAX movies, is an intense experience. You're bombarded with images on a five-story domed screen and sounds from a state-of-the-art digital system. Even though you know you're not moving, the engulfing sensations and steep pitch of the seating area will have you hanging on for dear life, whether the film is about whales, Mount Everest, or hurricanes and tornadoes. Features change every 4 to 6 months.

The **Charles Hayden Planetarium** takes you into space with daily star shows and shows on special topics that change several times a year. On weekends, rock-music laser shows take over. At the entrance is a hands-on astronomy exhibit, *Welcome to the Universe.*

The museum has a terrific gift shop, where toys and games promote learning without lecturing, and the ground-floor Galaxy Cafés have spectacular views of the skyline and river. There's a parking garage on the premises, but it's on a busy street, and entering and exiting can be harrowing.

New England Aquarium. Central Wharf. ☎ **617/973-5200.** www.neaq.org. Admission summer weekends and holidays, $14 adults, $12 seniors, $7.50 children 3–11; weekdays year-round and off-season weekends, $12.50 adults, $10.50 seniors, $6.50 children 3–11. Free for children under 3 and for those visiting only the outdoor exhibits, cafe, and gift shop. July–Labor Day Mon–Tues and Fri 9am–6pm; Wed–Thurs 9am–8pm; Sat–Sun and holidays 9am–7pm. Day after Labor Day–June Mon–Fri 9am–5pm; Sat–Sun and holidays 9am–6pm. T: Blue or Orange Line to State (or Blue Line to Aquarium if it's open).

This entertaining complex is home to more than 7,000 fish and aquatic mammals. At busy times in the summer, it seems to contain at least that many people—in July and August, try to make this your first stop of the day, especially on weekends. Consider investing in a Boston CityPass (see the chapter introduction for details), which allows you to skip the ticket line. Inside, buy an exhibit guide and plan your route as you commune with the penguin colony.

The focal point of the main building is the aptly named **Giant Ocean Tank.** A four-story spiral ramp encircles the cylindrical glass tank, which contains 187,000 gallons of salt water, a replica of a Caribbean coral reef, and a conglomeration of sea creatures who seem to coexist amazingly well. Other exhibits show off freshwater specimens, the Aquarium medical center, denizens of the Amazon, and the ecology of Boston Harbor. At the **Edge of the Sea** exhibit, you're encouraged to touch the sea stars, sea urchins, and horseshoe crabs in the tide pool. Be sure to leave time for a show at the floating marine mammal pavilion, **Discovery,** where sea lions perform every 90 minutes throughout the day. (Don't wait, because the ongoing expansion project you'll see near the entrance is likely to force out the sea lions.)

The aquarium is growing; the first stage of its expansion is the dramatic West Wing, which echoes the waves on adjacent Boston Harbor. It holds exhibit space, the gift shop, and a cafe with views of the city and the harbor. The complex is scheduled to gain an **IMAX theater** with 3-D capability in 2001; call for admission fees.

The aquarium runs **harbor tours** that teach "Science at Sea" daily in the spring, summer, and fall. Tickets are $9 for adults, $7 for seniors and youths 12 to 18, and $6.50 for children under 12. Discounts are available when you combine a visit to the aquarium with a harbor tour or a whale watch (see "Organized Tours," below).

THE FREEDOM TRAIL

As a line of red paint or red brick on the sidewalk, the 3-mile Freedom Trail links 16 historical sights. First painted in 1958, it has undergone a modest transformation over the past few years, with the installation of prominent markers and plaques to make the stops easier to identify. The nonprofit **Freedom Trail Foundation** (☎ **617/227-8800;** www.thefreedomtrail.org) makes an excellent jumping-off point while you're planning your visit. Call for a guide or, even better, check out the interactive Web site. If you're interested, it's the only way to rub gravestones legally. The trail begins at the **Boston Common Information Center,** 146 Tremont St., on the Common. The center is open Monday to Saturday from 8:30am to 5pm and Sunday from 9am to 5pm, and offers pamphlets to help you along your self-guided tour.

You can also explore the **Black Heritage Trail** from here. Sites include stations on the Underground Railroad and homes of famous citizens as well as the African Meeting House, the oldest standing black church in the country. A 2-hour guided tour of this trail starts at the Visitor Center, 46 Joy Street (☎ **617/742-5415;** www.nps.gov/boaf).

Space doesn't permit me to detail every stop on the Freedom Trail, but here's a concise listing.

- **Boston Common.** In 1634, when their settlement was just 4 years old, the town fathers paid the Rev. William Blackstone £30 for this property. In 1640 it was set aside as common land. Be sure to stop at Beacon and Park streets to visit the **memorial** designed by Augustus Saint-Gaudens to celebrate the deeds (indeed, the very existence) of Col. Robert Gould Shaw and the Union Army's 54th Massachusetts Colored Regiment, who fought in the Civil War. You may remember the story of the first American army unit made up of free black soldiers from the movie *Glory.*
- **Massachusetts State House** (☎ **617/727-3676**). Charles Bulfinch designed the "new" State House, and Gov. Samuel Adams laid the cornerstone of the state capitol in 1795. Free tours (guided and self-guided) leave from the second floor.

- **Park Street Church,** 1 Park St. (☎ **617/523-3383**). Consult the plaque at the corner of Tremont Street for a description of this Congregational church's storied past. From late June through August, it's open from 9:30am to 4pm Tuesday to Saturday. Sunday services are at 9 and 10:45am and 5:30pm year-round.
- **Old Granary Burying Ground.** This cemetery, established in 1660, contains the graves of—among other notables—Samuel Adams, Paul Revere, John Hancock, and the wife of Isaac Vergoose, believed to be "Mother Goose" of nursery rhyme fame. It's open daily from 8am to 5pm (3pm in the winter).
- **King's Chapel,** 58 Tremont St. (☎ **617/523-1749**). Completed in 1754, this church was built by erecting the granite edifice around the existing wooden chapel. The **burying ground** (1630), facing Tremont Street, is the oldest in Boston. It's open daily from 8am to 5:30pm (3pm in the winter).
- **Site of the First Public School.** Founded in 1634, the school is commemorated with a colorful mosaic in the sidewalk on (of course) School Street. Inside the fence is the 1856 statue of **Benjamin Franklin,** the first portrait statue in Boston.
- **3 School St.** This is the former Old Corner Bookstore. Built in 1712, it's on a plot of land that was once home to the religious reformer Anne Hutchinson.
- **Old South Meeting House,** 310 Washington St. (☎ **617/ 482-6439**). Originally built in 1670 and replaced by the current structure in 1729, it was the starting point of the Boston Tea Party. It's open daily, April through October from 9am to 5:30pm, November through March weekdays from 10am to 4pm, weekends from 10am to 5pm. Admission is $3 for adults, $2.50 for seniors, $1 for children 6 to 12, free for children under 6.
- ✪ **Old State House,** 206 Washington St. (☎ **617/720-3290;** www.bostonhistory.org). Built in 1713, it served as the seat of colonial government in Massachusetts before the Revolution, and as the state capitol until 1797. It houses the Bostonian Society's museum of the city's history, open daily from 9am to 5pm. Admission is $3 for adults, $2 for seniors and students, $1 for children 6 to 18, and free for children under 6.
- **Boston Massacre Site.** On a traffic island in State Street, across from the T station under the Old State House, a ring of cobblestones marks the location of the skirmish of March 5, 1770.

✪ **Faneuil Hall.** Built in 1742 (and enlarged using a Charles Bulfinch design in 1805), it was a gift to the city from the merchant Peter Faneuil. National Park Service rangers give free 20-minute talks every half hour from 9am to 5pm in the second-floor auditorium.

✪ The **Paul Revere House,** 19 North Sq. (☎ **617/523-2338;** www.paulreverehouse.org). The oldest house in downtown Boston (built around 1680) presents history on a human scale. Revere bought it in 1770, and it became a museum in the early 20th century. It's open daily April 15 to October 31 from 9:30am to 5:15pm, and November 1 to April 14 from 9:30am to 4:15pm; closed Mondays January through March, January 1, Thanksgiving, and December 25. Admission is $2.50 for adults, $2 for seniors and students, $1 for children 5 to 17, and free for children under 5.

• The **Old North Church,** 193 Salem St. (☎ **617/523-6676;** www.oldnorth.com). Paul Revere saw a signal in the steeple when he set out on his "midnight ride." Officially known as Christ Church, this is the oldest church building in Boston; it dates to 1723. It's open daily from 9am to 5pm; Sunday services (Episcopal) are at 9 and 11am and 4pm. The quirky gift shop and museum, in a former chapel, are open daily from 9am to 5pm, and proceeds go to support the church. Donations are appreciated.

• **Copp's Hill Burying Ground,** off Hull Street. The second-oldest cemetery (1659) in the city, it contains the graves of Cotton Mather and his family and of Prince Hall, who established the first black Masonic lodge. It's open daily from 9am to 5pm (until 3pm in winter).

✪ USS *Constitution* (☎ **617/242-5670**), Charlestown Navy Yard. Active-duty sailors in 1812 dress uniforms give free tours of "Old Ironsides" daily between 9:30am and 3:50pm. The adjacent **USS *Constitution* Museum** (☎ **617/426-1812;** www.ussconstititionmuseum.org) is open daily May through October from 9am to 6pm, November to April from 10am to 4pm; closed January 1, Thanksgiving, and December 25. A program that makes admission free to all has been extended until further notice.

• **Bunker Hill Monument** (☎ **617/242-5644**), Breed's Hill, Charlestown. The 221-foot granite obelisk honors the memory of the men who died in the Battle of Bunker Hill (actually fought on Breed's Hill) on June 17, 1775. The top is 295 stairs up. National Park Service rangers staff the monument, which is open daily from 9am to 4:30pm. Admission is free.

2 More Museums & Attractions

○ **Fenway Park.** 4 Yawkey Way, at Brookline Ave. ☎ **617/267-8661** for ticket information, 617/236-6666 for tour information, 617/267-1700 for tickets, 617/482-4SOX for touch-tone ticketing. www.redsox.com. Tickets $14 and up. Tours $5 adults, $4 seniors, $3 for children under 16. Tours May–Sept Mon–Fri 10am, 11am, noon, 1pm. No tours on holidays or before day games. T: Green Line D to Fenway, or B, C, or D to Kenmore.

No other experience in sports matches watching the **Boston Red Sox** play at Fenway Park, which they do from early April to early October, and later if they make the playoffs. The quirkiness of the oldest park in the major leagues (1912) and the fact that (at press time) the team last won the World Series in 1918 only add to the mystique. The Green Monster, or left-field wall, contains a hand-operated scoreboard (watch carefully during a pitching change— the left fielder from either team might suddenly disappear into the darkness to cool off), and the wall itself is such a celebrity that it's often called simply The Wall. It's 37 feet tall and irresistibly tempting to batters who ought to know better.

Practical concerns: Compared with its modern brethren, Fenway is tiny. Tickets go on sale in January, and the earlier you order, the better chance you'll have of landing seats during your visit. Forced to choose between a low-numbered grandstand section (say, 10 or below) and bleacher seats, go for the bleachers. They can get rowdy during night games, but the view is better from there than from the deep right-field corner. Throughout the season, a limited number of standing-room tickets go on sale the day of the game, and presold tickets sometimes are returned. It can't hurt to check, especially if the team isn't playing well.

One way is to take a **Fenway Park tour,** which includes a walk on the warning track and may be your only way inside the gates if the team is on the road or games sell out during your visit.

The Institute of Contemporary Art. 955 Boylston St. ☎ **617/266-5152.** www.icaboston.org. Admission $6 adults, $4 students and seniors, free for children under 12; free to all Thurs 5–9pm. Wed and Sat–Sun noon–5pm; Thurs noon–9pm; Fri noon–7pm. Closed major holidays. T: Green Line B, C, or D to Hynes/ICA.

Across from the Hynes Convention Center, the ICA hosts rotating exhibits of 20th-century art, including painting, sculpture, photography, and video and performance art. The institute also offers films, lectures, music, video, poetry, and educational programs for children and adults. "Docent Teens"—participants in the institute's nationally recognized program for urban youth—lead tours on Thursday afternoons, and staff members lead tours on Friday at 12:30pm. The 1886 building, originally a police station, is a showpiece in its own right.

In 2000, the ICA's proposal won a competition to select an arts institution for the South Boston waterfront, near the new federal courthouse on Fan Pier. Check here for details and updates as the project proceeds.

Mapparium. World Headquarters of the First Church of Christ, Scientist, 250 Mass. Ave. (at Huntington Ave.). ☎ **617/450-3793.** www.tfccs.com. Free admission. Mon–Sat 10am–4pm. Mother Church Sun 11:15am–2pm; Mon–Sat 10am–4pm. Closed major holidays. MBTA: Green Line E to Symphony or Orange Line to Mass. Ave.

One of Boston's most unusual attractions is undergoing renovation; it's scheduled to reopen in 2001. The Mapparium offers a real insider's view of the world . . . from inside. The unique hollow globe 30 feet across is a work of both art and history. The 608 stained-glass panels are connected by a bronze framework and surrounded by electric lights. Because sound bounces off the nonporous surfaces, the acoustics are as unusual as the aesthetics. As you cross the glass bridge just south of the equator, you'll see the political divisions of the world from 1932 to 1935, when the globe was constructed.

3 Parks & Gardens

Green space is an important part of Boston's appeal, and the public parks are hard to miss. The best-known park, for good reason, is the spectacular ✪ **Public Garden,** bordered by Arlington, Boylston, Charles, and Beacon streets. Something lovely is in bloom at the country's first botanical garden at least half the year. The spring flowers are particularly impressive, especially if your visit happens to coincide with the first really warm day of the year. It's hard not to enjoy yourself when everyone around you seems ecstatic just to be seeing the sun.

For many people, the official beginning of spring coincides with the return of the **swan boats** (☎ 617/522-1966; www.swanboats.com). The pedal-powered vessels—the attendants pedal, not the passengers—plunge into the lagoon on the Saturday before Patriots Day (the third Monday of April). Although they don't move fast, they'll transport you. They operate daily 10am to 5pm in the summer; daily 10am to 4pm in the spring; weekdays noon to 4pm and weekends 10am to 4pm from Labor Day to mid-September. The cost for the 15-minute ride is $1.75 for adults, $1.50 for seniors, 95¢ for children under 13.

Across Charles Street is **Boston Common,** the country's first public park. The property was purchased in 1634 and officially set aside as public land in 1640, so if it seems a bit run-down (especially compared to the Public Garden), it's no wonder. The Frog Pond, where there really were frogs at one time, makes a pleasant spot to splash around in the summer and skate in the winter. At the Boylston Street side is the **Central Burying Ground,** where you can see the grave of famed portraitist Gilbert Stuart. There's also a bandstand where you might take in a free concert, and many beautiful shade trees.

4 Cambridge

Boston and Cambridge are so closely associated that many people believe they're the same—a notion both cities' residents and politicians would be happy to dispel. Cantabrigians are often considered more liberal and better educated than Bostonians, which is another idea that's sure to get you involved in a heated discussion. Take the Red Line across the river and see for yourself.

For an overview, begin at the main Harvard T entrance. At the **information booth** (☎ **617/497-1630**) in the middle of Harvard Square at the intersection of Mass. Ave., John F. Kennedy Street, and Brattle Street, trained volunteers dispense maps and brochures and answer questions Monday through Saturday from 9am to 5pm and Sunday from 1 to 5pm. From mid-June through Labor Day, there are guided tours that include the entire old Cambridge area. Check at the booth for rates, meeting places, and times, or call ahead. If you prefer to sightsee on your own, you can buy an Old Cambridge or East Cambridge walking guide prepared by the **Cambridge Historical Commission** (☎ **617/349-4683**).

Whatever you do, spend some time in **Harvard Square.** It's a hodgepodge of college and high school students, instructors, commuters, street performers, and sightseers. Near the information booth are two well-stocked newsstands, **Nini's Corner** and **Out of Town News** (where you can find out what's happening at home from the extensive collection of newspapers and magazines), and the **Harvard Coop.** There are restaurants and stores along all three streets that spread out from the center of the square and on the streets that intersect them. If you follow **Brattle Street** to the residential area just outside the square, you'll come to a part of town known before and during the American Revolution as **"Tory Row"** because the residents were loyal to King George.

By the time you read this, the ravishing yellow mansion at 105 Brattle St. should have reopened after extensive refurbishment. The house is the ✪ **Longfellow National Historic Site** (☎ 617/ 876-4491; www.nps.gov/long), where the books and furniture have remained intact since the poet Henry Wadsworth Longfellow died there in 1882. Now a unit of the National Park Service, during the siege of Boston in 1775–76 the house served as the headquarters of Gen. George Washington, with whom Longfellow was fascinated. The poet first lived there as a boarder in 1837. When he and Fanny Appleton married in 1843, her father made it a wedding present. On a tour—the only way to see the house—you'll learn about the history of the building and its famous occupants.

The house is open from mid-March through mid-December. Tours are offered Wednesday through Sunday at 10:45 and 11:45am, and 1, 2, 3, and 4pm from June to October and on weekends from mid-March to May and November to mid-December, and Wednesday through Friday spring and fall at 12:30, 1:30, 2:30, and 3:30pm. Admission is $2 for adults, free for children under 17 and seniors.

HARVARD UNIVERSITY

Free, student-led tours leave from the **Events & Information Center** in Holyoke Center, 1350 Mass. Ave. (☎ 617/495-1573), during the school year twice a day on weekdays and once on Saturday, except during vacations, and during the summer four times a day Monday to Saturday and twice on Sunday. Call for exact times; reservations aren't necessary. The Events & Information Center has maps, illustrated booklets, and self-guided walking-tour directions, as well as a bulletin board where campus activities are publicized. You may want to check out the university Web site (www.harvard.edu) before your trip.

The best-known part of the university is **Harvard Yard,** actually two large quadrangles. The **John Harvard statue,** a rendering of one of the school's original benefactors, is in the Old Yard, which dates to the college's founding in 1636. Most

Harvard Square Attractions

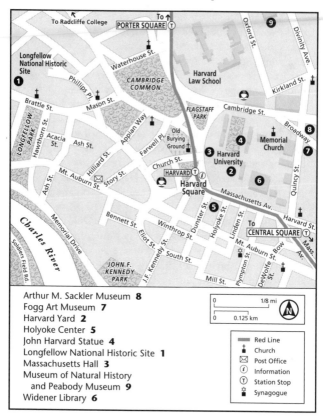

Arthur M. Sackler Museum **8**
Fogg Art Museum **7**
Harvard Yard **2**
Holyoke Center **5**
John Harvard Statue **4**
Longfellow National Historic Site **1**
Massachusetts Hall **3**
Museum of Natural History
    and Peabody Museum **9**
Widener Library **6**

0   1/8 mi
0   0.125 km

━━━ Red Line
✝ Church
⊠ Post Office
ⓘ Information
Ⓣ Station Stop
✡ Synagogue

first-year students live in the dormitories here—even in the school's oldest building, **Massachusetts Hall** (1720). The other side of the Yard (sometimes called Tercentenary Theater because the college's 300th-anniversary celebration took place there) is home to the imposing **Widener Library,** named after a Harvard graduate who perished when the *Titanic* sank.

Also on campus are two engaging museum complexes:

Harvard University Art Museums. 32 Quincy St. and 485 Broadway (at Quincy St.). ☎ **617/495-9400.** www.artmuseums.harvard.edu. Admission to all 3 museums $5 adults, $4 seniors, $3 students, free for children under 18; free to all Wed 10am–5pm, Sat 10am–noon. Open Mon–Sat 10am–5pm; Sun 1–5pm. Closed major holidays. T: Red Line to Harvard. Cross Harvard Yard diagonally from the T station and cross Quincy St., or turn your back on the Coop and follow Mass. Ave. to Quincy St., then turn left.

The Harvard art museums house a total of about 150,000 works of art in three collections: the Fogg Art Museum, the Busch–Reisinger Museum, and the Arthur M. Sackler Museum. The exhibit spaces also serve as teaching and research facilities. You can take a 1-hour guided tour on weekdays September through June, and Wednesdays only in July and August.

The **Fogg Art Museum** (32 Quincy St., near Broadway) centers on an impressive 16th-century Italian stone courtyard, with two floors of galleries opening off it. You'll see something different in each of the 19 rooms—17th-century Dutch and Flemish landscapes, 19th-century British and American paintings and drawings, French paintings and drawings from the 18th century through the Impressionist period, contemporary sculpture, and changing exhibits.

The **Busch–Reisinger Museum** in Werner Otto Hall (enter through the Fogg) is the only museum in North America devoted to the painting, sculpture, and decorative art of northern and central Europe, specifically Germany. Its encyclopedic collection also includes prints and illustrated books. Particularly notable are the early–20th-century collections, including works by Klee, Feininger, Kandinsky, and artists and designers associated with the Bauhaus.

The **Arthur M. Sackler Museum** (485 Broadway, at Quincy St.) houses the university's collections of Asian, ancient, and Islamic art. Included is an assemblage of Chinese jades and cave reliefs that's considered the best in the world, as well as Korean ceramics, Roman sculpture, Greek vases, and Persian miniature paintings and calligraphy.

Harvard Museum of Natural History. 26 Oxford St. ☎ **617/495-3045.** www.hmnh.harvard.edu.

Peabody Museum of Archaeology & Ethnology. 11 Divinity Ave. ☎ **617/ 496-1027.** www.peabody.harvard.edu. Admission to both $5 adults, $4 seniors and students, $3 children 3–13, free for children under 3; free to all Sat 9am–noon. Mon–Sat 9am–5pm; Sun 1–5pm. T: Red Line to Harvard. Cross Harvard Yard, keeping John Harvard statue on right, and turn right at Science Center. First left is Oxford St.

These fascinating museums house the university's collections of items and artifacts related to the natural world. The world-famous academic resource offers interdisciplinary programs and exhibitions that tie in elements of all the associated fields. You'll certainly find something interesting here, be it a dinosaur skeleton, a hunk of meteorite, a Native American artifact, or the world-famous Glass Flowers.

The Museum of Natural History comprises three institutions. The best-known is the **Botanical Museum,** whose most popular display is the **Glass Flowers,** 3,000 models of more than 840 plant species devised between 1887 and 1936 by the German father-and-son team of Leopold and Rudolph Blaschka. You might have heard about them, and you might be skeptical, but it's true: They look real. Children love the **Museum of Comparative Zoology,** where the dinosaurs share space with preserved and stuffed insects and animals that range in size from butterflies to giraffes. The **Mineralogical & Geological Museum** is the most specialized—hold off unless there's an interesting interdisciplinary display or you're really into rocks.

Young visitors also enjoy the dollhouselike "Worlds in Miniature" display at the **Peabody Museum of Archaeology & Ethnology,** which represents people from all over the world in scaled-down homes. The museum also boasts the **Hall of the North American Indian,** where 500 artifacts representing 10 cultures are on display. The museum also has a terrific gift shop (☎ **617/495-2248**) packed with reasonably priced folk art and crafts.

MASSACHUSETTS INSTITUTE OF TECHNOLOGY (MIT)

The public is welcome at the Massachusetts Institute of Technology campus, a mile or so from Harvard Square, across the Charles River from Beacon Hill and the Back Bay. Visit the **Information Office,** 77 Mass. Ave. (☎ **617/253-4795**), to take a free guided tour (weekdays, 10am and 2pm), or pick up a copy of the "Walk Around MIT" map and brochure. At the same address, the **Hart Nautical Galleries** (open daily 9am to 5pm) contain ship and engine models that trace the development of marine engineering. The school has an excellent outdoor sculpture collection, which includes works by Picasso and Alexander Calder, and notable modern architecture by Eero Saarinen and I. M. Pei. Even more modern are the holography displays at the **MIT Museum,** 265 Mass. Ave. (☎ **617/253-4444;** http://web.mit.edu/museum), where you'll also find works in more conventional mediums. The museum is open Tuesday through Friday from 10am to 5pm, weekends from noon to 5pm; it's closed on major holidays. Admission is $5 for adults, $3 for students and seniors, $1 for children 5 to 18.

To get to MIT, take the MBTA Red Line to Kendall/MIT. The scenic walk from the Back Bay takes you along Mass. Ave. over the river straight to the campus. By car from Boston, cross the river at the Museum of Science, Cambridge Street, or Mass. Ave. and follow signs to Memorial Drive, where you can usually find parking during the day.

5 Especially for Kids

What can the children do in Boston? A better question might be "What *can't* the children do in Boston?" Just about every major destination in the city either is specifically designed to appeal to youngsters or can easily be adapted to do so.

I wouldn't ordinarily make such an insulting suggestion, but experience tells me that some parents need reminding: Please allow your kids some input while you're planning your trip. A great deal of anecdotal evidence tells me that incorporating suggestions (especially from teenagers) cuts down on eye-rolling and sighing. And the college tour, whale watch, or day trip that you wouldn't have considered might turn out to be one of the highlights of your vacation.

The following attractions are covered extensively elsewhere in this chapter; here's the boiled-down version for busy parents.

Destinations with something for every member of the family include **Faneuil Hall Marketplace** (☎ **617/338-2323**) and the **Museum of Fine Arts** (☎ **617/267-9300**), which offers special weekend and after-school programs.

Hands-on exhibits are a big draw at the **Boston Tea Party Ship & Museum** (see below) and the **New England Aquarium** (☎ **617/973-5200**). The **Museum of Science** (☎ **617/723-2500**) not only is a hands-on paradise, but also is home to the Hayden Planetarium and the Mugar Omni Theater. And you might get your hands on a baseball at a **Red Sox game** (see "More Museums & Attractions," above).

The allure of seeing people the size of ants draws young visitors to the **John Hancock Observatory** (☎ **617/572-6429**) and the **Prudential Center Skywalk** (☎ **617/859-0648**). And they can see actual ants—although they may prefer dinosaurs—at the Museum of Comparative Zoology, part of the **Harvard University Museum of Natural History** (☎ **617/495-3045**).

Older children who have studied modern American history will enjoy a visit to the **John F. Kennedy Library and Museum**

(☎ **617/929-4523**). Middle-schoolers who enjoyed Esther Forbes's *Johnny Tremain* might get a kick out of the **Paul Revere House** (☎ **617/523-2338**). Young visitors who have read Robert McCloskey's children's classic *Make Way for Ducklings* will relish a visit to the **Public Garden,** and fans of E. B. White's *The Trumpet of the Swan* certainly will want to ride on the **swan boats** (☎ **617/522-1966;** see "Parks & Gardens," above). Considerably less tame and much longer are **whale watches** (see "Organized Tours," below).

The walking-tour company ✪ **Boston by Foot,** 77 N. Washington St. (☎ **617/367-2345,** or 617/367-3766 for recorded information; www.bostonbyfoot.com), has a special program, "Boston by Little Feet," that's geared to children 6 to 12 years old. The 60-minute walk gives a child's-eye view of the architecture along the Freedom Trail and of Boston's role in the American Revolution. Children must be accompanied by an adult, and a map is provided. Tours run from May through October and meet at the statue of Samuel Adams on the Congress Street side of Faneuil Hall, Saturday at 10am, Sunday at 2pm, and Monday at 10am, rain or shine. The cost is $6 per person.

The **Historic Neighborhoods Foundation** (☎ **617/ 426-1885**) offers a 90-minute "Make Way for Ducklings" tour ($7 adults, $5 children, free for children under 5). The tour follows the path of the Mallard family described in Robert McCloskey's famous book and ends at the Public Garden.

✪ **Children's Museum.** 300 Congress St. (Museum Wharf). ☎ **617/ 426-8855.** www.bostonkids.org. Admission $7 adults, $6 children 2–15 and seniors, $2 children age 1, free for children under 1; Fri 5–9pm $1 for all. June–Aug Mon–Thurs 10am–7pm, Fri 10am–9pm, Sat–Sun 10am–5pm; Sept–May Sat–Thurs 10am–5pm, Fri 10am–9pm. T: Red Line to South Station. Walk north on Atlantic Ave. 1 block (past Federal Reserve Bank), turn right onto Congress St., walk 2 blocks (across bridge). Call for information about discounted parking.

As you approach the Children's Museum, don't be surprised to see adults suddenly being dragged by the hand when their young companions realize how close they are and start running. You know the museum is near when you see the 40-foot-high red-and-white milk bottle out front. It makes both children and adults look small in comparison—which is probably part of the point. No matter how old, everyone behaves like a little kid at this delightful museum.

Children can stick with their parents or wander on their own, learning, doing, and role-playing. The centerpiece of the renovated warehouse building is a new two-story-high maze, the **New Balance Climb,** which incorporates motor skills and problem-solving. Other favorites include **Grandparents' Attic,** a souped-up version of playing in Grandma's closet; **Under the Dock,** an environmental exhibit that teaches about the Boston waterfront and allows youngsters to dress up in a crab suit; hands-on physical experiments (such as creating giant soap bubbles) in **Science Playground;** and **Boats Afloat,** which has an 800-gallon play tank and a replica of the bridge of a working boat. **Supermercado** is a marketplace that immerses children in Hispanic culture, surrounding them with Spanish newspapers, ethnic food products, and salsa music. You can also explore a Japanese house and subway train from Kyoto (Boston's sister city) and learn about young adults in **Teen Tokyo.** Children under 4 and their caregivers have a special room, **Playspace,** that's packed with toys and activities.

Call or surf ahead for information about traveling exhibitions, KidStage participatory plays, and special programs. And be sure to check out the excellent gift shop (as if you have a choice).

Boston Tea Party Ship & Museum. Congress Street Bridge. ☎ **617/ 338-1773.** www.historictours.com/boston/teaparty.htm. Admission $8 adults, $7 students, $4 children 4–12, free for children under 4. Mar–Nov daily 9am–dusk (about 6pm in summer, 5pm in spring and fall). Closed Dec–Feb. T: Red Line to South Station. Walk north on Atlantic Ave. 1 block, past the Federal Reserve Bank, turn right onto Congress St., and walk 1 block.

On December 16, 1773, a public meeting of independent-minded Bostonians led to the symbolic act of resistance commemorated here. The brig *Beaver II* is a full-size replica of one of the three merchant ships loaded with tea that stood at anchor that night. After assembling at the Old South Meeting House, colonists poorly disguised as Indians emptied the vessels' cargo into the harbor. The ship sits alongside a museum with exhibits on the "tea party." The audio and video displays (including a 15-minute film), dioramas, and information panels tell the story of the uprising. You can dump a bale of tea into Boston Harbor—a museum staffer retrieves it—and drink some complimentary tax-free tea (iced in summer, hot in winter).

6 Organized Tours

ORIENTATION TOURS

GUIDED WALKING TOURS   Even if you usually explore on your own, consider an excellent walking tour with ✪ **Boston by**

Foot, 77 N. Washington St. (☎ **617/367-2345,** or 617/ 367-3766 for recorded information; www.bostonbyfoot.com). From May through October, the nonprofit educational corporation conducts historical and architectural tours that focus on particular neighborhoods or themes. The rigorously trained guides are volunteers who encourage questions. Buy tickets ($8 per person) from the guide; reservations are not required. The 90-minute tours take place rain or shine. *Note:* All excursions from Faneuil Hall start at the statue of Samuel Adams on Congress Street.

The **"Heart of the Freedom Trail"** tour starts at Faneuil Hall Tuesday through Saturday at 10am. Tours of **Beacon Hill** begin at the foot of the State House steps on Beacon Street weekdays at 5:30pm, Saturday at 10am, and Sunday at 2pm. **"Boston Underground"** looks at subterranean technology, including crypts, the subway, and the depression of the Central Artery. It starts at Faneuil Hall Sunday at 2pm. Other tours and meeting places are **Victorian Back Bay,** on the steps of Trinity Church, 10am Friday and Saturday; the **Waterfront,** at Faneuil Hall, Friday at 5:30pm and Sunday at 10am; and the **North End,** at Faneuil Hall, Saturday at 2pm.

Once a month, a special tour ($9) covers a particular theme or area. Special theme tours—they include "Great Women of Boston," "Literary Landmarks," and a Chinatown tour—can be scheduled if there are enough requests. Off-season tours for groups only (minimum 10 people; $10 per person) are available.

The **Society for the Preservation of New England Antiquities** (☎ 617/227-3956; www.spnea.org) offers a fascinating tour that describes and illustrates life in the mansions and garrets of Beacon Hill in 1800. "Magnificent and Modest," a 2-hour program, costs $10 and starts at the Harrison Gray Otis House, 141 Cambridge St., at 11am on Saturday and Sunday from May through October. The price includes a tour of the Otis House, and reservations are recommended.

The **Historic Neighborhoods Foundation** (☎ 617/426-1885) offers 90-minute walking tours in several neighborhoods, including Beacon Hill, the North End, Chinatown, the Waterfront, and the Financial District. Schedules change with the season, and reservations are required. The programs highlight points of interest to visitors while covering history, architecture, and topographical development. Tours usually cost about $6 per person; check ahead for schedules and meeting places.

Boston by Sea: The Maritime Trail (☎ 617/574-5950; www.bostonbysea.org) is a walk near the Waterfront with a costumed guide. The 45-minute land-only version is currently free. The 90-minute boat trip around the harbor, subtitled "Living History in Story, Sites, and Songs," includes a thorough account of the city's maritime legacy, video clips, and even some tunes (namely, sea chanteys). Tickets cost $25 for adults, $20 seniors and students, $10 children under 13. Tours leave Long Wharf daily at 1 and 3pm through early October. For reservations, call **Boston Harbor Cruises** (☎ 617/227-4321).

The **Boston Park Rangers** (☎ 617/635-7383; www.ci.boston.ma.us/parks) offer free guided walking tours. The best-known focus is the **Emerald Necklace,** a loop of green spaces designed by pioneering American landscape architect Frederick Law Olmsted. You'll see and hear about the city's major parks and gardens, including Boston Common, the Public Garden, the Commonwealth Avenue Mall, the Muddy River in the Fenway, Olmsted Park, Jamaica Pond, the Arnold Arboretum, and Franklin Park. The full 6-hour walk includes a 1-hour tour of any of the sites. Call for schedules. The **MDC Charles River Rangers** (☎ 617/727-9650, ext. 445) occasionally lead tours that focus on the river and the issues that affect it.

TROLLEY TOURS   A narrated tour on a trolley (actually a bus chassis with a trolley body) can give you an overview before you focus on specific attractions (remember: each tour is only as good as its guide), or you can use the all-day pass to hit as many places as possible in 8 hours or so. Because Boston is so pedestrian friendly, a trolley tour isn't the best choice for the able-bodied and unencumbered making a long visit. In some neighborhoods, notably the North End, the trolleys stop a long way away from the attractions, so don't believe a ticket-seller who tells you otherwise. But if you're unable to walk long distances, or traveling with children, a trolley tour can be worth the money.

Each tour is only as good as its guide, and quality varies widely—every few years a TV station or newspaper runs an "exposé" of the wacky information a tour guide is passing off as fact. Have a grain of salt ready.

Trolley tickets cost $18 to $24 for adults, $12 or less for children. Boarding spots are at hotels, historic sites, and tourist information centers. There are busy waiting areas near the New England Aquarium, the Park Street T stop, and the corner of

Boylston Street and Charles Street South. Each company paints its cars a different color. Orange-and-green **Old Town Trolleys** (☎ 617/269-7150; www.historictours.com) are the most numerous. Minuteman Tours' **Boston Trolley Tours** (☎ 617/867-5539; www.historictours.com) are blue; **Beantown Trolleys** (☎ 800/343-1328 or 617/236-2148) say "Gray Line" but are red; and **CityView Luxury Trolleys** (☎ 617/363-7899, or 800/525-2489 outside 617) are silver. The **Discover Boston Multilingual Trolley Tours** (☎ 617/742-1440) vehicle is white; it conducts tours in Japanese, Spanish, French, German, and Italian.

"DUCK" TOURS   The most unusual way to see Boston is with ✪ **Boston Duck Tours** (☎ 800/226-7442 or 617/723-DUCK; www.bostonducktours.com). The tours, offered only from April to November, are pricey but great fun. Sightseers board a "duck," a reconditioned Second World War amphibious landing craft, on the Boylston Street side of the Prudential Center. The 80-minute narrated tour begins with a quick but comprehensive jaunt around the city. Then the duck lumbers down a ramp, splashes into the Charles River, and goes for a spin around the basin.

Tickets, available at the Prudential Center, are $21 for adults, $18 for seniors and students, $11 for children 4 to 12, and 25¢ for children under 4. Tours run every 30 minutes from 9am to 1 hour before sunset. Reservations are not accepted (except for groups of 16 or more), and tickets usually sell out, especially on weekends. Try to buy same-day tickets early in the day, or plan ahead and ask about the limited number of tickets available 2 days in advance.

SIGHTSEEING CRUISES

Take to the water for a taste of Boston's rich maritime history or a daylong break from walking and driving. You can cruise around the harbor or go all the way to Provincetown or Gloucester. The season runs from **April through October,** with spring and fall offerings often restricted to weekends. If you're traveling in a large group, call ahead for information about reservations and discounted tickets. If you're prone to seasickness, check the size of the vessel for your tour before buying tickets; larger boats provide more cushioning and comfort than smaller ones.

The largest company is **Boston Harbor Cruises,** 1 Long Wharf (☎ 617/227-4321; www.bostonboats.com). It runs 30-minute lunchtime cruises on weekdays at 12:15pm; tickets are $2. Ninety-minute **historic sightseeing cruises,** which tour the Inner and Outer Harbor, depart daily at 1 and 3pm, at 7pm (the sunset cruise), and at 11am on weekends and holidays. Tickets are $15 for adults, $12 for seniors, $10 for children under 12. The 45-minute *Constitution* **cruise** takes you around the Inner Harbor and docks at the Charlestown Navy Yard so that you can go ashore and visit "Old Ironsides." Tours leave Long Wharf hourly from 10:30am to 4:30pm, and on the hour from the Navy yard from 11am to 5pm. The cruise is $8 for adults, $7 for seniors, and $6 for children.

Massachusetts Bay Lines (☎ **617/542-8000;** www.massbaylines.com) offers 55-minute **harbor tours** from Memorial Day through Columbus Day. Cruises leave from Rowes Wharf on the hour from 10am to 6pm; the price is $8 for adults, $5 for children and seniors. The 90-minute sunset cruise departs at 7pm. Tickets are $15 for adults, $10 for children and seniors.

The **Charles Riverboat Company** (☎ **617/621-3001;** www.charlesriverboat.com) offers 55-minute narrated cruises around the **lower Charles River basin** and in the opposite direction, through the **Charles River locks to Boston Harbor.** Boats depart from the CambridgeSide Galleria mall; river tours leave on the hour from noon to 5pm, harbor tours once a day, at 10:30am. Tickets for either tour are $8 for adults, $6 for seniors, and $5 for children 2 to 12.

WHALE WATCHING

The **New England Aquarium** (☎ **617/973-5281;** see "The Top Attractions," above) runs whale watches daily from May through mid-October and on weekends in April and late October. You'll travel several miles out to sea to Stellwagen Bank, the feeding ground for the whales as they migrate from Newfoundland to Provincetown. Tickets (cash only) are $26 for adults, $21 for senior citizens and college students, $19 for youths 12 to 18, and $16.50 for children 3 to 11. Children must be 3 years old and at least 30 inches tall. Reservations are strongly recommended and can be held with a MasterCard or Visa.

Boston Harbor Whale Watch (☎ **617/345-9866;** www.bostonwhale.com) promises more time watching whales than trying to find them. Tours depart from Rowes Wharf beginning in mid-June and operate Friday through Sunday until the end of the month. From July through early September, there's daily service. Departure times are 10am on weekdays, 9am and 2pm on weekends. Expect to spend about 4½ hours at sea. Tickets are $21 for adults, $18 for seniors and children under 13. Reservations are suggested.

SPECIALTY TOURS

THE LITERARY TRAIL   A tour of pertinent sites in Boston, Cambridge, and Concord, the Literary Trail (☎ 617/574-5950; www.Lit-Trail.org) is a narrated trolley tour. You can also explore on your own, using a guide that's available at local bookstores. The 4-hour, 20-mile trolley excursion begins and ends at the Omni Parker House hotel (you can also exit in Harvard Square). It explores locations associated with authors and poets such as Emerson, Thoreau, Longfellow, and Louisa May Alcott, among others. The fare is $35 for adults, $31.50 for students and children under 18; reservations are required.

FOR HORROR-MOVIE FANS   "**Ghosts and Gravestones**" covers burial grounds and other shiver-inducing areas in a trolley and on foot. Presented by **Minuteman Tours** (☎ 617/269-3626; www.historictours.com), the 2-hour tour starts at dusk on summer and fall weekends. It costs $28 for adults, $15 for children.

MORE SPECIAL-INTEREST TOURS   Boston's busiest operator of theme tours is **Old Town Trolley** (☎ 617/269-7150; www.historictours.com). Schedules and offerings vary according to the season and level of visitor interest. Prices vary according to what's included but are usually at least $20 for adults, a little less for seniors and children. Call ahead for reservations, meeting places, and details of the tours. At press time, options included **"JFK's Boston"** (with stops at John F. Kennedy's birthplace in Brookline and the presidential library), separate tours for **seafood** lovers and **chocolate** lovers, a tour that stops at several **brew pubs,** and a December **"Holiday Lights"** tour.

6

Shopping

*B*oston's shopping scene is a harmonious blend of classic and contemporary. You'll find intimate boutiques and sprawling malls, esoteric bookshops and national chain stores, classy galleries and snazzy secondhand-clothing outlets. In this chapter I'll point you to areas that are great for shop-hopping, and specific destinations that are great for specific items.

1 The Shopping Scene

One of the best features of shopping in Massachusetts is that there's no sales tax on clothing priced below $175, or on food. Just about every store will ship your purchases home for a fee, but if it's part of a chain that operates in your home state, you'll probably be subject to that sales tax. Be sure to ask first. All other items are taxed at 5% (as are restaurant meals and takeout food).

In the major shopping areas, stores usually open at 10am on weekdays and Saturday. Malls keep their own hours (noted below); smaller shops stay open weeknights and Saturday until 6 or 7pm, and Sunday until 5 or 6pm. Winter open days and Sunday open hours may vary. The state no longer prohibits stores from opening before noon on Sunday, but many still wait till noon or don't open at all. If a business sounds too good to pass up, call to make sure it's open before venturing out.

GREAT SHOPPING AREAS

The area's premier shopping area is Boston's **Back Bay.** Dozens of classy galleries, shops, and boutiques make **Newbury Street** a world-famous destination. Nearby, the **Shops at Prudential Center** and **Copley Place** (linked by a weatherproof walkway across Huntington Avenue), **Neiman Marcus, Lord & Taylor,** and **Saks Fifth Avenue** form the backbone of a giant retail complex.

Another popular destination is **Faneuil Hall Marketplace.** The shops, boutiques, and pushcarts at Boston's busiest attraction sell everything from cosmetics to costume jewelry, sweaters to souvenirs.

Back Bay & Beacon Hill

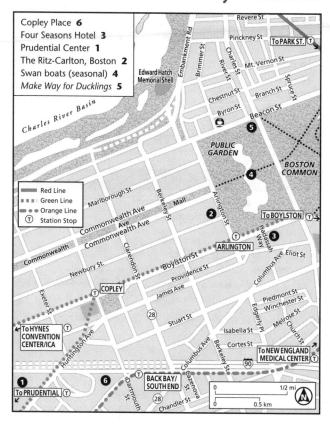

Copley Place **6**
Four Seasons Hotel **3**
Prudential Center **1**
The Ritz-Carlton, Boston **2**
Swan boats (seasonal) **4**
Make Way for Ducklings **5**

If the prospect of the hubbub at Faneuil Hall is too much for you, stroll over to **Charles Street,** at the foot of Beacon Hill. It's a short but commercially dense (and picturesque) street noted for its gift shops and antiques dealers.

One of Boston's oldest shopping areas is **Downtown Crossing.** The traffic-free pedestrian mall along Washington, Winter, and Summer streets near Boston Common is home to two major department stores (**Filene's** and **Macy's**), tons of smaller clothing and shoe stores, food and merchandise pushcarts, outlets of two major bookstore chains (**Barnes & Noble** and **Borders**), and the original **Filene's Basement** (see below).

Harvard Square in Cambridge, with its bookstores, boutiques, and T-shirt shops, is about 15 minutes from downtown Boston by subway. Over the neighborhood association's objections, chain stores have swept into "the Square," driving up rents and driving out many of the businesses that contributed to its legendary bohemian atmosphere. Today you'll find a mix of national and regional outlets, and more than a few persistent independent retailers.

For a less generic experience, stroll along shop-lined **Massachusetts Avenue** in either direction to the next T stop (**Porter Square** to the north, **Central Square** to the southeast). The walk takes an hour or so—time well spent for dedicated consumers.

2 Shopping A to Z

Here we've singled out establishments we especially like and neighborhoods that suit shoppers interested in particular types of merchandise. Unless otherwise indicated, addresses are in Boston.

ANTIQUES & COLLECTIBLES

No antiques hound worthy of the name will leave Boston without an expedition along both sides of **Charles Street** from Cambridge Street to Beacon Street.

✪ **Boston Antique Cooperative I & II.** 119 Charles St. ☎ **617/227-9810.** T: Red Line to Charles/MGH.

Merchandise from Europe, Asia, and the United States fills these shops. They specialize in furniture, vintage clothing and photographs, jewelry, and porcelain, but you might come across just about anything. The traffic is heavy and the turnover rapid, so if you see something you like, buy it immediately or risk losing out.

Danish Country Antique Furniture. 138 Charles St. ☎ **617/227-1804.** T: Red Line to Charles/MGH.

Owner James Kilroy specializes in Scandinavian antique furnishings dating from the 1700s onward. You'll also see folk art, crafts, Royal Copenhagen porcelain, and 19th-century Chinese furniture and home accessories.

Shreve, Crump & Low. 330 Boylston St. ☎ **800/324-0222** or 617/267-9100. T: Green Line to Arlington.

This Boston institution, founded in 1796, is best known for new jewelry, china, silver, crystal, and watches. The antiques department specializes in 18th- and 19th-century American and English furnishings, British and American silver, and Chinese porcelain.

ART

Everyone has to start somewhere, and the artists whose work you'll find in the big museums years from now might be showing at galleries in Boston today. You'll find the greatest concentration of galleries along ✪ **Newbury Street** (remember to look up for galleries on higher floors). Browsers and questions are welcome. Most galleries are open Tuesday through Sunday from 10 or 11am to 5:30 or 6pm. For specifics, check with the **Newbury Street League** (☎ 617/267-7961; www.newbury-st.com).

Tremont Street and Harrison Avenue in the South End make a budding gallery area, as is the Leather District around South Street (between South Station and Chinatown), which is muddling through the Big Dig. You'll find galleries, but you're equally likely to see bulldozers.

One excellent way to see artists at work is to check listings in the *Globe* and *Herald* for information about neighborhood **open studio** days. The artists' communities in the South End, the Fort Point Channel area, Somerville, and even tony Brookline stage the weekend events once or twice a year. You may be asked to make a contribution to charity in exchange for a map of the studios.

Alpha Gallery. 14 Newbury St., 2nd floor. ☎ **617/536-4465.** E-mail: alphagall@aol.com. T: Green Line to Arlington.

Directed by Joanna E. Fink, daughter of founder Alan Fink, Alpha Gallery specializes in contemporary American paintings, sculpture, and works on paper, as well as modern master paintings and prints.

Barbara Krakow Gallery. 10 Newbury St., 5th floor. ☎ **617/262-4490.** www.barbarakrakowgallery.com. T: Green Line to Arlington.

This prestigious gallery, established more than 30 years ago, specializes in paintings, sculpture, drawings, and prints created after 1945.

Gallery NAGA. 67 Newbury St. ☎ **617/267-9060.** www.gallerynaga.com. T: Green Line to Arlington.

In the neo-Gothic Church of the Covenant, Gallery NAGA exhibits contemporary painting, prints, sculpture, photography, furniture, and works in glass. A stop here is a must if you want to see holography (trust me, you do).

✪ **Gargoyles, Grotesques & Chimeras.** 262 Newbury St. ☎ **617/536-2362.** T: Green Line B, C, or D to Hynes/ICA.

Gargoyles of all sizes decorate this intentionally gloomy space. You'll also see plaster reproductions of details on the facades of famous cathedrals and other buildings, non-gargoyle home decorations, and haunting photographs that set the Gothic mood.

Haley & Steele. 91 Newbury St. ☎ **617/536-6339.** www.haleysteele.com. T: Green Line to Arlington.

If you prefer traditional to contemporary, this is the place. You'll find maritime, military, botanical, ornithological, and historical prints, and 19th-century oil paintings and British sporting prints.

✪ **International Poster Gallery.** 205 Newbury St. ☎ **617/375-0076.** www.internationalposter.com. T: Green Line to Copley.

This extraordinary gallery's Italian vintage poster collection is the largest anywhere, and the thousands of other pieces include posters and ephemera from around the world. The accommodating staff will comb its databases (cyber and cerebral) to help you find the exact image you want. Prices start at $50, with most in the $500 to $2,000 range.

✪ **Nielsen Gallery.** 179 Newbury St. ☎ **617/266-4835.** www.nielsengallery.com. T: Green Line to Copley.

Owner Nina Nielsen personally selects the artists who exhibit in her gallery (which has been here for more than 35 years), and she has great taste. You might come across the work of a young, newly discovered talent or that of a more established artist.

✪ **Pucker Gallery.** 171 Newbury St. ☎ **617/267-9473.** www.puckergallery.com. T: Green Line to Copley.

Pucker Gallery's eclectic offerings include Inuit, African, and Israeli art; contemporary paintings, prints, drawings, and ceramics by regional and international artists; and excellent photographs. The staff is eager to show off and discuss the art, which spreads over four floors.

Robert Klein Gallery. 38 Newbury St., 4th floor. ☎ **617/267-7997.** www.robertkleingallery.com. T: Green Line to Arlington.

For 19th- and 20th-century photography, head to Robert Klein Gallery. Among the artists represented are Diane Arbus, Robert Mapplethorpe, Man Ray, and Ansel Adams.

Vose Galleries of Boston. 238 Newbury St. ☎ **617/536-6176.** www.voseartgalleries.com. T: Green Line B, C, or D to Hynes/ICA.

One of the specialties here is Hudson River School paintings—fitting, because the business and the mid–19th-century movement are about the same age. The oldest continuously operating gallery in the United States opened in 1841 and is still run by the Vose family (now in its fifth generation). You'll see works of the Boston School and American Impressionists among the 18th-, 19th-, and early–20th-century American paintings.

BOOKS

Avenue Victor Hugo Bookshop. 339 Newbury St. ☎ **617/266-7746.** www.avenuevictorhugobooks.com. T: Green Line B, C, or D to Hynes/ICA.

This two-story shop buys, sells, and trades new and used books and estate libraries. The stock of 150,000 books is comprehensive; the primary specialty is science fiction. You'll also find periodicals, with back issues of magazines that date to 1850, and a selection of general fiction titles that's billed as the largest north of New York City.

Barnes & Noble. 395 Washington St. ☎ **617/426-5184.** www.barnesandnoble.com. T: Red or Orange Line to Downtown Crossing.

The downtown branch of the national chain carries a large selection of local-interest titles and has a huge periodicals section. Barnes & Noble runs the bookstore operations at Boston University and Harvard (see "College Paraphernalia," below). There's also a branch at 325 Harvard St., Coolidge Corner, Brookline (☎ **617/232-0594**).

Borders Books & Music. 24 School St. ☎ **617/557-7188.** www.borders.com. T: Orange or Blue Line to State.

Two levels of books and one of music, plus an in-house cafe and occasional author appearances, make this sprawling store near Downtown Crossing a popular destination.

✪ **Brattle Book Shop.** 9 West St. ☎ **800/447-9595** or 617/542-0210. E-mail: brattle@tiac.net. T: Red or Orange Line to Downtown Crossing or Green Line to Boylston.

This marvelous store near Macy's buys and sells used, rare, and out-of-print titles, and owner Kenneth Gloss does free appraisals. Be sure to check the carts out front (in all but the nastiest weather) for good deals on books of all ages. *Warning:* Book lovers and collectors who make this their first stop may not get any other shopping done.

Globe Corner Bookstore. 500 Boylston St. ☎ **617/859-8008.** www.globecorner.com. T: Green Line to Copley. 28 Church St., Cambridge. ☎ 617/497-6277. T: Red Line to Harvard.

These overstuffed stores (offspring of the dear departed original on the Freedom Trail) carry huge selections of travel guides and essays, maps, atlases, globes, and nautical charts.

✪ **Harvard Book Store.** 1256 Mass. Ave., Cambridge. ☎ **800/542-READ** outside 617, or 617/661-1515. www.harvard.com. E-mail: hbs-info@harvard.com. T: Red Line to Harvard.

The excellent scholarly selection and discounted best-sellers attract shoppers to the main level of this independent bookstore, and the basement is the draw for those in the know. Prices on remainders are good, and used paperbacks (many bought for classes and hardly opened) are 50% off their original price.

Schoenhof's Foreign Books. 76A Mt. Auburn St., Cambridge. ☎ **617/ 547-8855.** www.schoenhofs.com. E-mail: info@schoenhofs.com. T: Red Line to Harvard.

Schoenhof's stocks books for both children and adults in more than two dozen languages, as well as dictionaries and language-learning materials for more than 300 languages and dialects. After a recent expansion, it also carries gifts, greeting cards, calendars, and the like. The multilingual staff arranges special orders at no extra charge.

✪ **WordsWorth Books.** 30 Brattle St., Cambridge. ☎ **800/899-2202** or 617/354-5201. www.wordsworth.com. E-mail: info@wordsworth.com. T: Red Line to Harvard.

This sprawling store stocks more than 100,000 volumes, all (except textbooks) discounted at least 10%. It's a great place for browsing; if you prefer, the information desk staff will brainstorm with you until the database generates the title you want. The excellent selection of children's books and gifts is up the street at ✪ **Curious George Goes to WordsWorth,** 1 John F. Kennedy St. (☎ **617/498-0062;** www.curiousg.com).

COLLEGE PARAPHERNALIA

The centrally located big names are BU and Harvard (you'll see Boston College merchandise downtown, too), but why stop there? Look like a real insider with a T-shirt from the **Emerson College Book Store,** 80 Boylston St. (☎ **617/728-7700;** T: Green Line to Boylston); the **MIT Coop,** 3 Cambridge Center (☎ **617/ 499-3200;** T: Red Line to Kendall/MIT); the **Northeastern University Bookstore,** 360 Huntington Ave. (☎ **617/373-2286;** T: Green Line E to Northeastern); or the **Suffolk University Bookstore,** 148 Cambridge St., Beacon Hill (☎ **617/227-4085;** T: Blue Line to Bowdoin).

Barnes & Noble at Boston University. 660 Beacon St. ☎ **617/267-8484.** www.bkstore.com/bu. T: Green Line B, C, or D to Kenmore.

The BU crest, mascot (a terrier), or name appears somewhere on at least a floor's worth of clothing and just about any other item with room for a logo. The author series (☎ **617/236-7421**) brings writers to campus year-round.

The Harvard Coop. 1400 Mass. Ave., Cambridge. ☎ **617/499-2000.** www.thecoop.com. T: Red Line to Harvard.

The Coop (rhymes with *hoop*), or Harvard Cooperative Society, is student-oriented but not a run-of-the-mill college bookstore. You'll find Harvard insignia merchandise, stationery, prints and posters, and music. As at BU, Barnes & Noble runs the book operation.

✪ **The Harvard Shop.** 52 John F. Kennedy St., Cambridge. ☎ **617/ 864-3000.** T: Red Line to Harvard.

Kids in shopping malls from Jacksonville to Juneau wear Harvard shirts in every color and outlandish pattern under the sun. Visit this shop for authentic gear in the shadow of the school.

CRAFTS

✪ **The Artful Hand Gallery.** Copley Place. ☎ **617/262-9601.** T: Orange Line to Back Bay or Green Line to Copley.

The Artful Hand specializes, as you might guess, in handcrafted items. It shows and sells work by an excellent roster of artists. You'll see wonderful jewelry, ceramics, blown glass, wood pieces (including boxes), and sculpture, plus furniture, folk art, and books.

✪ **Society of Arts and Crafts.** 175 Newbury St. ☎ **617/266-1810.** www.societyofcrafts.org. T: Green Line to Copley.

Contemporary American work, much created by New Englanders, is the focus at the oldest nonprofit craft organization in the country. The jewelry, furniture, home accessories, glass, and ceramics range from practical to purely decorative. The **Downtown Crossing** branch, open on weekdays only, is on the second floor of 101 Arch St. (☎ **617/345-0033**), off Summer Street.

DEPARTMENT STORES

There's so much else going on in the Back Bay that you might forget it's home to branches of three elegant chains. We particularly like **Lord & Taylor,** 760 Boylston St. (☎ **617/262-6000**), for its great sales and costume jewelry. **Filene's,** 426 Washington St. (☎ **617/357-2100**), has an exceptional cosmetics department, and **Macy's,** 450 Washington St. (☎ **617/357-3000**)—across Summer Street from Filene's—bears the hallmarks of the New York–based chain, including excellent selections of housewares, china, and silver. The high-end **Saks Fifth Avenue,** Prudential Plaza (☎ **617/262-8500**), would be the classiest department store in town if not for **Neiman Marcus,** 5 Copley Place (☎ **617/536-3660**), which charges Texas-size prices for the trappings of true luxury.

FASHION
ADULTS

Anne Fontaine. Heritage on the Garden, 318 Boylston St. ☎ **617/423-0366.** T: Green Line to Arlington.

This is the first U.S. outlet for the designer's "perfect white blouse collection from Paris." We wanted to laugh, but then we saw for ourselves—almost every item *is* a perfect (for one reason or another) white blouse. A few darker tops have sneaked in, too. Prices start at $80.

Dakini. 1704 Mass. Ave., Cambridge. ☎ **617/864-7661.** www.dakini.com. T: Red Line to Porter.

Come here for fleece in every imaginable incarnation, from shearlinglike jackets to velvety gloves, high-fashion women's separates to kids' pullovers. It's not cheap, but it's top quality, and the regular sales can make you feel both toasty and thrifty.

Louis Boston. 234 Berkeley St. ☎ **800/225-5135** or 617/262-6100. www.louisboston.com. T: Green Line to Arlington.

This ultraprestigious store (with prices to match) sells designer men's suits that can be coordinated with handmade shirts, silk ties, and Italian shoes. Louis, Woman, at the same address, caters to an equally elegant female clientele. Also on the premises are a full-service hair salon and Café Louis, which serves lunch and dinner.

CHILDREN

Calliope. 33 Brattle St., Cambridge. ☎ **617/876-4149.** T: Red Line to Harvard.

The must-see window displays at this Harvard Square shop use stuffed animals, clothes, and toys to illustrate sayings and proverbs, often twisted into hilarious puns. The merchandise inside—clothing, shoes, and a huge selection of plush animals—is equally delightful.

Oilily. 31 Newbury St. ☎ **800/964-5459** or 617/247-9299. www.oilily.nl. T: Green Line to Arlington.

At this end of Newbury Street, even kids must be *au courant.* Lend a hand with a visit to the Boston branch of the chichi international chain, which specializes in brightly colored fashions and accessories for ages newborn to 14 years. There's also a women's store at 32 Newbury St. (☎ **617/247-2386**).

Saturday's Child. 1762 Mass. Ave., Cambridge. ☎ **617/661-6402.** T: Red Line to Porter.

Never mind the nursery rhyme—"Saturday's child works hard for a living," my foot. You won't want your little angel lifting a finger in these precious (in both senses of the word) outfits. You'll also find top-quality shoes, accessories, and toys.

Varese Shoes. 285 Hanover St. ☎ **617/523-6530.** T: Green or Orange Line to Haymarket.

One window holds men's shoes, but that's not why you hear oohing and aahing all the way from the Freedom Trail (10 steps away). The other window is full of the most adorable Italian leather children's shoes. So they're not necessarily practical—are all of *your* shoes practical?

FOOD

Cardullo's Gourmet Shoppe. 6 Brattle St., Cambridge. ☎ **617/491-8888.** T: Red Line to Harvard.

A veritable United Nations of fancy food, Cardullo's carries specialties (including a huge variety of candy) from just about everywhere. If you can't afford the big-ticket items, order a tasty sandwich to go.

✪ **Dairy Fresh Candies.** 57 Salem St. ☎ **800/336-5536** or 617/742-2639. www.dairyfreshcandies.com. T: Green or Orange Line to Haymarket.

This North End hole-in-the-wall is crammed with decadent sweets and other delectables, from bagged nuts and dried fruit to imported Italian specialties. Before sweet-tooth–oriented holidays (especially Easter), it's irresistible. The store is too small for turning the children loose, but they'll be happy they waited outside when you return with confections to fortify them along the Freedom Trail.

J. Pace & Son. 42 Cross St. ☎ **617/227-9673.** T: Green or Orange Line to Haymarket.

Imported Italian food items, from fine meats and cheeses to pasta and cookies, overflow the shelves and cases at this bustling market on the threshold of the North End. Prices are good, especially for olive oil, and there's never a dull moment at the front counter. Order a sandwich if you don't feel like hauling groceries around—you can eat outside with the Big Dig workers.

Savenor's Supermarket. 160 Charles St. ☎ **617/723-6328.** T: Red Line to Charles/MGH.

Long a Cambridge institution (and a Julia Child favorite), Savenor's moved to Beacon Hill after a fire in 1993. It's the perfect place to load up on provisions before a concert or movie on the nearby Esplanade. And it's *the* local purveyor of exotic meats—if you crave buffalo or rattlesnake meat, this is the place.

GIFTS & SOUVENIRS

The Flat of the Hill. 60 Charles St. ☎ **617/619-9977.** E-mail: theflatofthehill@ juno.com. T: Red Line to Charles/MGH.

A folk-art wooden dog stands watch at the door of this jam-packed shop, which overflows with fun tchotchkes—home accessories, picture frames, stuffed animals, toys, and all manner of candles.

✪ **Joie de Vivre.** 1792 Mass. Ave., Cambridge. ☎ **617/864-8188.** T: Red Line to Porter.

Joie de Vivre's selection of gifts and toys for adults and sophisticated children is beyond compare. The kaleidoscope collection alone is worth the trip to this shop outside Porter Square; you'll also find salt and pepper shakers, jewelry, note cards, and puzzles.

Koo De Kir. 34 Charles St. ☎ **617/723-8111.** www.koodekir.com. T: Red Line to Charles/MGH.

In the heart of 19th-century Beacon Hill, Koo De Kir is a splash of the 21st century. Its selection of contemporary home accessories, furniture, lighting, and sculpture ranges from classics-to-be to downright whimsical.

Museum of Fine Arts Gift Shop. Copley Place. ☎ **617/536-8818.** T: Orange Line to Back Bay or Green Line to Copley. South Market Building, Faneuil Hall Marketplace. ☎ **617/720-1266.** T: Green or Blue Line to Government Center.

For those without the time or inclination to visit the museum, the satellite shops carry posters, prints, cards and stationery, books, educational toys, scarves, mugs, T-shirts, and reproductions of jewelry in the museum's collections. You might even be inspired to pay a call on the real thing.

The Shop at the Union. 356 Boylston St. ☎ **617/536-5651.** T: Green Line to Arlington.

This large, crowded store has a wide selection of high-quality home, garden, and personal accessories. You'll see jewelry, greeting cards, antiques, needlework, handmade children's clothes, toys, and confections. Most of the merchandise is manufactured by women or by woman-owned firms. Proceeds benefit the human services programs of the Women's Educational and Industrial Union, a nonprofit educational and social-service organization founded in 1877.

HOME & GARDEN

La Ruche. 168 Newbury St. ☎ **617/536-6366.** T: Green Line to Copley.

If you've never dreamed of living in a birdhouse, that might be because you've never been to this boutique. It stocks European and American glassware and pottery (including the complete line of Mackenzie–Childs majolica ware), unusual home and garden accessories, hand-painted furnishings, and dazzling architectural birdhouses.

Stoddard's. 50 Temple Place. ☎ **617/426-4187.** T: Red or Orange Line to Downtown Crossing.

The oldest cutlery shop in the country (since 1800), Stoddard's is full of items you don't know you need until you see them. You'll find sewing scissors, nail scissors, scissors for any other use you can think of, knives of all descriptions—including a spectacular selection of Swiss army knives—shaving brushes, binoculars, fishing tackle, and fly rods. There's also a branch at Copley Place (☎ **617/536-8688**).

Sweet Peas Home. 216 Clarendon St. ☎ **617/247-2828.** www. sweetpeashome.com. T: Green Line to Copley.

Just off Newbury Street, this little shop carries engagingly funky home and bath accessories, picture frames, lamps, candles, and furniture. You'll see a lot of faux rustic items, many made or painted by hand.

JEWELRY & WATCHES

Beadworks. 23 Church St., Cambridge. ☎ **617/868-9777.** T: Red Line to Harvard.

The jewelry here will suit you exactly—you make it yourself. Prices for the dazzling variety of raw materials start at 5¢ a bead, fittings (hardware) are available, and you can assemble your finery at the in-store worktable.

High Gear Jewelry. 139 Richmond St. ☎ **617/523-5804.** T: Green or Orange Line to Haymarket.

Don't be put off by the sign that says this little shop around the corner from the Paul Revere House (and right on the Freedom Trail) is a wholesale outlet. Retail shoppers are welcome to peruse the impressive selection of reasonably priced costume jewelry and watches.

✪ **John Lewis, Inc.** 97 Newbury St. ☎ **617/266-6665.** T: Green Line to Arlington.

John Lewis's imaginative women's and men's jewelry—crafted on the premises—suits both traditional and trendy tastes, and the staff is cordial and helpful. The pieces that mark you as a savvy Bostonian are earrings, necklaces, and bracelets made of hammered silver or gold circles.

MALLS & SHOPPING CENTERS

CambridgeSide Galleria. 100 CambridgeSide Place, Cambridge. ☎ **617/621-8666.** T: Green Line to Lechmere, or Red Line to Kendall/MIT and free shuttle bus (every 10 to 20 min.).

This three-level mall has two large department stores—**Filene's** (☎ **617/621-3800**) and **Sears** (☎ **617/252-3500**)—and more than 100 specialty stores. Pleasant but quite generic, it might be just the bargaining chip you need to lure your teenager to the nearby Museum of Science. Open Monday through Saturday 10am to 9:30pm, Sunday 11am to 7pm. Garage parking rates start at $1 for an hour.

✪ **Copley Place.** 100 Huntington Ave. ☎ **617/369-5000.** T: Orange Line to Back Bay or Green Line to Copley.

Copley Place has set the standard for upscale shopping in Boston since 1985. Connected to the Westin and Marriott hotels and the

Flying Lobsters

If you relished the fresh seafood in Boston and want to share some with a friend, you can send a top-quality live lobster and make someone at home very happy. **James Hook & Co.,** 15 Northern Ave. at Atlantic Avenue (☎ **617/423-5500;** T: Red Line to South Station), and **Legal Seafoods Fresh by Mail,** Logan Airport Terminal C (☎ **800/477-5342** or 617/569-4622; T: Blue Line to Airport) will handle the overnight shipping.

Prudential Center, it's a crossroads for office workers, moviegoers, out-of-towners, and enthusiastic consumers. You can while away a couple of hours or a whole day shopping and dining here and at the adjacent Shops at Prudential Center (see below) without ever going outdoors. Some of Copley Place's 100-plus shops will be familiar from the mall at home, but this is emphatically not a suburban shopping complex that happens to be in the city. There's also an 11-screen movie theater, but beware: Some of the screens are almost comically tiny.

Open Monday through Saturday 10am to 8pm, Sunday noon to 6pm. Some stores have extended hours, and the theaters and some restaurants are open through late evening.

By car, the Massachusetts Turnpike eastbound has a Copley exit. Park in the **Copley Place Garage** (☎ **617/375-4488**), off Huntington Avenue at Exeter Street. To pay a reduced rate, have your ticket validated when you make a purchase. Time limits may apply during the day.

Faneuil Hall Marketplace. Between North, Congress, and State sts. and I-93. ☎ **617/338-2323.** T: Green or Blue Line to Government Center or Orange Line to Haymarket.

The original festival market is both wildly popular and widely imitated, and Faneuil Hall Marketplace changes constantly to appeal to visitors as well as natives wary of its touristy reputation. The original part of **Faneuil Hall** itself dates to 1742, and the lower floors take it back to its retail roots. The **Quincy Market Colonnade,** in the central building, houses a gargantuan selection of food and confections. The bars and restaurants always seem to be crowded, and the shopping is terrific, if a tad generic. Many long-term leases expired in 1999 and 2000, so turnover has been high recently—look for grand-opening and going-out-of-business sales.

In and around the five buildings surrounded by brick-and-stone plazas, the shops combine "only in Boston" with "only at every mall in the country." **Marketplace Center** and the ground floors of the **North Market and South Market buildings** have lots of chain outlets—a magnet for many, a distraction to some. Most of the unique offerings are under **Quincy Market's canopies** on the pushcarts piled high with crafts and gifts, and upstairs or downstairs in the market buildings. The only way to find what suits you is to explore.

Shop hours are Monday through Saturday from 10am to 9pm and Sunday from noon to 6pm. The Colonnade opens earlier, and most bars and restaurants close later. If you must drive, there's parking in the Government Center garage off Congress Street and the marketplace's own crowded garage off Atlantic Avenue.

The Garage. 36 John F. Kennedy St., Cambridge. No phone. T: Red Line to Harvard.

Wander up the corkscrew ramp to the boutiques and shops (a record store, a clothing store, a jewelry store, and two stores carrying sci-fi paraphernalia) on the upper levels of this little mall. On the main floor, you can have a light or filling meal at **Formaggio's** (☎ **617/547-4795**) or **Bruegger's Bagel Bakery** (☎ **617/661-4664**).

The Shops at Prudential Center. 800 Boylston St. ☎ **800/SHOP-PRU** or 617/267-1002. T: Green Line to Copley, E to Prudential, or B, C, or D to Hynes/ICA.

The main level of the city's second-tallest tower holds this sprawling complex. In addition to **Lord & Taylor** (☎ **617/262-6000**) and **Saks Fifth Avenue** (☎ **617/262-8500**), there are more than 40 shops and boutiques, a food court, a "fashion court," a post office, and five restaurants.

Hours are Monday through Saturday 10am to 8pm, Sunday 11am to 6pm. The restaurants and food court stay open later.

MARKETS

Farmers' Markets. City Hall Plaza, Mon and Wed. T: Green or Blue Line to Government Center. Copley Sq., Tues and Fri. T: Green Line to Copley or Orange Line to Back Bay.

Massachusetts farmers and growers under the auspices of the state **Department of Food and Agriculture** (☎ **617/227-3018**) dispatch trucks filled with whatever's in season to the heart of the city from July through November. Depending on the time of year, you'll have your pick of berries, herbs, tomatoes, squash, pumpkins, apples, corn, and more, all fresh and reasonably priced.

MEMORABILIA

✪ **Boston City Store.** Faneuil Hall, lower level. ☎ **617/635-2911**. T: Green or Blue Line to Government Center.

A great, wacky idea, the Boston City Store sells the equivalent of the contents of the municipal attic and basement, from old street signs (look for your name) to used office equipment and furniture. The selection changes regularly according to what has outlived its usefulness or been declared surplus, but you'll always find lucky horseshoes from the mounted police for $5 apiece. Closed Sunday.

✪ **Nostalgia Factory.** 51 N. Margin St. ☎ **800/479-8754** or 617/720-2211. www.nostalgia.com. T: Green or Orange Line to Haymarket.

The Nostalgia Factory has gained national attention for its million-piece collection of posters and advertising pieces. Long a Newbury Street fixture, the store moved to the North End in 1997 and gained more room for its enormous collections. They include original movie posters of all ages and in many languages, vintage war and travel posters, and political memorabilia.

MUSIC

Looney Tunes Records & Tapes. 1106 Boylston St. ☎ **617/247-2238.** T: Green Line B, C, or D to Hynes/ICA. 1001 Mass. Ave., Cambridge. ☎ **617/786-5624.** T: Red Line to Harvard.

Where there are college students, there are pizza places, copy shops, and used-record (and CD) stores. These two specialize in jazz and classical, and they have tons of other tunes at excellent prices.

Newbury Comics. 332 Newbury St. ☎ **617/236-4930.** www.newbury.com. T: Green Line B, C, or D to Hynes/ICA.

You'll find a wide selection of CDs, tapes, posters, and T-shirts—and, of course, comics—at the branches of this funky chain. The music is particularly cutting-edge, with lots of independent labels and imports. There are also stores at 1 Washington Mall, near City Hall (☎ **617/248-9992**), and in Harvard Square at 36 John F. Kennedy St., in the Garage mall (☎ **617/491-0337**).

Tower Records. 360 Newbury St. (at Mass. Ave.). ☎ **617/247-5900.** www.towerrecords.com. T: Green Line B, C, or D to Hynes/ICA.

One of the largest record stores in the country, Tower boasts three floors of records, tapes, CDs, videos, periodicals, and books. It's open until midnight every night. The Harvard Square branch, 95 Mount Auburn St. (☎ **617/876-3377**), is smaller but still quite impressive.

PERFUME & COSMETICS

✪ **Colonial Drug.** 49 Brattle St., Cambridge. ☎ **617/864-2222.** T: Red Line to Harvard.

The perfume counter at this family business puts the "special" in "specialize." You can choose from more than 1,000 fragrances—plus cosmetics, soap, and countless other body-care products—with the help of the gracious staff members. They remain unflappable even during Harvard Square's equivalent of rush hour, Saturday afternoon.

E6 Apothecary. 167 Newbury St. ☎ **800/664-6635** or 617/236-8138. www. e6apothecary.com. T: Green Line to Copley.

This place is the exact opposite of scary department store cosmetic counters. The friendly staffers can guide you toward the right formula for your face, and they're equally helpful if you're spending 5 bucks or 500. E6 is the exclusive Boston supplier of Shu Uemura and Lorac products, and it carries many other brands that are hard (or impossible) to find north of New York.

TOYS & GAMES

FAO Schwarz. 440 Boylston St. (at Berkeley St.). ☎ **617/262-5900.** T: Green Line to Copley.

The giant teddy bear out front is the first indication that you're in for a rollicking good time, and a teddy bear wouldn't steer you wrong. A branch of the famed New York emporium, FAO Schwarz stocks top-quality toys, dolls, stuffed animals, games, books, and vehicles (motorized and not).

The Games People Play. 1100 Mass. Ave., Cambridge. ☎ **800/696-0711** or 617/492-0711. T: Red Line to Harvard.

Just outside Harvard Square, this 25-year-old business carries enough board games to outfit every country, summer, and beach house in New England. There are puzzles, playing cards, and backgammon sets, too.

The Magic Hat. Marketplace Center, Faneuil Hall Marketplace. ☎ **617/ 439-8840.** T: Green or Blue Line to Government Center or Orange Line to Haymarket.

Bring your Houdini fantasies to this small shop with a big "wow" factor. At least one staff member practices sleight-of-hand at the counter, and the stock of props, tricks, gifts, and other fun merchandise is (literally) incredible.

7

Boston After Dark

*T*he nightlife scene in Boston and Cambridge is, to put it mildly, not exactly world-class—you can be back from a night of club-hopping when your friends in New York are still drying their hair. The spirited performing-arts community takes up some of the slack, but if your definition of vacation includes "party all night," you're in for a surprise (and not the good kind). Closing time for clubs is 2am, which means packing a lot into 4 hours or so.

For up-to-date entertainment listings, consult the "Calendar" section of the Thursday *Boston Globe* (www.boston.com/globe), the "Scene" section of the Friday *Boston Herald* (www.bostonherald.com), and the Sunday arts sections of both papers. The free weekly *Boston Phoenix* (www.bostonphoenix.com) has especially good club listings, and the free biweekly *Improper Bostonian* offers extensive live music listings. Before your visit, you can check with Boston's tourism offices (see "Visitor Information" in chapter 2), to see if big events are scheduled during your visit.

GETTING TICKETS   Some companies and venues sell tickets over the phone or the Internet; many will refer you to a ticket agency.

The major agencies that serve Boston are **Ticket Master** (☎ 617/931-2000; www.ticketmaster.com), **Next Ticketing** (☎ 617/423-NEXT; www.nextticketing.com), and **Tele-charge** (☎ 800/447-7400; www.telecharge.com, click on "across the USA"). They calculate service charges per ticket, not per order. To avoid the charge, visit the box office in person. If you wait until the day before or the day of a performance, you'll sometimes have access to tickets that were held back for one reason or another and have just gone on sale.

1 The Performing Arts

Year-round, you can find a performance that fits your taste and budget, be it a touring theater company or a children's chorus.

Yankee thrift gains artistic expression at the ✪ **BosTix** booths at Faneuil Hall Marketplace (on the south side of Faneuil Hall) and in Copley Square (at the corner of Boylston and Dartmouth streets). Same-day tickets to musical and theatrical performances are half price, subject to availability. A **coupon book** with discounted and two-for-one admission to many area museums is available, too. Credit cards are not accepted, and there are no refunds or exchanges. Check the board for the day's offerings.

BosTix (☎ **617/482-2849;** www.boston.com/artsboston) also offers full-price advance tickets; discounts on more than 100 theater, music, and dance events; and tickets to museums, historic sites, and attractions in and around town. The booths are Ticket Master outlets, too. They're open Tuesday through Saturday from 10am to 6pm (half-price tickets go on sale at 11am), and Sunday from 11am to 4pm. The Copley Square location is also open Monday from 10am to 6pm.

CONCERT HALLS & AUDITORIUMS

The ✪ **Hatch Shell** on the Esplanade (☎ **617/727-9547,** ext. 450) is an amphitheater best known as the home of the Boston Pops' Fourth of July concerts. Almost every night in the summer, free music and dance performances and films take over the stage to the delight of crowds on the lawn.

The **Emerson Majestic Theatre,** 219 Tremont St. (☎ **617/ 824-8000;** www.emerson.edu/majestic), may be under renovation as you read this. The popular dance and music performance space also handles Emerson College student productions.

Berklee Performance Center. 136 Mass. Ave. ☎ **617/266-1400,** ext. 8820. www.berklee.edu/calen/database.html. T: Green Line B, C, or D to Hynes/ICA.

The Berklee College of Music's theater features the work of faculty members, students, and professional recording artists (many of them former Berklee students). Offerings are heavy on jazz and folk, with plenty of other options.

Boston Center for the Arts. 539 Tremont St. ☎ **617/426-7700** (events line) or 617/426-2787 (box office). www.bcaonline.org. T: Orange Line to Back Bay.

Five performance spaces and an anything-goes booking policy make the BCA a leading venue for contemporary theater, music and dance performances, visual arts exhibitions, and poetry and prose readings.

Jordan Hall. 30 Gainsborough St. ☎ **617/536-2412,** or 617/262-1120, ext. 700 (concert line). www.newenglandconservatory.edu/jordanhall. T: Green Line E to Symphony.

The New England Conservatory of Music's auditorium features both students and professionals; it presents classical instrumental and vocal soloists, chamber music, and occasionally, contemporary artists.

Sanders Theatre. 45 Quincy St. (corner of Cambridge St.), Cambridge. ☎ **617/496-2222.** www.fas.harvard.edu/~memhall. T: Red Line to Harvard.

In Memorial Hall on the Harvard campus, Sanders Theatre was a multipurpose facility before there was such a thing. It's a lecture hall and a performance space that features big names in classical, folk, and world music, as well as student performances.

Symphony Hall. 301 Mass. Ave. (at Huntington Ave.). ☎ **617/266-1492** or 617/CONCERT (program information). SymphonyCharge ☎ **888/266-1200** (from outside the 617 area code) or 617/266-1200. www.bso.org. T: Green Line E to Symphony, or Orange Line to Mass. Ave.

Acoustically perfect Symphony Hall is home to the Boston Symphony Orchestra. When the orchestra is away, top-notch classical and chamber music artists from elsewhere take over.

Wang Theatre. 270 Tremont St. ☎ **617/482-9393** or 800/447-7400 (Tele-charge). www.boston.com/wangcenter. T: Green Line to Boylston or Orange Line to New England Medical Center.

Also known as the Wang Center, this art deco palace is home to Boston Ballet, and books numerous and varied national companies. On some Monday evenings in the winter, it reverts to its roots as a movie theater and shows classic films on its enormous screen.

CLASSICAL MUSIC

✪ **Boston Pops.** Performing at Symphony Hall, 301 Massachusetts Ave. (at Huntington Ave.). ☎ **617/266-1492** or 617/CONCERT (program information). SymphonyCharge ☎ 888/266-1200 (outside 617) or 617/266-1200. www.bso.org. Tickets $33–$45 for tables; $12.50–$28 for balcony seats. T: Green Line E to Symphony.

From early May to early July, members of the Boston Symphony Orchestra lighten up. Tables and chairs replace the floor seats at Symphony Hall, and drinks and light refreshments are served.

The Pops play a range of music from light classical to show tunes to popular music (hence the name), sometimes with celebrity guest stars. Conductor Keith Lockhart is so popular that he could almost give the orchestra its name all by himself. Performances are Tuesday through Sunday evenings. Special holiday performances in late December ($18 to $65) usually sell out well in advance, but it can't hurt to check.

The regular season ends with a week of free outdoor concerts at the Hatch Shell on the Charles River Esplanade, including the traditional Fourth of July concert, which features fireworks.

✪ **Boston Symphony Orchestra.** Symphony Hall, 301 Mass. Ave. (at Huntington Ave.). ☎ **617/266-1492** or 617/CONCERT (program information). SymphonyCharge ☎ 888/266-1200 (outside 617) or 617/266-1200. www.bso.org. Tickets $24–$79. Rush tickets $8 (on sale 9am Fri; 5pm Tues, Thurs). Rehearsal tickets $14.50. T: Green Line E to Symphony.

The Boston Symphony Orchestra, one of the world's greatest, was founded in 1881. The repertoire includes contemporary music, but classical is the BSO's calling card—you may even want to schedule your trip to coincide with a particular performance, or with a visit by a celebrated guest artist or conductor. Seiji Ozawa, the latest in a line of distinguished conductors, has announced that he'll end his tenure as music director in 2003— so you may unwittingly be watching an audition.

The season runs from October through April, with performances most Tuesday, Thursday, and Saturday evenings; Friday afternoons; and some Friday evenings. Half-hour talks (included in the ticket price) precede some performances; check ahead to see if yours is one. If you couldn't get tickets in advance, check at the box office 2 hours before show time, when returns from subscribers go on sale. A limited number of rush tickets (one per person) are available on the day of the performance for Tuesday and Thursday evening and Friday afternoon programs. Wednesday evening and Thursday morning rehearsals are sometimes open to the public.

✪ **Handel & Haydn Society.** 300 Mass. Ave. ☎ **617/266-3605.** www.handelandhaydn.org. Tickets $25–$65. T: Green Line E to Symphony.

The Handel & Haydn Society uses period instruments and techniques in its orchestral and choral performances, yet is as cutting-edge as any other ensemble in town. Established in 1815, it's the oldest continuously performing arts organization in the country.

Under the direction of Christopher Hogwood, the society prides itself on its creative programming of "historically informed" concerts. The season runs year-round, with most performances at Symphony Hall and Jordan Hall.

The society was the first American group to perform Handel's *Messiah,* in 1818, and made it an annual holiday tradition in 1854. If you'll be in town in December, check for ticket availability as soon as you start planning your trip.

CONCERT SERIES

The biggest names in classical music, dance, theater, jazz, and world music appear as part of the **FleetBoston Celebrity Series,** 20 Park Plaza, Boston, MA 02116 (☎ **617/482-2595,** or 617/ 482-6661 for Celebrity Charge; www.celebrityseries.org). It's a subscription series that also offers tickets to individual events, which take place at Symphony Hall, Jordan Hall, the Wang Theatre, and other venues.

Free (or Almost Free) Concerts

Radio station–sponsored outdoor music is a summer staple. Specifics change from year to year, but you can count on hearing jazz, classical, oldies, and sometimes pop at various convenient venues, including City Hall Plaza, Copley Square, and the Hatch Shell, at lunch, after work, and in the evening. Check the papers when you arrive, or just follow the crowds and the music.

Federal Reserve Bank of Boston. 600 Atlantic Ave. ☎ **617/973-3453.** www.bos.frb.org. T: Red Line to South Station.

Local groups and artists perform jazz, classical, and contemporary music in the bank's ground-floor auditorium on Thursdays and some Fridays at 12:30pm.

Fridays at Trinity. Trinity Church, Copley Sq. ☎ **617/536-0944.** Donations accepted. T: Green Line to Copley or Orange Line to Back Bay.

This landmark church features organ recitals by local and visiting artists on Fridays at 12:15pm. Take advantage of the chance to look around this architectural showpiece.

King's Chapel Noon Hour Recitals. 58 Tremont St. ☎ **617/227-2155.** $2 donation requested. T: Red or Green Line to Park St.

Organ, instrumental, and vocal solos fill this historic building with music and make for a pleasant break along the Freedom Trail. Concerts are at 12:15pm on Tuesdays.

MUSIC IN THE MUSEUMS

A treat for the eyes and the ears, live music could be the offering that helps you schedule your visit to a museum.

✪ **Isabella Stewart Gardner Museum.** 280 The Fenway. ☎ **617/734-1359.** www.boston.com/gardner. Tickets (including museum admission) $16 adults, $11 seniors, $9 students with ID, $7 youths 12–17, $5 children 5–11. T: Green Line E to Museum.

This gorgeous museum, originally a home modeled after a 15th-century Venetian palace, features soloists, local students, chamber music, and sometimes jazz in the Tapestry Room. Performances are Saturday and Sunday at 1:30pm, from late September to early May.

Museum of Fine Arts. 465 Huntington Ave. ☎ **617/267-9300** or 617/369-3300. Tickets $14, $12 seniors and students, $5 children under 12. T: Green Line E to Museum.

The "Concerts in the Courtyard" series brings folk and jazz artists to the MFA on Wednesday evenings from June through September at 7:30pm. The courtyard opens to picnickers at 6pm; bring dinner, or buy it there. Chair seating is limited, and you're encouraged to bring a blanket or lawn chair.

ROCK & POP CONCERTS

✪ **FleetBoston Pavilion.** 290 Northern Ave., Wharf 8, South Boston. ☎ **617/374-9000,** or 617/931-2000 (Ticket Master). www.bankbostonpavilion.com.

One of the most congenial venues in the area is this giant white tent. The 5,000-seat pavilion schedules pop, rock, country, rap, folk, and jazz performers on evenings from May through September. Call ahead for information about water transportation and shuttle buses from South Station.

FleetCenter. 1 FleetCenter (Causeway St.). ☎ **617/624-1000** (events line), or 617/931-2000 (Ticket Master). www.fleetcenter.com. T: Orange or Green Line to North Station.

The state-of-the-art FleetCenter opened in 1995, replacing legendary Boston Garden. It's the home of the Bruins (hockey), the Celtics (basketball), the circus (in October), ice shows (at least once a year), and touring rock and pop artists of all stripes. Concerts are in the round or in the arena stage format.

Orpheum Theater. 1 Hamilton Place. ☎ **617/679-0810,** or 617/423-NEXT for tickets. www.dlclive.com/orpheum.html. T: Red or Green Line to Park St.

Although it's old (the building went up in 1852) and cramped, the Orpheum offers an intimate setting for big-name performers.

Most of the time, it books top local acts and national artists such as Sheryl Crow, Elvis Costello, Sting, and Smash Mouth. Each fall, the "Comics Come Home" charity event attracts top talent (the live show is taped for Comedy Central). Hamilton Place is off Tremont Street, across from the Park Street Church.

DANCE

✪ **Boston Ballet.** 19 Clarendon St. ☎ **617/695-6955** or 800/447-7400 (Tele-charge). www.bostonballet.org. Performing at the Wang Theatre, 270 Tremont St., and Shubert Theatre, 265 Tremont St. (both box offices, Mon–Sat 10am–6pm). Tickets $23–$73. Student rush tickets (1 hr. before curtain) $12.50, except for *The Nutcracker.* T: Green Line to Boylston.

Boston Ballet's reputation seems to jump a notch every time someone says, "So it's not just *The Nutcracker.*" The country's fourth-largest dance company is a holiday staple, and during the rest of the season (October through May), it presents an eclectic mix of classic story ballets and contemporary works. Because the Wang was built as a movie theater, the pitch of the seats makes the top two balconies less-than-ideal locations—paying more for a better seat is a good investment.

Dance Umbrella. 515 Washington St., 5th floor. ☎ **617/482-7570** or 617/824-8000 (MajesTix). www.danceumbrella.org. Tickets $17–$50; students and children $15.

Contemporary dance aficionados will want to check out the latest offerings sponsored by Dance Umbrella. It commissions and presents international, culturally diverse works—a broad definition that covers everything from acrobats and jazz tap dancers to well-known groups such as the Mark Morris and Bill T. Jones/Arnie Zane companies. Performances take place at venues in Boston, most often at the **Emerson Majestic Theatre,** 219 Tremont St.

THEATER

Local and national companies, professional and amateur actors, classic and experimental drama combine to make the theater scene in Boston and Cambridge a lively one, and in the past few years it has positively exploded. Listed here are the big names, but smaller names and venues abound. Call ahead or check the papers or BosTix (see "Let's Make a Deal," above) after you arrive—you're sure to find something of interest.

Boston is one of the last cities for pre-Broadway tryouts, allowing an early look at a classic (or classic flop) in the making. It's also a popular destination for touring companies of established Broadway hits. You'll find most of the shows headed to or coming from Broadway in the Theater District, at the **Colonial Theatre,** 106 Boylston St. (☎ 617/426-9366); the **Shubert Theatre,** 265 Tremont St. (☎ 617/482-9393); the **Wang Theatre,** 270 Tremont St. (☎ 617/482-9393); and the **Wilbur Theater,** 246 Tremont St. (☎ 617/423-4008).

The excellent local theater scene boasts the **Huntington Theatre Company,** which performs at the Boston University Theatre, 264 Huntington Ave. (☎ 617/266-0800; www.bu.edu/huntington), and the **American Repertory Theatre** (**ART**), which makes its home at Harvard University's Loeb Drama Center, 64 Brattle St., Cambridge (☎ 617/547-8300; www.amrep.org). Both stage classic and contemporary productions; the ART is more likely to put on the work of a living playwright.

FAMILY THEATER/AUDIENCE PARTICIPATION

The Charles Playhouse, 74 Warrenton St. (☎ 617/426-5225) is home to the off-Broadway sensation **Blue Man Group** (www. blueman.com) and *Shear Madness* www.shearmadness.com), the longest-running nonmusical play in theater history.

Blue Man Group began selling out as soon as it arrived on the Charles Playhouse's Stage I in 1995. Famous for reducing even the most eloquent theatergoer to one-syllable sputtering, the troupe of three cobalt-colored entertainers backed by a rock band uses music, percussion, food, and audience members in its overwhelming performance art. Shows are at 8pm Wednesday and Thursday, 7 and 10pm Friday and Saturday, and 3 and 6pm Sunday. Tickets, available at the box office and through Ticket Master, are $49 and $39.

Shear Madness, on Stage II (downstairs), is a zany "comic murder mystery" that has turned the stage into a unisex hairdressing salon for over 20 years (it opened in January 1980), and the show's never the same twice. One of the original audience-participation productions, the play changes at each performance as spectator-investigators question suspects, reconstruct events, and then name the murderer. Performances are Tuesday through Friday at 8pm, Saturday at 6:30 and 9:30pm, and Sunday at 3 and 7:30pm.

2 The Club & Music Scene

The Boston-area club scene is multifaceted and constantly changing, and somewhere out there is a good time for everyone, regardless of age, musical taste, or budget. Check the "Calendar" section of the Thursday *Globe,* the "Scene" section of the Friday *Herald,* the *Phoenix,* or the *Improper Bostonian* while you're making plans.

A night on the town in Boston is relatively brief: Most bars close by 1am, clubs close at 2am, and the T shuts down around 12:30am. The drinking age is 21; a valid driver's license or passport is required as proof of age, and the law is strictly enforced, especially near college campuses.

COMEDY CLUBS

✪ **Comedy Connection at Faneuil Hall.** Quincy Market, Upper Rotunda. ☎ **617/248-9700.** go.boston.com/comedyconnection. Cover $8–$30. T: Green or Blue Line to Government Center or Orange Line to Haymarket.

A large room with a clear view from every seat, the oldest original comedy club in town (established in 1978) draws top-notch talent from near and far. Big-name national acts lure enthusiastic crowds, and the openers are often just as funny but not as famous—yet. Shows are nightly at 8pm, plus Friday and Saturday at 10:15pm. The cover charge seldom tops $12 during the week but jumps for a big name appearing on a weekend. The Backstage restaurant-club next door, under the same ownership, offers dinner-show packages that include preferred seating.

Comedy Studio. At the Hong Kong restaurant, 1236 Mass. Ave., Cambridge. ☎ **617/661-6507.** Cover $5–$7. T: Red Line to Harvard.

Nobody here is a sitcom star—yet. With a growing reputation for ferreting out undiscovered talent, the no-frills Comedy Studio draws connoisseurs, college students, and network scouts. It's not just setup-punchline-laugh, either; sketches and improv spice up the standup.

DANCE CLUBS

Many clubs are in the areas surrounding Boston's **Kenmore Square** (especially along Lansdowne Street) and the **Alley,** off Boylston Street near Tremont Street. That makes club-hopping easy, but it also means students overrun the neighborhoods on Friday and Saturday. If you don't feel like dealing with huge crowds of loud teenagers and recent college grads, stick to slightly more upscale and isolated nightspots. If you do like loud teenagers, seek out a place where admission is 18- or 19-plus (policies change regularly, sometimes from night to night, so call ahead).

✪ **Avalon.** 15 Lansdowne St. ☎ **617/262-2424.** Cover $5–$15. T: Green Line B, C, or D to Kenmore.

A cavernous space divided into several levels, with a full concert stage, private booths and lounges, large dance floors, and a spectacular light show, Avalon is either great fun or sensory overload. It recently expanded, allowing more concert bookings (the Chemical Brothers, Semisonic, and Fiona Apple have played recently); when the stage is not in use, DJs take over.

Friday is **"Avaland,"** with national names in the booth and costumed house dancers on the floor. On Saturday (suburbanites' night out), expect more mainstream dance hits. The dress code calls for jackets, shirts with collars, and no jeans or athletic wear. The crowd is slightly older than at Axis. Open Thursday (international night) to Sunday (gay night) 10pm to 2am.

Axis. 13 Lansdowne St. ☎ **617/262-2437.** Cover $7–$10. T: Green Line B, C, or D to Kenmore.

Progressive rock at bone-rattling volume and "creative dress"—break out the leather—attract a young crowd. There are special nights for alternative rock, house, techno, soul, and funk music, and for international DJs. Open Tuesday through Sunday (gay night with adjoining Avalon) 10pm to 2am.

The Big Easy Bar. 1 Boylston Place. ☎ **617/351-7000.** Cover $7–$10. T: Green Line to Boylston.

Buttoned-up Boston meets let-it-all-hang-out New Orleans—it could get ugly. Not here, however, in a large, inviting space with a balcony (great for people watching), a billiard room, a dance floor, and music by top local DJs that runs from soul to alternative rock. Tuesday is international night. The lower level is the **Sugar Shack;** at both, the crowd tends to be on the young (collegiate and post-) side. No ripped jeans or athletic shoes.

Karma/Mambo Lounge. 5 Lansdowne St. ☎ **617/421-9595.** Cover $5–$15. T: Green Line B, C, or D to Kenmore.

Dancing machines, this one's for you. Pack something eye-catching, but not too fancy, and your dancing shoes. Thursday is Top 40 hip-hop night; big-name DJs take over on Friday (American) and Saturday (international) night.

✪ **The Roxy.** In the Tremont Boston hotel, 279 Tremont St. ☎ **617/338-7699.** www.gbcx.com/roxy. Cover $10–$15. T: Green Line to Boylston.

This former hotel ballroom boasts excellent DJs and live music, a huge dance floor, a concert stage, and a balcony (perfect for checking out the action below). Occasional concerts take good advantage of the acoustics and sight lines. Call for the latest schedule—swing recently yielded to disco on Fridays, and specific offerings change regularly. Open 8pm (entertainment starts at 10) to 2am Thursday to Saturday, and some Wednesdays and Sundays for special events. No jeans or athletic shoes.

ECLECTIC

✪ **Johnny D's Uptown Restaurant & Music Club.** 17 Holland St., Davis Sq., Somerville. ☎ **617/776-2004** or 617/776-9667 (concert line). www. johnnyds.com. Cover $2–$16, usually $5–$10. T: Red Line to Davis.

This family-owned and -operated establishment is one of the best in the area. Live-music aficionados, you'll kick yourself if you don't at least check out who's performing while you're in town. Johnny D's draws a congenial crowd for acts on international tours and acts that haven't been out of eastern Massachusetts. The music ranges from zydeco to rock, rockabilly to jazz, blues to ska. The food's even good (try the weekend brunch). This place is worth a long trip, but it's only two stops past Harvard Square on the Red Line, about a 15-minute ride at night. Open daily from 11:30am to 1am. Brunch starts at 9am on weekends; dinner runs from 4:30 to 9:30pm Tuesday through Saturday, with lighter fare until 11pm.

Kendall Café. 233 Cardinal Medeiros Way, Cambridge. ☎ **617/661-0993.** Cover $5–$10. T: Red Line to Kendall/MIT.

This friendly neighborhood bar near the 1 Kendall Square office-retail complex showcases three up-and-coming artists each night. Folk predominates, and you might also hear rock, country, or blues in the tiny back room. Or just stay at the bar—you won't be able to see, but it's such a small place that you'll have no trouble hearing. Shows are Monday through Saturday at 8pm, Sunday at 4pm.

The Western Front. 343 Western Ave., Cambridge. ☎ **617/492-7772.** Cover $5–$10. T: Red Line to Central.

A 30-ish friend swears by this legendary reggae club for one reason: "You're never the oldest one there." A casual spot on a nondescript street south of Central Square, it attracts an integrated crowd for world-beat music, blues, and especially reggae. Sunday is dance-hall reggae night, and the infectious music makes every night dancing night. Open Tuesday through Sunday from 5pm to 2am; live entertainment begins at 9pm.

FOLK

Boston is one of the only cities where folk musicians consistently sell out larger venues that usually book rock and pop performers. If an artist you want to see is out touring, check ahead for Boston-area dates. The music listings in the "Calendar" section of the Thursday *Globe* include information about **coffeehouses,** which are the main area outlets for folk. Curiously, the streets around Harvard Square are another promising venue—Tracy Chapman is just one famous "graduate" of the scene. Also check the papers to see whether the **Nameless Coffee House** is open during your visit. A local legend for 30 years, the Nameless pops up periodically from September to June at the First Parish in Cambridge, 3 Church St. (☎ **617/864-1630**).

✪ **Club Passim.** 47 Palmer St., Cambridge. ☎ **617/492-7679.** Cover $5–$22; most shows $12 or less. T: Red Line to Harvard.

Passim has launched more careers than the mass production of acoustic guitars—Joan Baez, Suzanne Vega, and Tom Rush started out here. In a basement on the street between buildings of the Harvard Coop, this coffeehouse (which doesn't serve alcohol) enjoys an international reputation built on more than 30 years of nurturing new talent and showcasing established musicians. Patrons who have been regulars since day one mix with college students. There's live music 4 to 6 nights a week and Sunday afternoons, and coffee and light meals are available all the time. Tuesday is open-mike poetry night. Open Sunday through Thursday from 11am to 11pm, Friday and Saturday from 11am to 4am.

JAZZ & BLUES

If you're partial to these genres, consider timing your visit to coincide with the **Boston Globe Jazz & Blues Festival** (☎ **617/267-4301;** www.boston.com/jazzfest), usually scheduled for the third week of June. Constellations of jazz and blues stars (large and small) appear at events, some of them free, many of them outdoors. The festival wraps up with a free Sunday-afternoon program at the Hatch Shell.

On summer Fridays at 6:30pm, the ✪ **Waterfront Jazz Series** (☎ **617/635-3911**) brings amateurs and professionals to Christopher Columbus Park on the waterfront for a refreshing interlude of music and cool breezes.

Cantab Lounge. 738 Mass. Ave., Cambridge. ☎ **617/354-2685.** Cover $3–$6. T: Red Line to Central.

Follow your ears to this friendly neighborhood bar, which attracts a three-generation crowd. When the door swings open at night, deafening music (usually R&B or rock, sometimes jazz) spills out. The source on weekends often is Little Joe Cook and the Thrillers, headliners since the early '80s whose catchy tunes you'll dance to all night and hum all the next day—because your ears will still be ringing. Downstairs is the Third Rail, where you can hear blues and, on Wednesday, poetry.

✪ **House of Blues.** 96 Winthrop St., Cambridge. ☎ **617/491-2583**, or 617/497-2229 for tickets. Dining reservations (☎ 617/491-2100) accepted only for parties of 25 or more. www.hob.com. Cover $7–$30; Sat matinee $5. T: Red Line to Harvard.

The original House of Blues, a blue clapboard house near Harvard Square, packs them in every evening and on weekend afternoons. It attracts tourists, music buffs, and big names—Mighty Sam McClain, Junior Brown, NRBQ, and the Fabulous Thunderbirds have played recently. And there's no telling when an audience member will turn out to be someone famous who winds up onstage jamming. The restaurant is open 11:30am to 11pm Monday to Saturday, 4:30 to 11pm on Sunday; the music hall until 1am Sunday to Wednesday, 2am Thursday to Saturday. ✪ **Sunday gospel buffet brunch** seatings are at 10am, noon, and 2pm; advance tickets ($26 adults, $13 children) are highly recommended.

✪ **Regattabar.** In the Charles Hotel, 1 Bennett St., Cambridge. ☎ **617/661-5000** or 617/876-7777 (Concertix). Tickets $6–$25. T: Red Line to Harvard.

The Regattabar's selection of local and international artists is considered the best in the area—a title that Scullers (see below) is happy to dispute. Tito Puente, the Count Basie Orchestra, McCoy Tyner, Rebecca Parris, and Karen Akers have appeared recently. The large third-floor room holds about 200 and, unfortunately, sometimes gets a little noisy. Buy tickets in advance from Concertix (there's a $2 per ticket service charge), or try your luck at the door an hour before performance time. Open Tuesday through Saturday and some Sundays, with one or two performances per night.

Ryles Jazz Club. 212 Hampshire St., Inman Sq., Cambridge. ☎ **617/876-9330.** www.rylesjazz.com. Cover $5 weeknights; $7–$15 weekends.

This popular spot books local, regional, and national acts—Maynard Ferguson played recently. Hard-core music buffs of every stripe turn out for a wide variety of first-rate jazz, R&B, world beat, and Latin in two rooms. Both levels offer top-notch music and a friendly atmosphere. The Sunday jazz brunch runs from 10am to 3pm. Open Tuesday through Sunday; shows start at 9pm.

✪ **Scullers Jazz Club.** In the Doubletree Guest Suites hotel, 400 Soldiers Field Rd. ☎ **617/562-4111** or 617/931-2000 (Ticket Master). www.scullersjazz.com. Tickets $10–$35.

Overlooking the Charles River, Scullers is a lovely, comfortable room that books top singers and instrumentalists—recent notables include Branford Marsalis, Abbey Lincoln, Livingston Taylor, and (quite a coup) Bobby Short. Patrons tend to be more hard-core and quieter than the crowds at the Regattabar, but it really depends on who's performing. There are usually two shows a night from Tuesday through Saturday; the box office is open those days from 11am to 6:30pm. Ask about dinner packages, which include preferred seating.

ROCK

Bill's Bar. 5½ Lansdowne St. ☎ **617/421-9678.** Cover $5–$10. T: Green Line B, C, or D to Kenmore.

Long known as the only real hangout on Lansdowne Street, Bill's has transformed itself into a live-music destination and kept its friendly atmosphere and great beer menu. It books locals and touring up-and-comers or DJs most nights at 9:30 or 10pm. Monday is hard-rock night; Tuesday is hip-hop, funk, and soul. Open nightly 8pm to 2am.

Lizard Lounge. 1667 Mass. Ave., Cambridge. ☎ **617/547-0759.** Cover $2–$7. T: Red Line to Harvard.

In the basement of the Cambridge Common restaurant, the Lizard Lounge features well-known local rock and folk musicians who draw a postcollegiate-and-up crowd (Harvard Law School is next door). Shows Wednesday through Saturday at 10pm; Sunday is open-mike poetry jam night.

Rock of Ages

Bring an ID, bring an ID, bring an ID—you must be 21 to drink alcohol, and the law is strictly enforced. Even if you look older, bouncers won't risk a fine or license suspension, especially at 18-plus shows.

✪ The Middle East. 472–480 Mass. Ave., Central Sq., Cambridge. ☎ **617/ 864-EAST** or 617/931-2000 (Ticket Master). www.mideastclub.com. Cover $7–$15. T: Red Line to Central.

The Middle East books an impressive variety of progressive and alternative rock in two rooms (upstairs and downstairs) every night. Showcasing top local talent as well as bands with international reputations—keep an eye out for the Mighty Mighty Bosstones, who usually pass through in December—it's a popular hangout that gets crowded, hot, and *loud*. There's also Middle Eastern food and gallery space with rotating art exhibits. The bakery next door, under the same management, features acoustic artists most of the time and belly dancers on Wednesdays. Some music shows are all ages (most are 18-plus); the age of the crowd varies with the performer.

T.T. the Bear's Place. 10 Brookline St., Cambridge. ☎ **617/492-0082** or 617/492-BEAR (concert line). www.mindspring.com/~ttthebears. Cover $3–$15, usually less than $10. T: Red Line to Central.

This no-frills spot generally attracts a young crowd, but 30-somethings will feel comfortable, too. Bookings range from cutting-edge alternative rock and roots music to ska and funk shows to up-and-coming pop acts. New bands predominate early in the week, with more established artists on weekends. Open Monday 7pm to midnight, Tuesday through Sunday 6pm to 1am.

3 The Bar Scene

Bostonians had some quibbles with the TV show "Cheers," but no one ever complained that the concept of a neighborhood bar where the regulars practically lived was implausible. This tends to be a fairly insular scene—as a stranger, don't expect to be welcomed with open arms. This is one area where you can and probably should judge a book by its cover. If you poke your head in the door and see people who look like you and your friends, give it a whirl.

BARS & LOUNGES

The Bay Tower. 60 State St. ☎ **617/723-1666.** www.baytower.com. No cover. T: Green or Orange Line to State.

The view from the 33rd floor of any building is bound to be amazing; sitting atop 60 State St., you'll be mesmerized by the harbor, the airport, and Faneuil Hall Marketplace directly below.

There's dancing to live music Monday through Saturday (piano on weeknights, jazz quartet Friday and Saturday). No denim or athletic shoes.

The Black Rose. 160 State St. ☎ **617/742-2286.** www.irishconnection.com. Cover $3–$5. T: Orange or Blue Line to State.

Purists might sneer at the Black Rose's touristy location, but performers don't. Sing along with the authentic Irish entertainment—you might be able to make out the tune on a fiddle over the din—at this jam-packed pub and restaurant at the edge of Faneuil Hall Marketplace.

Bull & Finch Pub. 84 Beacon St. ☎ **617/227-9605.** www.cheersboston.com. T: Green Line to Arlington.

If you're out to impersonate a native, try not to be shocked when you walk into "the 'Cheers' bar" and realize that inside it looks nothing like the bar on the TV show. (The outside does, though—bring a camera.) The Bull & Finch really is a neighborhood bar, but today it's far better known for attracting legions of out-of-towners, who find good pub grub, drinks, and plenty of souvenirs. Food is served from 11am to 1:15am, and there's a kids' menu ($3.50 to $4.50).

✪ **Casablanca.** 40 Brattle St., Cambridge. ☎ **617/876-0999.** T: Red Line to Harvard.

Students and professors jam this legendary Harvard Square watering hole, especially on weekends. You'll find excellent food (see chapter 4), an excellent jukebox, and excellent eavesdropping.

Green Street Grill/Charlie's Tap. 280 Green St., Cambridge. ☎ **617/876-1655.** No cover for music. T: Red Line to Central.

This atmospheric Central Square hangout draws a congenial crowd for live blues, rock, and jazz on weekends and, on Tuesdays (we kid you not), magicians. Blues and jazz aficionados will find perhaps the best jukebox on the planet, and there's also excellent food. Open nightly until 1am.

Harvard Gardens. 320 Cambridge St. ☎ **617/523-2727.** T: Red Line to Charles/MGH.

A new incarnation of a run-down Beacon Hill standby, Harvard Gardens remains a neighborhood favorite. In this neighborhood, that means students, yuppies, and medical professionals of every stripe (Mass. General Hospital is across the street). It's more lounge than tavern, with plenty of beers on tap, great margaritas, and food until 11pm (midnight on weekends).

✪ **Mr. Dooley's Boston Tavern.** 77 Broad St. ☎ **617/338-5656.** Cover $3 Fri–Sat. T: Blue or Orange Line to State.

Sometimes an expertly poured Guinness is all you need. If one of the nicest bartenders in the city pours it, so much the better. This Financial District spot also offers a wide selection of imported beers on tap, live music, and a menu of "pub favourites."

Purple Shamrock. 1 Union St. ☎ **617/227-2060.** Cover $3–$6 Thurs–Sat. T: Green or Blue Line to Government Center, or Orange Line to Haymarket.

Across the street from Faneuil Hall Marketplace, the Purple Shamrock packs in wall-to-wall 20-somethings. This is a rowdy, fun place that schedules DJs, cover bands, and, I'm obliged to report, karaoke (on Tuesday).

Radius. 8 High St. ☎ **617/426-1234.** No cover. T: Red Line to South Station.

The high-tech bar at this hot, *haute* restaurant offers almost everything the dining room does—the chic crowd, the noise, the perfect martinis—without the sky-high food bill.

Top of the Hub. Prudential Center. ☎ **617/536-1775.** No cover. T: Green Line E to Prudential.

Boasting a panoramic view of greater Boston, Top of the Hub is 52 stories above the city; the view is especially beautiful at sunset. There is music and dancing nightly. Dress is casual but neat. Open until 1am Sunday through Wednesday, 2am Thursday to Saturday. (See chapter 6 for restaurant listing.)

BREW PUBS

Boston Beer Works. 61 Brookline Ave. ☎ **617/536-2337.** T: Green Line B, C, or D to Kenmore.

Across the street from Fenway Park, this cavernous, cacophonous space is even more frantic before and after Red Sox games. Don't plan to be able to hear anything your friends are saying. It has a full food menu and 14 brews on tap, including excellent bitters and ales, and seasonal concoctions such as Red Oktoberfest: lager with blueberries floating in it (not as dreadful as it sounds). Especially good are the cask-conditioned offerings, seasoned in wood till they're as smooth as fine wine. Sweet-potato fries make a terrific snack. Open daily from 11:30am to 1am.

✪ **Brew Moon Restaurant & Microbrewery.** 115 Stuart St. ☎ **617/ 742-BREW.** T: Green Line to Boylston.

Handcrafted beer meets tasty edibles at this popular Theater District spot, where bar food, sandwiches, and salads accompany freshly made brews. The Munich Gold won a gold medal at the 1996 Great American Beer Festival; if you're looking for something lighter, try the Grasshopper IPA or the out-of-this-world house-brewed root beer. Open daily from 11:30am to 2am. The equally busy Harvard Square branch, at 50 Church St. (☎ **617/ 499-BREW**), stays open till 1am (midnight on Sunday). Both have live music at the ✪ **Sunday jazz brunch,** 11am to 3pm.

John Harvard's Brew House. 33 Dunster St., Cambridge. ☎ **617/868-3585.** www.johnharvards.com. No cover. T: Red Line to Harvard.

This subterranean Harvard Square hangout pumps out terrific English-style brews in a clublike setting (try to find the sports figures in the stained-glass windows) and prides itself on its food. The beer selection changes regularly; it includes at least one selection from each "family" (ambers, porters, seasonals, and more), all brewed on the premises. Order a sampler if you can't decide. Open daily from 11:30am to 1:30am; food is served until 11:30pm.

Samuel Adams Brew House. In the Lenox Hotel, 710 Boylston St. ☎ **617/ 536-2739.** T: Green Line to Copley.

This dark, sometimes noisy spot boasts excellent pretzels, friendly service, and the signature local brew, guaranteed to be served fresh. Choose from the dozen beers on tap or order a sampler of four. Open daily from 11:30am to 1:30am.

HOTEL BARS

The Atrium. Bostonian Hotel, at Faneuil Hall Marketplace, 40 North St. ☎ **617/523-3600.** T: Green or Blue Line to Government Center or Orange Line to State.

The floor-to-ceiling windows of this ground-floor room across the street from Faneuil Hall Marketplace allow for great people watching. There is champagne by the glass, live piano music on weeknights, and cushy furnishings that encourage lingering. This is one of the only places in Boston that allows cigar-smoking, so it can be smoky. Open daily until midnight.

Boston Harbor Hotel. 70 Rowes Wharf (entrance on Atlantic Ave.). ☎ **617/439-7000.** T: Red Line to South Station (or Blue Line to Aquarium if it's open).

You have two appealing options on the ground floor: **Intrigue,** which looks like a comfortable living room and boasts a harbor view, and the **Rowes Wharf Bar,** with a serious businesslike atmosphere and serious martinis.

A Multimedia Experience

The owners of ✪ **Jillian's Boston,** 145 Ipswich St. (☎ **617/437-0300;** www.jilliansboston.com), revived an interest in pool in Boston and continue expanding their horizons as entertainment technology becomes more sophisticated. The 70,000-square-foot complex, which anchors the Lansdowne Street strip, contains a 52-table pool parlor, a virtual-reality movie "ride," slot machines (for fun, not profit), and an interactive aviation game. The 250-game video midway includes classic arcade games. There are dartboards, a table tennis area, a dance club, five full bars, and a restaurant. If you can't scare up some fun here, check your pulse.

Jillian's is open Monday through Saturday 11am to 2am, Sunday noon to 2am. Children under 18 accompanied by an adult are admitted before 7pm. Pool costs $12 an hour for 1 or 2 people, $14 for 3 or more. Valet parking is available Wednesday to Sunday after 6pm except during Red Sox games. T: Green Line B, C, or D to Kenmore.

✪ **Bristol Lounge.** 200 Boylston St. (in the Four Seasons Hotel). ☎ **617/351-2053.** T: Green Line to Arlington.

This is a perfect choice after the theater, after work, or after anything else. An elegant room with soft lounge chairs, a fireplace, and fresh flowers, it features a fabulous Viennese Dessert Buffet on weekend nights. There's live jazz every evening. An eclectic menu is available until 11:30pm (12:30am on Friday and Saturday).

Oak Bar. In the Fairmont Copley Plaza Hotel, Copley Sq. ☎ **617/267-5300.** T: Green Line to Copley or Orange Line to Back Bay.

This paneled, high-ceilinged room is a haven for cigar smokers. The lighting is muted, the leather seating soft and welcoming, the oyster bar picture-perfect. There's live entertainment nightly. Proper dress is required. Open Sunday through Thursday 4:30pm to 12:30am, Friday and Saturday until 1am.

GAY & LESBIAN CLUBS & BARS

In addition to the clubs listed below, there's a weekly gay night at some mainstream clubs. On Sunday, **Avalon** and **Axis** play host to the largest gathering of gay men in town. On Thursday and Sunday nights, women congregate and play pool upstairs at the

Hideaway Pub, 20 Concord Lane, off Fresh Pond Parkway, Cambridge (☎ **617/661-8828**). For up-to-date listings, check *Bay Windows* (www.baywindows.com) and the monthly *Phoenix* supplement "One in 10."

Club Café. 209 Columbus Ave. ☎ **617/536-0966.** T: Green Line to Arlington or Orange Line to Back Bay.

This trendy South End spot draws a chic crowd of men and women for conversation (the noise level is reasonable), dining, live music in the front room, and video entertainment in the back room. Open daily from 2pm to 1am; lunch is served weekdays from 11:30am to 2:30pm, and dinner from 5:30 to 10pm Sunday through Wednesday, and until 11pm Thursday through Saturday. Sunday brunch starts at 11:30am.

Fritz. In the Chandler Inn Hotel, 26 Chandler St. ☎ **617/482-4428.** T: Orange Line to Back Bay.

This popular South End hangout is a neighborhood favorite. The friendly crowd bonds over sports—there's even a satellite dish.

Jacques. 79 Broadway, Bay Village. ☎ **617/426-8902.** T: Green Line to Arlington.

The only drag venue in town, Jacques draws a friendly crowd of gay and straight patrons who mix with the "girls" and sometimes engage in a shocking activity—that's right, disco dancing. The eclectic entertainment includes live bands, performance artists, and, of course, drag shows. Open daily from noon to midnight.

Man-Ray. 21 Brookline St., Cambridge. ☎ **617/864-0400.** Cover $3–$10. T: Red Line to Central.

The area's best goth scene is at Man-Ray, which has regular fetish nights and an appropriately gloomy atmosphere. Thursday is "Campus" night, when the crowd is 21-plus and mostly men. Open Wednesday until 1am, Thursday through Saturday until 2am.

Paradise. 180 Mass. Ave., Cambridge. ☎ **617/494-0700.** No cover. T: Red Line to Central, 10-min. walk.

Not to be confused with the Boston rock club (well, you can, but it won't be quite the same experience), the Paradise attracts an all-ages male crowd. It's also a good place to see strippers. Thursday is college night. Open daily 5pm to 1am.

See also Accommodations and Restaurant indexes below.

ACCOMMODATIONS INDEX

RESTAURANT INDEX

NOTES

NOTES

FROMMER'S® COMPLETE TRAVEL GUIDES

Alaska
Amsterdam
Arizona
Atlanta
Australia
Austria
Bahamas
Barcelona, Madrid &
  Seville
Beijing
Belgium, Holland &
  Luxembourg
Bermuda
Boston
British Columbia & the
  Canadian Rockies
Budapest & the Best of
  Hungary
California
Canada
Cancún, Cozumel &
  the Yucatán
Cape Cod, Nantucket &
  Martha's Vineyard
Caribbean
Caribbean Cruises & Ports
  of Call
Caribbean Ports of Call
Carolinas & Georgia
Chicago
China
Colorado
Costa Rica
Denmark
Denver, Boulder & Colorado
  Springs
England
Europe

European Cruises & Ports
  of Call
Florida
France
Germany
Greece
Greek Islands
Hawaii
Hong Kong
Honolulu, Waikiki & Oahu
Ireland
Israel
Italy
Jamaica
Japan
Las Vegas
London
Los Angeles
Maryland & Delaware
Maui
Mexico
Montana & Wyoming
Montréal & Québec City
Munich & the Bavarian
  Alps
Nashville & Memphis
Nepal
New England
New Mexico
New Orleans
New York City
New Zealand
Nova Scotia, New Brunswick
  & Prince Edward Island
Oregon
Paris
Philadelphia & the
  Amish Country

Portugal
Prague & the Best of the
  Czech Republic
Provence & the Riviera
Puerto Rico
Rome
San Antonio & Austin
San Diego
San Francisco
Santa Fe, Taos & Albuquerque
Scandinavia
Scotland
Seattle & Portland
Shanghai
Singapore & Malaysia
South Africa
Southeast Asia
South Florida
South Pacific
Spain
Sweden
Switzerland
Thailand
Tokyo
Toronto
Tuscany & Umbria
USA
Utah
Vancouver & Victoria
Vermont, New Hampshire
  & Maine
Vienna & the Danube Valley
Virgin Islands
Virginia
Walt Disney World &
  Orlando
Washington, D.C.
Washington State

FROMMER'S® DOLLAR-A-DAY GUIDES

Australia from $50 a Day
California from $60 a Day
Caribbean from $70 a Day
England from $70 a Day
Europe from $70 a Day

Florida from $70 a Day
Hawaii from $70 a Day
Ireland from $60 a Day
Italy from $70 a Day
London from $85 a Day

New York from $80 a Day
Paris from $80 a Day
San Francisco from $60 a Day
Washington, D.C.,
  from $70 a Day

FROMMER'S® PORTABLE GUIDES

Acapulco, Ixtapa &
  Zihuatanejo
Alaska Cruises & Ports of Call
Bahamas
Baja & Los Cabos
Berlin
California Wine Country
Charleston & Savannah
Chicago
Dublin

Hawaii: The Big Island
Las Vegas
London
Los Angeles
Maine Coast
Maui
Miami
New Orleans
New York City
Paris

Puerto Vallarta, Manzanillo
  & Guadalajara
San Diego
San Francisco
Sydney
Tampa & St. Petersburg
Venice
Washington, D.C.

FROMMER'S® NATIONAL PARK GUIDES

Family Vacations in the
  National Parks
Grand Canyon

National Parks of the
  American West
Rocky Mountain

Yellowstone & Grand Teton
Yosemite & Sequoia/
  Kings Canyon
Zion & Bryce Canyon

FROMMER'S® MEMORABLE WALKS

Chicago
London

New York
Paris

San Francisco
Washington, D.C.

FROMMER'S® GREAT OUTDOOR GUIDES

New England
Northern California

Southern California & Baja
Southern New England

Washington & Oregon

FROMMER'S® BORN TO SHOP GUIDES

Born to Shop: France
Born to Shop: Italy

Born to Shop: London
Born to Shop: New York

Born to Shop: Paris

FROMMER'S® IRREVERENT GUIDES

Amsterdam
Boston
Chicago
Las Vegas

London
Los Angeles
Manhattan
New Orleans

Paris
San Francisco
Seattle & Portland
Vancouver

Walt Disney World
Washington, D.C.

FROMMER'S® BEST-LOVED DRIVING TOURS

America
Britain
California

Florida
France
Germany

Ireland
Italy
New England

Scotland
Spain
Western Europe

THE UNOFFICIAL GUIDES®

Bed & Breakfasts in
  California
Bed & Breakfasts in
  New England
Bed & Breakfasts in
  the Northwest
Bed & Breakfasts in
  Southeast
Beyond Disney
Branson, Missouri

California with Kids
Chicago
Cruises
Disneyland
Florida with Kids
Golf Vacations in the
  Eastern U.S.
The Great Smoky &
  Blue Ridge
  Mountains

Inside Disney
Hawaii
Las Vegas
London
Miami & the Keys
Mini Las Vegas
Mini-Mickey
New Orleans
New York City
Paris

San Francisco
Skiing in the West
Southeast with Kids
Walt Disney World
Walt Disney World
  for Grown-ups
Walt Disney World
  for Kids
Washington, D.C.

SPECIAL-INTEREST TITLES

Frommer's Britain's Best Bed & Breakfasts and
  Country Inns
Frommer's Britain's Best Bike Rides
The Civil War Trust's Official Guide
  to the Civil War Discovery Trail
Frommer's Caribbean Hideaways
Frommer's Adventure Guide to Central America
Frommer's Adventure Guide to South America
Frommer's Adventure Guide to Southeast Asia
Frommer's Food Lover's Companion to France
Frommer's Gay & Lesbian Europe
Frommer's Exploring America by RV
Hanging Out in Europe

Israel Past & Present
Mad Monks' Guide to California
Mad Monks' Guide to New York City
Frommer's The Moon
Frommer's New York City with Kids
The New York Times' Unforgettable
  Weekends
Places Rated Almanac
Retirement Places Rated
Frommer's Road Atlas Britain
Frommer's Road Atlas Europe
Frommer's Washington, D.C., with Kids
Frommer's What the Airlines Never Tell You